PRINCE

of

DRONES

THE REGINALD DENNY STORY

KIMBERLY PUCCI

BearManor Media

2019

Prince of Drones: The Reginald Denny Story

© 2019 Kimberly Pucci

All rights reserved.

Front cover photo credit: Reginald Denny with one of his scale models on MGM set of *Romeo and Juliet* (1936). Courtesy of Marc Wanamaker/Bison Archives.

Cover design by Lindy Martin.

Kimberly Pucci at Santa Barbara Polo Club with one of her grandfather's early inspirations. Photo credit Brooke Daniels.

Published in the United States of America by:

BearManor Media

4700 Millenia Blvd.
Suite 175 PMB 90497
Orlando, FL 32839

bearmanormedia.com

Printed in the United States.

Typesetting and layout by John Teehan

ISBN—978-1-62933-488-2

TABLE OF CONTENTS

Acknowledgements ix

Prologue: Drone Tales.. 1

Chapter 1: The Forsaken Prince 5

Chapter 2: India 'n' a Jones...................................... 11

Chapter 3: The Snipe 15

Chapter 4: War Vet On Broadway............................. 21

Chapter 5: The Reckless Age 29

Chapter 6: Up and Away... 41

Chapter 7: Universal Appeal 45

Chapter 8: Fast and Furious 55

Photo Section I 62

Chapter 9: Motherland 127

Chapter 10: Denny Swansong.................................. 135

Chapter 11: I'm Forever Blowing Bubbles................ 145

Chapter 12: Of Human Bondage.............................. 153

Chapter 13: Dennymite 163

Chapter 14: Radioplane 173

Photo Section II 181

Chapter 15: Target Drone Denny 235

Chapter 16: Goodbye Norma Jeane, Hello
        Jack Northrop 245

Chapter 17: Flareplane and Fair Lady 255

Chapter 18: His Reprise 267

Chapter 19: Leaving a Legacy on Wings Home 277

Chapter 20: Remote Possibilities 283

Photo Section III 287

Epilogue 333

Appendix A: Radioplane Brochure 1945 335

Appendix B: Flareplane Patent 359

Appendix C: Flareplane Proposal 365

Bibliography 379

Index 381

About the Author 397

*Dedicated to
Grandpa and his
Great-Grandson Jeremy*

ACKNOWLEDGEMENTS

FOR THEIR BELIEF, INSPIRATION, AND SUPPORT in helping bring my vision to life, I extend a very special "Thank You" to:

Academy of Motion Picture Arts and Sciences, Emmajane and Simon Albertini, Gerry Albertini, Mark Albertini, Buzz Aldrin, Greg Banas, Kevin Brownlow, John Bruner, Canada Aviation and Space Museum, Stephanie Carlisi, Tony Chong, Allison Cohen, Cheryl Crane and Josh LeRoy, Cynthia Curiel, Izzy Davidson, Deluxe Digital Media, Diane and Reginald Denny, Wendy and Pen Densham, Edwards Air Force Base Flight Test Nation, Major General David J. Eichhorn, Brandon Florian, Gia Galligani, Adam Gross, Steven K. Hill, Bob Hohman, Holloman Air Force Base, Robin Hutton, Holly and Anthony Jackson, Laurie Jacobson and Jon Provost, Andrea Kalas, Laura La Plante, Kayla Lea, George Lewis, Patrick Loughney and the team at Packard Humanities Institute, George Lucas, Frank Lupo, A.C. Lyles, Meredith Mingledorf, Marianne Moloney, Northrop Grumman Corporation, Ben Ohmart, Bruce Orriss, Archive and Post Production Team at Paramount Pictures, Christine Forsyth-Peters, Jon Peters, Rick Pratt and Eric Blum Productions, Alan Purwin, Lynne Quarterman, Laurel Robinson, Jason Rohr, Henry Root, Adriana Rotaru, Royal Air Force Museum, Kevin Russen and Fagan Fighters WWII Museum, Tonya and Burt Rutan, Mike Satren, Chip Schutzman, Janice Simpson and the team at Universal Pictures, Post Production Team at Sony Pictures Entertainment, Debbie Speckmeyer, Steven Spielberg, Mike Strickler, John Teehan, Turner Classic Movies, Adam Ugolnik, United States Air Force, United States Army, United States Marine Corp, United States Navy, UCLA Film & Television Archive, Brahm Vaccarella, Tom Vice and his team at Northrop Grumman Corporation, Laura Wagner, Marc Wanamaker, Jay Weissberg, Dony West, and Wright-Patterson Air Force Base. Most special thanks to Bubbles and her daughter, my dear mother Joanie, for sharing magical memories with me. I love you, always and forever, my eternal Angels.

"It's a transmitter. It's a radio for speaking to God. And it's within my reach."

– *Raiders of the Lost Ark*

PROLOGUE: DRONE TALES

ONE RAINY FEBRUARY NIGHT IN 1964, I walked into the den of our Studio City home to join the family as they watched The Beatles make their U.S. debut performance on *The Ed Sullivan Show*. I was six years old and thrilled my favorite grandparents had come to live with us after their stay in New York; they brought magic back into our home much like Mary Poppins and Bert did for the Banks household. Over the droning screams of teenage girls and Dad grumbling about those "beatniks and their long hair," I noticed Grandpa sitting alone at the corner of the couch. The seventy-two-year-old man looked more like a bored little boy to me, as though he'd rather be doing anything but staring at that RCA television set. Curious, I stepped up to him, put my arm around him, and smiled. He patted the couch beside him and in his refined British accent beamed, "My Little Princess, come sit and I'll tell you a story."

Grandpa's blue eyes came to life as he led me on a journey outside that black-and-white den into a colorful world with fascinating tales of a young boy who flew a futuristic aircraft; not by sitting inside the plane, but with a magical box and his fly-away imagination. Like Superman, the boy soared to far-away places to save the world from dastardly villains, only this hero stayed safely on the ground while the airplane did the good deed. My eyes widened as flying machines with a mind of their own came to the rescue. With the sharing of his wild chronicles and science fiction adventures, Grandpa painted a picture that no television show ever could. Over the next few years I looked forward to spending these fantastical moments with the pipe-smoking dreamer. What I didn't realize then was how real Grandpa's stories would turn out to be, and what an important role he played in making them come true.

From the time I was two years old, I attended Grandpa's plays and watched him on television acting as another character, but I was eight when I realized that he was "famous." My parents and grandparents were getting ready to leave for what seemed like a Royal Ball. Mom looked like Audrey Hepburn in her short pixie haircut and long pink gown; Dad was dapper as a penguin in his black tux. Like a proud parent of kids going to the prom, I snapped pictures of them with our Kodak Instamatic camera. Later that night, as I watched the *Academy Awards* on television with my sister and our babysitter, I noticed Mom, Dad, Grandma, and Grandpa on the screen. There they were, seated in the audience surrounded by applauding movie stars with a caption below that read "Reginald Denny."

I tilted my head and wondered. *Why are they there? And why do they single him out as though he's somebody important?*

Years later and now in my early twenties, I moved to Hawaii to embark on my dream of working with sea mammals. I was ecstatic to leave the mainland to spend my days swimming with dolphins and whales in paradise at Oahu's Sea Life Park. There, I also acquired the duty of caring for abandoned wild sea birds. I found great joy in educating the park's guests about our rescued infant frigatebirds, who spent their days in viewing pens located near the animated penguins. Holding the downy baby birds, I'd look up to see their adult counterparts circling overhead alongside hang gliders who danced upon thermals over the ocean. The sight of the large pterodactyl-looking seabirds flying with the gliders was surreal. In a hypnotic trance I watched man and prehistoric bird circle slowly together, way up in the sky.

I'd then snap back to reality, returning to earth and back to work.

After putting the baby frigatebirds in their protective cages for the night, I'd feed the Pacific bottlenose dolphins and false killer whales and then quickly shower alongside their holding tanks to get ready for my night job at Café Kahala. On the road that curved around Makapu'u Point, I again noticed the hang gliders above and wished I could soar along with them off into the sunset instead of going to work again for the night.

If I had to have a second job, Café Kahala was the place to be. The nouveau French restaurant was owned by Ma Maison's Patrick Terrail with restaurateurs Cheryl Crane and Josh LeRoy, who taught me how to own the role of maître d' as though I was hosting a party at my own fabulous home. All in a day's work, I balanced caring for wild animals in the tropical sunshine with greeting Hollywood royalty by night at the popular hotspot.

This particular evening as I started my shift, I realized there were herring scales still stuck to my hands from feeding the cetaceans their tasty dinner earlier. As I discretely peeled the round transparent stickers into the trash can, the first wave of attendees arrived at my party. Before I could finish, Cheryl's mom Lana Turner, her good friend Mitzi Gaynor, and two gentlemen approached my hostess stand.

As I seated the group, Lana turned to her guests and boasted, "This is Kimberly; she's Reginald Denny's granddaughter!"

I hid my right scaled hand behind my back while the men introduced themselves as friends of my grandfather's and claimed they knew my family well.

"He was a magnificent actor. I was so sorry to hear of his passing," one gentleman said. He turned to Lana. "But you know, his real claim to fame was the radio-controlled airplanes he designed for the military."

He nodded to me, "You know about the drones he invented, don't you?"

Drones?

This man who held a key into my locked-up heritage informed me that he and my grandfather had worked together many years ago. He gave me his phone number should I ever return to the mainland. I thanked him and motioned for the waiter to pour our VIP guests Dom Perignon while I escaped to the restroom to scrape the remaining fish scales off my hands.

As months flew by at the sea park, the baby frigatebirds grew to juveniles and the transfer from viewing pen to their night cages became quite a lifting experience; one on each arm, their large talons wrapped around my wrists and wingspan now spreading six feet. As they flapped their powerful wings for balance when the Hawaiian trade winds crossed our path, I'd lose my once steady footing and be lifted off the ground. It was exhilarating yet scary at the same time as I felt I'd be joining the gliders above, but not know how to get back down to the ground. I decided it was time for my feathered friends to join their airborne relatives without me.

The day we released them to the skies was a magical one. Watching the adolescent frigates take off on their maiden voyage to finally soar high above with the rest of the flyers gave me such a sense of freedom that I felt I could actually fly across the ocean myself, somewhere over the tropical rainbow. As they flew, I glanced across and noticed some guys standing above at the edge of the cliffs. They were holding black boxes with antennas on them and appeared to be guiding radio-controlled airplanes. Intrigued with these airborne craft that flew remotely and remembering what Lana's restaurant guest had said about Grandpa, I hopped in my car and headed up the road to investigate.

The two University of Hawaii students welcomed me as an inquisitive newcomer and demonstrated how they used remote control devices to guide the flying wings across the sky. I watched their sailplanes soar like seabirds, dive swiftly down to the sea, then loop up and around in aerial acrobatics. One of the guys kept his eyes on the plane in focused concentration while he adjusted the "transmitter." The other explained to me that they were testing "drones" to help monitor illegal fishing and hunting of sea mammals.

There's that word again.

"But aren't these really radio-controlled airplanes?" I asked.

"Drones are radio-controlled airplanes with a job, on a mission." He showed me how he could see through a camera wherever the plane went.

I looked at the screen he had set up on a rock and was amazed at what I saw—my frigates in flight! It was as though we were flying right alongside them, up close and personal, high in the sky.

So, this is what a drone does!

I asked if I could give it a try and he hesitantly handed me the controls. Thinking it was as easy as he made it look, I attempted to fly the remote-control plane. The power I felt in my hands while watching the plane soar was spectacular, but I started to feel a little sea sick from trying to navigate it in the air above a moving sea. Without warning, the wind grabbed the plane and I feared I would lose control, so I handed the transmitter back over to the drone operator just before the craft crashed into the ocean. He lifted the drone back up with ease to circle once again alongside my frigates.

I couldn't sleep that night. What a day, what an experience! Just as fascinating as it was to set the frigates free and fly the planes, I now felt the need to find out what those guys at the restaurant were talking about. If my grandfather actually had something to do with this aerial art of flying a plane remotely, on a mission to help the animals I loved, I wanted to learn more. I'd seen photos of my much younger Grandpa with airplanes, but now I was curious about this "remote control" thing. Apparently, there was more to Grandpa and his stories than had met my childish eyes. I was compelled to delve deeper into his life, so I decided to get back to Los Angeles where I could learn more about him. I also wanted to find out why this invention of his was kept a secret instead of celebrated.

Upon returning to Southern California, I met a handsome young actor with the striking blue eyes of Grandpa's and who was just beginning his quest into Hollywood. While chugging down oyster shooters and tequila shots on our first date at a beachfront restaurant in Del Mar, I told him the reason I left my paradise in Hawaii was to write a book about my extraordinary grandfather. He was blown away by what I told him and encouraged me to do it, but his charmed enthusiasm turned out to be more distracting than motivating. Rather than continuing my research, I blew off writing and instead focused on the man who would become my husband and the father of my wonderful son. We spent the next couple of decades rocking and rolling La La Land while he became a television star and I played supporting roles to iconic Hollywood figures.

Needless to say, much has changed in the past thirty-five years, including the emergence of drones. In 1984, not many people knew about RPVs or UAVs, myself included. Now they've literally taken off and I've awoken from someone else's nightmare to uncover a hidden treasure chest of glittering history. Through my extensive research, I discovered that the birth of our flying robots wasn't conceived by a high-tech guru, rocket scientist, computer whiz, or brilliant physicist, or a governmental figure trying to get an edge on war. Rather, its story plays out like a romantic and thrilling movie much like the adventures of Indiana Jones, with the discovery of the ark—or rather an *arc*—all through an artist's dream beginning in the heart of Hollywood with my grandfather as its leading man. While Howard Hughes designed and flew his manned aircraft, Grandpa took aviation to a realm where no man, airplane, or machine had gone before him, while he too soared with the stars.

It's been a heartwarming adventure as I've dug into the past and the timing is finally right for me to bring this colorful tale of the amazing man who I've known as Grandpa to life, and to share his-story of unmanned flight with the world.

Without further ado, I am proud to introduce to you Reginald Denny. Not the unfortunate truck driver of the 1992 Los Angeles Riots, but rather the "Prince of Drones."

1 THE FORSAKEN PRINCE

HE WAS BORN REGINALD LEIGH DUGMORE on the twentieth day of November 1891. Raised in the picturesque riverside resort of Richmond Surrey, young "Reggie" was the scion of England's oldest theatrical family with five generations of performances in his genes. His great-grandfather was the outstanding theatrical Shakespearean figure of his generation who performed at the old Sadler's Wells Theatre in London during the 1700s, and his grandmother Mrs. Henry Leigh was the heroine of the famous *Drury Lane* melodramas during the 1800s. Reggie's father had been given the birth name of William Henry Dugmore; however, he changed his Irish surname to the stage name of "W.H. Denny" upon gaining notoriety as a baritone singer with the Savoy Opera. W.H. earned his fame as a comedy player with W.S. Gilbert and Arthur Sullivan by portraying the original Shadbolt the Jailer in Savoy's *The Yeomen of the Guard* (1888), and Don Alhambra del Bolero in *The Gondoliers* (1889).

With his father frequently away on tour, most of Reggie's youth was spent at home on the River Thames with his mother Georgina Pike Dugmore and his five siblings. Reggie became the little man of the house where he took his first role of entertaining the family. Complemented by his infectious grin, he made up amusing stories, sang tunes from his daddy's operettas, and carved model boats to sail upon the river. He was a chip off the old block with the brilliant blue eyes of his father, only much better looking than the comedic player.

Notable actor and director George Bellamy first took notice of the young wunderkind and discovered him for the stage. "It was whilst W.H. Denny and I were playing in *Her Royal Highness* at the Vaudeville in 1898 that he suggested I should go with him to his home in Richmond. Here, I first saw the young Denny and was greatly impressed by the kiddie. He had inherited his mother's good looks, and altogether, he struck me as one of the most handsome and one of the cleverest looking boys I had ever seen. Sometime later, Dion Boucicault decided to run *A Royal Family* at the Court Theatre, the author being Captain Robert Marshall. They badly needed a handsome boy to play the youthful prince and searched all the London agencies without success. They mentioned the subject to me, and I immediately thought of the wonderful Denny boy. Boucicault laughed. 'Surely Denny can't have a handsome son!' he said. 'Wait until you see him,' I retorted. Next day I went down to Richmond, saw Mrs. Dugmore and she immediately fell in with my suggestion. We took Reginald with us and as soon as Boucicault and Marshall saw him, they both agreed their search had ended."

When Boucicault asked for permission to cast the seven-year-old in his play, W.H. complied but only if they used the stage name of "Denny" to avoid any confusion with his son's theatrical heritage. Master Reginald Denny, as he was billed, played Prince Charles Ferdinand in *A Royal Family* which opened at London's new Court Theatre on October 14, 1899. The *Sun and Daily Mail* newspaper praised him stating, "One of the chief factors in the popularity and long run of the play is the fine acting of the youthful Prince." Queen Victoria showed up to see the small handsome boy perform in his very first stage role. Famous actors as Sir Henry Irving, Julia Neilson, and Sir Herbert Beerbohm Tree also came to get a glimpse of the young sensation. Reggie's mother Georgina would bring him to rehearsals and showed up proudly for each of her son's stellar performances.

Reggie was such a hit in *A Royal Family* that the following year he was cast in *Lady Huntsworth's Experiment* (1900) with Gertrude Elliott at London's Criterion Theatre, then as Peter Cratchit in *Scrooge* (1901) at the Vaudeville Theatre in Sandringham London for their first Command Performance given before King Edward VII. Following these noble performances, the ten-year-old played a midshipman in *The President* (1902) at the Prince of Wales Theatre. Rave reviews rolled in as Reggie thrived on stage. Already in his heritage, the theater became his family.

At home, Reggie's mother was overwhelmed with the task of managing six kids on her own. W.H. was off in Australia, carrying on as a traveling player, when one of Reggie's sisters became critically ill and died suddenly. Debilitating grief over the death of her child compounded with Georgina's exhaustion landed her with a severe case of pneumonia. Eleven-year-old Reggie, with his older brother Gerald, and three sisters Nora, Mona, and Madge, did their best to care for mummy; but she wasn't strong enough to recover. Georgina died at the young age of forty, with the children at her bedside. On her deathbed, Georgina whispered to her special son, "Reggie, you have the gift of talent. Continue to perform, sing, and make others laugh. Keep your eyes to the sky and don't let anything make you look down."

W.H returned for his wife's funeral; however, instead of staying home with the children, he sold the family residence, sent Gerald off to a university, and his daughters away to a convent. He put Reggie on a train headed for Devonport, Devonshire, to live in the country with his Aunt and Uncle Pike. Still recovering from the loss of mummy, torn from the rest of his family, and realizing his distant touring father didn't have time to care for him, left the forsaken child actor feeling heartbroken and alone.

At the farm, Reggie spent time in the barn where he performed for a captive audience of animals. His two male cousins mocked his singing and teased him for such absurdities, so he took off alone and gathered wood to carve small model boats. Jealousy drove Reggie's cousins to further tease him, break his precious vessels and sink them in the farm pond. Having been raised in a nurturing environment and exposed to professionalism on stage, Reggie was confused, bored, and frustrated with such displays of pettiness and utter disregard. Too brilliant to relate to the regular, Reggie debated with his elders who regarded him "too much to handle." Deemed a burden on the family, Reggie was sent by his aunt off on yet another train to a Catholic boarding school in Mayfield Sussex. The happy childhood days of family and theater faded into a memory.

At St. Francis Xavier College, Reggie survived like an old-fashioned Harry Potter; an abandoned English boy who had to find his own magical methods to cope in the confines of an orphanage with evil sorcerers at every turn. When Reggie arrived at the all-boys school, with his bright blue eyes and long hair, his classmates made fun of him for being such a "pretty lassie." He was different, more mature and smarter than the others. To deflect the teasing, Reggie took on the role of a princely jokester to try and assimilate, but his peers laughed at him instead of with him.

One of the Brothers there was a falconer and observed the jeering Reggie endured. He took the boy aside and demonstrated how he trained his falcon to take off, hunt for its prey, and return back to its wing master. Reggie was fascinated by the raptor bird and intrigued with Nikola Tesla's new concept of telemetry, by which a small transmitter was attached to the falcon's talons to track its whereabouts when it went out of sight. Reggie was more interested in exploring the avian arts than commonplace schoolwork. Often, he retreated to his room, studied aerodynamics, and sketched the falcon on the pages of his journal. His imagination flew wild and provided an escape from the prison walls of the lonely institution.

Reggie's desire to flee the school propelled him to study fervently. Beyond his years academically, he took the prestigious Society of Arts Exam, passed it with flying colors, and earned an A.A. degree at the early age of fifteen. With his sights on college, he prepped for the London Matriculation Exam but was distracted from his studies when his fag-master ordered him to do a series of demeaning and outrageous chores for him, as a Cinderella-type slave. Fagging was a tradition practiced at British boys' boarding schools where the juvenile "fags" paid service to the older students, or "fag-masters." Fags weren't there solely for menial tasks such as boot polishing, laundry, and cooking, but for any service the senior requested and at any time. This slavery system often resulted in physical, emotional, and sexual abuse. If the younger pupils didn't obey their masters, they were beaten or worse. The senior to whom Reggie was assigned demanded oral sex. An affair typical to the era in such institutions, this humiliating act continued until one evening after dinner when the senior called Reggie to his dormitory and ordered him to remove his clothing. Fed up and boiling with suppressed anger, when his fag-master began the routine buggery, Reggie pushed him away and darted out the room to the headmaster's office. In response to Reggie's reporting of injustice, instead of disciplining the senior boy, the headmaster priest told Reggie that he must obey his master. When the man of the cloth and the fag-master attempted to restrain him into conformity, Reggie used his fists and knocked the senior boy out cold. He beat the priest into a heap on the ground and made his getaway. That was it. The frightened yet emboldened teen scaled the walls to freedom and fled to a nearby forest, narrowly escaping the howling hound dogs sent after him by police.

It was now fight and flight for the young prince. Unlike the trained falcons, the sixteen-year-old hastily flew the coop with no intention of returning. He jumped aboard a freight train headed for London in a desperate quest to reconnect with his family. Contacting his father was out of the question because he knew he'd be sent back to the orphanage. Trying to find Gerald or going to the convent where his sisters lived weren't promising options either. Reggie was better off homeless than to return to an abusive environment. He vowed never to return to school or the Catholic religion as an enslaved altar boy.

On the streets of London, Reggie learned that his eighty-five-year-old grandmother was acting in *The Great Millionaire* (1907) at the old Drury Lane Theatre. He made his way in and watched her perform from the back row of the theater but was kicked out when he attempted to go backstage after the curtain fell. Looking like a vagabond in his tattered clothing, Reggie waited outside the theater for his grandmother, vying for a lifeline, but was shooed away by an escort who cleared the path for his grandmother to step into her impressive automobile. By contrast, the homeless teen was now alone and begging for every meal to survive. There were gangs and criminals at every turn and Reg concluded that if he was to live, he'd better learn to fight. He longed to train at England's most swagger boxing club, the National Sporting Club, but without one of its members to sponsor him he couldn't even get inside its sacred portals. After being severely beaten by a street gang, the hardening runaway sneaked into the private pugilist club where he watched the professional boxers trade punches in the ring. The fighters took notice of his interest and asked him if he wanted to take a try. Reg jumped into the ring and put on the gloves. While making his punches, the president of the National Sporting Club and Fifth Earl of Lonsdale, Hugh Lowther, arrived. When Lord Lonsdale saw the homeless teen throw his mighty punches and stand up to his own seasoned trainers, he took Reg in and assigned Harry Preston to teach the lad how to become a prizefighter.

Harry Preston was a bantamweight champ and years later he became the one of the few boxers to have been knighted. Preston adopted the youth as his protégé and took great joy in teaching young Denny the pugilist art like a true knight. Preston told Reg, "Boxing is an art. Pugilists don't just pound on each other. They strategize while they dance around the ring, look for an opening, then make a quick committed punch before their swift retreat." He took Reg off the streets and invited him to stay at his mansion where there was a gym for workouts and where he kept his racecars. They'd also go to the port where Preston kept his yacht and from there, they took swims in the English Channel to build strong muscles. The future knight incorporated his boxing training with the skills of a sportsman in preparing Reg to stay sharp and in shape for any battle. Under the tutelage of his excellent mentor, Reg forged his way to the very top of England's long line of amateur boxers. At age seventeen, he became a winning prizefighter at the prominent East End boxing hall, Wonderland. Then it was off to The Ring at Blackfriars where he fought in four fights and won all. In the next round, Reg got knocked out so severely that when he came to, he had a broken jaw.

Reg decided to return to stage work instead of being killed in the ring, so he hit the streets and used his long-lost father's name of Denny to land a job. He soon scored a walk-on part as an extra in Charles Frohman's original production of J.M. Barrie's *What Every Woman Knows* (1908) at the Duke of York's Theatre, then doubled up with a small role in an upcoming show of *Madame X* (1908). When Reg showed up for rehearsal at His Majesty's Theatre for *Madame X*, he received another blow. His father had just returned from New York and was cast in the same play as Parrisard the Blackmailer. W.H. had years before co-founded the Actors' Orphanage and was enraged to learn his own son had brutalized a priest, run away from the boarding school, and now had the audacity to show up on the London stage.

After watching his son rehearse, W.H. made a plea to Reg. "My son, I must ask you to give up the stage. You come from a long line of actors and we can't have the family name held up to ridicule. It's bad enough to be an actor, but it's unpardonable to be bad. Go back to school and earn your degree for a real profession."

The show lasted only a week and upon last curtain call, Reg immediately set about ignoring his old man's advice. He stayed in London and continued to cultivate his natural talents into an honest living. Charles Frohman asked Reg to join the chorus in another of his productions, John Galsworthy's *Strife* (1909). On March 9, the play opened at the Duke of York's Theatre and after six matinee performances the production was transferred to the Haymarket Theatre, and then to the Adelphi Theatre for evening performances where Reg earned an extra ten shillings to eat. The show attracted much attention and a reviewer for *The Times* wrote, "When an artist of Mr. Galsworthy's high endeavor, mental equipment and technical skills writes a play like *Strife*, he has done much more than write a play, he has rendered a public service."

Reg was happy to work with such stage pros once again in the medium that felt like home. He then secured his first big part as Prince Danilo in Pat Malone's No. 3 Company production of *The Merry Widow* (1909). The No. 3 Company took him on his first road tour to perform in various small villages throughout the United Kingdom. Singing and acting were in his genes and the eighteen-year-old six-foot pugilist soon found that audiences responded favorably to his developing baritone operatic voice, strong physique, and good looks. Young ladies of the various villages flocked to him like present-day groupies of a rock star. Surprised at the reaction he garnered from the girls, Reg blushed and flashed his now-crooked grin. When he sang, they melted. He had no interest in the opposite sex but found them to be entertaining and he liked to make them laugh. While on tour in Liverpool, Reg had gotten a hold of some sneezing powder on the streets. He ventured to the old Liverpool Zoo where he proceeded to the monkey's cage. When the monkeys flung their feces at him, Reg took out the snuff and swiftly blew the powder at them. The monkeys sneezed furiously, screamed and madly scolded him. A crowd gathered to see about the commotion. When the zookeepers caught the teen in front of the monkeys' cage entertaining a group of giggling girls, they kicked him out of the zoo and told the scallywag never to return.

The Merry Widow tour lasted for almost a year. When it was over, Reg returned to London to look for work. Famous Broadway producer and theater owner Henry B. Harris was in town casting for his New York premiere of James Tolman Tanner's *The Quaker Girl*. Harris needed eight English chorus men for the Edwardian musical comedy. Once he heard the handsome nineteen-year-old sing, he cast Reg as one of them. Reg boarded the trans-Atlantic cruiser with Harris's No. 2 Company bound for his first trip to America. Rehearsals began onboard the ship where Harris closely observed the singing boxer. He liked Reg's look and developing baritone so much, he also assigned him as understudy to Lawrence Rae as the roguish French roué Prince Carlo.

On October 23, 1911, *The Quaker Girl* opened at the Park Theatre on Broadway. The production played three weeks before Lawrence Rae became seriously ill and presented an opportunity for his understudy to go for the gold. Reg became Broadway's youngest leading man. He may have been too green for the undertaking, but his determined practice compensated his lack of experience. The company tried out other actors for the part; they tried opera singers who couldn't act, and actors who couldn't sing. Reg was sort of an 'in between.' Once he owned the role, he stepped in and reveled in belting out the lyrics to the hit song of the show, "Come to the Ball," making his debut performance on Broadway opposite female leads Ina Claire and Elizabeth Brick.

Now making New York his home, Reg rented a room on 55th Street in a boarding house run by Mrs. Barnes. It was an inexpensive haven of refuge to the tired and hungry actor; his neighbors were Scottish actor Ernest Torrence, British actor Percy Marmont, and American stage actress Eulalie Jensen. Reg was curious about the new medium of film and after stage rehearsals, he snuck with his neighbors over to Flatbush where they did some "flickers" with the Vitograph Company. He used another name for shame of such a degrading exhibition.

The Quaker Girl was a huge success and ran two-hundred-forty performances into the spring months. After another sold-out evening performance, Reg and a couple of castmates were on their way back to the boarding house. In a back alley, they were approached by a notorious bunch of gangsters called the Gopher Gang. The hoodlums taunted the "pretty boy" and demanded the actors give them their earned money. Reg refused and instead used his handy boxing skills, nearly killing a couple of guys. When the police arrived, they arrested Reg and took him to the station where he was thrown in jail along with the street gang.

W.H. had been in New York performing for the Shuberts in *The Blue Bird* (1912). When he arrived at the jailhouse to bail his son out, he was once more disappointed with Reg's performance. "My son. Your grandmother was a fine actress and I am an excellent actor, and now you are going to ruin the family record with this audacious display."

While walking him out of the jailhouse, W.H. went on to lecture his son. "All great actors and artists die penniless and I shall die a poor man. But my boy, I have seen you act, and I am sure that you will die a very rich man. Leave the stage and return to London where you'll finish school instead of shaming the family name."

The rebellious young adult had no intention of listening to the insults of his remote father. Once free from jail, Reg returned to the Park Theatre to resume his princely role in *The Quaker Girl*. Henry Harris had been in England casting another of his stage productions. When it was time to return to New York, Harris and his wife boarded the *RMS Titanic* for its maiden voyage across the sea. Reg got another knock in the jaw when he learned that the ill-fated ship had hit an iceberg and had sunk in the North Atlantic, taking his producer and the show down with it. The party in New York was over. Reg decided to heed his father's advice and leave 55th Street and Broadway behind.

2

INDIA 'N' A JONES

Reg returned to Great Britain via *Titanic's* sister ship, the *RMS Olympic*. Instead of going back to school, he got a job in London playing a young British Army officer in a dramatic sketch called *Gentlemen: The King!* (1912). The production took him on the road where he toured the music halls of England for a few months until the playwright, Robert Barr, died of a heart attack.

When he returned to London, Reg learned that the Bandmann Opera Company was looking for men to sing in a number of light operas and musical comedies including those in which he'd previously starred, *The Merry Widow* and *The Quaker Girl*. As India was under British Raj, the company was about to tour India and the Far East taking a bunch of musical Brits with them. When Reg auditioned for Maurice Bandmann, he was considered for the job but with the condition that he remain professional and not pursue any of the troupe's young chorus girls while on the six-month tour. When Reg told Bandmann that he was "not apt to be interested in the opposite sex in his travels as he was so wholeheartedly wrapped up in his profession," he was hired for the ride.

On his twenty-first birthday, Reg boarded the boat bound for Bombay with the Bandmann Opera Company. Rehearsals were held onboard, and it became evident he'd bitten off more than he could chew. He was given the chance to sing lead baritone in an operetta called *Gipsy Love*; however, his baritone voice had not yet properly set. He didn't have enough experience and the music was too much for his voice, or his voice was too much for the music; in any event, his voice was not good enough for the part, so he was relegated to lesser roles.

One evening during rehearsals, Reg noticed a beautiful chorus girl from Kent. He made his way over to the seventeen-year-old brunette and learned her name was Irene Hilda Haisman, but she preferred being called by her nickname "Rene." "Quite an attractive youngster," Reg generously conceded after he had been introduced to her.

"Then we danced together. Rene's dancing is one of those things which a man may enjoy once in his lifetime if he is lucky. After I had once had this pleasure, there was no need for the entire ship's roster of passengers to be as fortunate as I had been, so I danced with her all the rest of the evening. Rene knew she was being discussed by the other and older members of the cast. Tongues were wagging briskly about the new girl. One woman said in a tone which carried to our ears, 'She may be little, but she is certainly wise.' Rene's dark eyes flashed. She straightened to her full five feet and flirted with me. She went on deck in the moonlight with me and that was how it all began. We had both heard that remark and without a word, mutually decided to give them something to talk about. Of course, neither of us had any idea it would ever be serious, and we laughed about it. The trip to India was perfect in so far as we were concerned. A full moon in the tropics is sufficient reason for anyone to fall in love. The older heads of the company came to Rene, warning her that I was never serious. She listened to this and pondered. There were other admirers on board, and she annexed a sufficient number of these to keep me on the anxious seat. The night before we arrived in India, we talked the whole thing over and Rene solemnly declared she feared we had both just been flirting. She thought that was the wise thing to do. I took the answer coolly enough, but it hurt my pride, so upon arriving in Calcutta I made no effort to see Rene except at rehearsals for about a week. It had the desired effect. To that they might discharge me, and the women of the company continued their warnings to Rene that she would regret such a hasty decision, I proposed to her."

The charismatic singer won the teen's heart and she heartily accepted Reg's proposal. On January 28, 1913, the two were secretly married at a marriage hall in Calcutta. The couple went on to perform together with Bandmann in Calcutta, Bombay, Rangoon, and then onto Singapore where they spent their romantic honeymoon. There, Rene was called in by Mr. Bandmann who had found out about her marriage. He reminded her of the clause in her contract stating that as she was underage, she could not marry without written permission of a parent or guardian. Being her husband and now her guardian, Reg approached Bandmann and insisted he change the silly marriage clause. Instead of providing an exception, the company immediately fired Reg along with Rene and issued the now-unemployed singers two return tickets back home.

The capricious newlyweds weren't quite ready to abandon this new adventure. The couple got housing with an Indian family in Singapore where they learned how to cook delicious curry dishes as well as learn about as the Hindu-Buddhist way of life. Constantly being told that he couldn't act or sing, first by his father and now by an opera company, Reg decided to give up the stage for good and pursue another walk of life. He soon secured the job of a "creeper" on a rubber plantation and the couple left Singapore on a boat headed to Java. Reg had been advised by some Brits not to mention the fact that he was married when applying for the job. When the couple arrived in Java, he found out why. Upon finally making it deep into the jungles of the Indonesian island, Reg discovered that creepers had to live in a chummery, or housing for men only. With another strike against them for being married, the couple decided to use those tickets and head back to England.

Reg and Rene boarded a banana boat heading north up the Indian Ocean and it stopped on the island of Sri Lanka. There, they were offered a job with a team doing the same songs and dances of the popular musical comedies they had been playing with Bandmann. They couldn't refuse as they needed the money, so they took the job as vaudeville performers at a "dinema" in Colombo for a month. After a performance one evening, they noticed a big crowd assembled outside watching a fight. The British jiu-jitsu champion of the world, Captain Leopold McLaglen, was conducting a demonstration of his martial arts moves. Reg approached McLaglen and told him he'd been a boxer in England and was intrigued with this method of Asian fighting. McLaglen told Reg he was in India teaching martial arts to the British military and showed him a few of his jiu-jitsu moves.

After his demonstration, McLaglen asked Reg if they'd like to team up with him and his female partner for a two-week tour in the Nilgiri Mountains of Southern India. McLaglen guaranteed an excellent financial return and said if Reg paid his own railroad fare and hotel expenses, he'd save their earnings into one big lump sum which would be divided and paid out at the end of the tour. More money sounded good to Reg, so he agreed to the terms.

The foursome left Colombo and went on tour into the Nilgiri Hills. Reg and Rene performed their vaudeville act as an opener to the fight while McLaglen's female partner acted as a human magnet seductively drawing in onlookers. Once the large crowd gathered, McLaglen gave a live jiu-jitsu demonstration and then challenged any five men to wrestle with him. He was a big man and so skilled in his Asian fighting technique that he severely injured many of the volunteers. Reg had a hard time watching McLaglen's brutal fighting methods, but it was earning them a lot of money. They drew huge crowds all over the Nilgiri Mountains and played Octacommund, then Wellington and ended up in Bangalore. The morning after the last show in Bangalore, Reg awoke to find McLaglen and his lady friend had disappeared taking all the tour's earnings. Reg felt a fool for falling for the scheme. Not only was he broke, but he owed a large hotel bill that he needed to pay or else be thrown in jail again.

Their show with Bandmann had previously been given at the United Services Club in Calcutta where Reg met the military secretary to the Maharajah of Mysore, Colonel Jones. Jones had mentioned to Reg that the Maharajah's celebration was to take place at the palace in Mysore and they needed performers for the important event. Reg remembered it would be that week, so he borrowed enough money to buy a ticket and quickly boarded the train to Mysore. Once he arrived at the station there, he learned the Grand Palace was ten miles away and there was no public transportation. Reg started the grueling hike in extreme heat and when he finally arrived at the gates of the palace, he was a deplorable looking figure with clothing that hung limply and a face streaked with dirt. Bravely he strode up the long flight of grand marble steps and asked the guard if he could please meet with Colonel Jones. When Jones saw the disheveled performer, he provided water, fed him, and got him cleaned up. Reg told Jones that he and his wife had a successful vaudeville act and they'd be delighted to accept his previous offer to perform for the Maharajah at his celebration.

Jones accepted Reg's proposal and agreed to pay him in silver bags of three thousand rupees. They sent for Rene and when she arrived at the palace, the couple was housed as special guests of Krishna Raja Wadiyar IV and his wife Maharani Pratapa Kumari Ammani. They entertained the man whom Mahatma Gandhi referred to as the "raja rishi" or saintly king. As part of their song-and-dance act, Reg and Rene introduced the popular British dance the "Gaby Glide" into India. The dance was considered hot stuff and quite shocking at the time, but the raja and his wife loved it and joined in on the fun.

During their stay at the palace, Reg and the High King got to know each other and shared discussion about their common passions for music and nature. The king was an accomplished musician and patronized fine arts. He played eight musical instruments: the flute, violin, saxophone, piano, mridangam, nadaswara, sitar, and veena. He was a philosopher-king and his followers described his rule as "Rama Rajya," an ideal kingdom.

During his reign, Mysore became the first Indian state to generate hydroelectric power in Asia and Bangalore was the first Asian city to have streetlights, first lit on August 5, 1905. Krishna Raja Wadiyar funded and began many schools including the Banaras Hindu University, the University of Mysore, and the Indian Institute of Science at Bangalore. *The Times* called him "a ruling prince second to none in esteem and affection inspired by both his impressive administration and his attractive personality." He was then one of the world's wealthiest men with a personal fortune estimated at $400 million in U.S. dollars, equivalent to $7 billion at today's prices. For these reasons, the raja rishi's reign is often described as the "Golden Age of Mysore."

In addition to housing several elephants at the golden sanctuary, the raja had a zoo of animals. The art of falconry was popular among royalty in India and the king employed raptor birds for pest control around the palace. Reg was again intrigued with the avian art and practiced falconry with the raja rishi. The maharajah saw the fire in Reg's blue eyes. He taught the singer about his religion, Hinduism. Reg had shared that he left the Catholic religion due to the secular rules he had to obey. The raja took the Brit aside and also taught the nervous man mediation with yoga sessions to calm his mind.

After spending years in South Africa, Mahatma Gandhi returned to India and arrived at the Mysore Palace just in time for the King's Celebration. Gandhi warned everyone about the disadvantages of British rule, that war was imminent, and declared that India should be freed of British dominance. Reg told Gandhi that from his personal experience he wholeheartedly agreed. Gandhi shared his words of wisdom with the British actor: "You must be the change you want to see in the world; whatever you do will be insignificant, but it is very important that you do it."

Just as Reg and Rene were getting comfortable with their stay at the palace, Colonel Jones informed them Great Britain had declared war on Germany. Reg decided it was time to leave India to avoid being stranded in a foreign country under British rule in the midst of war. As promised, Colonel Jones kept his word and handed Reg the silver bags as payment for their performances. The maharajah expressed his gratitude to Reg for such wonderful entertainment and shared a few words of kingly wisdom to complement those shared by Gandhi: "In a gentle way, you can shake the world. Keep singing with your smiling eyes to the sky."

Their train stopped in Bangalore where Reg paid his hotel bill. There, he also found the Dallas Comedy Company performing two plays, the farce comedy *Charley's Aunt* and J.M. Barrie's *What Every Woman Knows*. The company had just lost two of its members, so Reg signed himself and his wife up to join the troupe for some extra money. They toured the rest of India making their way north playing a repertoire of about six shows. Just as the tour finished, more rumors of war emerged. Reg thought it was finally time to leave, and from Bombay they sailed with the Dallas Comedy Company back to England.

It was a bad scene back home. Reg and Rene only remained in London for a couple weeks until the hostel in which they were staying got bombed. Reg thought they'd better leave while they could. With silver money in their pockets, the couple left the dangerous European scene and boarded a boat for the week-long journey to the safe-haven of America where theater was flourishing.

3

THE SNIPE

As war rumbled in Europe, Reg was relieved to be back in the States for a new start. He introduced Rene to Mrs. Barnes and the couple stayed at the boarding house where he'd previously lived and where many fellow British actors resided. The couple got straight to work and knocked on theatrical stage doors. The first job Reg landed was as a juvenile leading man with a stock company called The Carey Players, which earned him enough money to pay rent.

Rene and Reg soon teamed together again and secured roles in the new stage production of *Kitty MacKay* (1914) opening at the Shubert Theatre on 44th and Broadway. Rene was given the lead role of Kitty MacKay and used her maiden name for the American stage, while Reg played the supporting role of Lieutenant David Graham. Rene won rave reviews for her performance. *The Harvard Advocate* praised her in saying, "Ms. Irene Haisman is admirably fitted for the role of Kitty. She is evidently a real Scotch lassie and combines sparkle, youth, and beauty with a flexible voice, good stage presence, and considerable acting ability." Reg, on the other hand, didn't receive such a complimentary review. "Mr. Reginald Denny makes a passable hero being as handsome as the conventional college youth of the posters, with a manner almost as easy as that of John Drew. His main fault is an absolute lack of facial expression, a type of 'controlled acting' which can be carried too far." Reg's ego was bruised because his wife had outshone him, and the negative reviews again made him question whether or not he should perform.

Just as the *Kitty MacKay* tour finished, Reg found out two actors who played a married couple in a successful Broadway production had suddenly left and the producer was looking for replacements. Reg and Rene raced to the Harris Theatre where they auditioned for William Harris Jr's production of *Twin Beds* (1914-15) and instantly won the lead roles; Rene replaced Madge Kennedy as Blanch Hawkins and Reg replaced John Westley as Harry Hawkins. The play enjoyed a long run at both the Harris and Fulton Theatres; however, Rene once again received outstanding reviews, while Reg suffered the same "lack of facial expression and controlled acting" feedback. He feared his father was right; he should give up the stage for good.

As the world of motion pictures emerged, Reg decided to take another shot at the flickers. The recently formed Famous Players Film Company was casting supporting leads for a new comedy about a Greek statue that comes to life starring the famous "Pink Lady," Hazel Dawn. After a successful audition for director Hugh Ford, Reg was cast as

Cornelius Griffin to debut in his first official motion picture role with Famous Players' *Niobe*. Rene was cast as Beatrice Sillocks in the same film and they had a great time acting together on set in front of the new Bell and Howell moving picture camera. Distributed by the company's newly formed Paramount Pictures, *Niobe* (1915) premiered in New York on April 4 to excellent reviews.

That summer, Reg got another break when he landed the lead role of Charles Roche in J.M. Barrie's Shakespearean play *Rosalind* (1915) starring opposite famous actress Marie Tempest. During rehearsals, Reg received an urgent telegram from his sister Nora with news that their father had died suddenly from a heart attack and their brother, Gerald, had been killed. Reg was unaware his brother had joined the British Army and had been stationed in Africa where he was seriously injured in combat. While onboard a small naval boat heading to safety, Gerry was thrown overboard when a storm overturned the craft and sharks devoured his body before the military could rescue him. Reg was devastated to hear of his family losses, but he didn't have the time or money to travel to England for either funeral. He stayed in New York, went on with the show, and blocked all emotion for his long-lost family.

On September 2, 1915, *Rosalind* opened at the Lyceum Theatre in Rochester and ran for a month. Immediately after, Reg joined the Mabel Brownell-Clifford Stock Company in Newark and acted in supporting roles throughout the holidays. He was now a familiar face in theatrical circles. He and Rene hosted parties for fellow actors, writers, and musicians in their cozy apartment on 55th Street. They didn't have much money, and their measly savings were often depleted by Reg's bleeding-heart desire to help out struggling artists when they needed a loan. During a New Year's Eve celebration at their apartment, Rene happily announced she was pregnant. The couple was thrilled they were now settling in New York to start a family of their own.

Reg was even more thrilled when he was hired for the role of Captain Joseph Strangford in Edward Knoblauch's *Paganini* (1916) to play opposite George Arliss and Arliss' wife at the Criterion Theatre. It was a great opportunity to perform with one of the Broadway greats. On August 15 during rehearsal with Arliss, Reg was told Rene was in labor. He rushed to the hospital in time to be with his wife and welcome their beloved daughter whom they named Barbara. Having lost four immediate family members, Reg found comfort in having his wife and daughter by his side with their new theatrical family in America. He was determined now more than ever to make a success in life.

Paganini ran for just over a month. When it closed, Reg performed in two one-act plays by George Bernard Shaw at Shubert's Maxine Elliott Theatre in Manhattan. He replaced Leslie Austin as a young British Army officer in *Great Catherine* (1916), and then played a young Egyptian prince in *The Queen's Enemies* (1916) with George Abbott. Next, Reg was cast for the role of Henders in J.M. Barrie's *The Professor's Love Story* (1917) again starring George Arliss at the Knickerbocker Theatre. He was making a name on the boards of Broadway and getting the knack of performing on stage without the "controlled acting."

While appearing in *The Professor's Love Story*, Reg received an offer for a part in *The Cinderella Man* (1917) at the Alcazar Theatre in San Francisco. Richard Bennett, a great favorite at the Alcazar, had declined the role so the producers turned to the new Broadway actor to fill the lead. Rene was against the trip as she now had a baby, but Reg persuaded her to come as it was a good opportunity in California. They packed up bag and baggage, put most of their surplus money into railroad tickets, and started across country. When they finally made it to San Francisco, the theatrical producers regretted to inform Reg that Bennett had changed his mind and joined the production. The stage director apologized that there was no part for Reg and gave the again stranded actor two weeks' pay until they could get him another role.

One week passed and then another. They had no friends in the city and the baby was still very young and helpless so Rene couldn't work. All this moving around unsettled the new mother and she finally hit a breaking point. Rene had followed her husband all around India, England, and now America while giving up her stage career to be a wife and mother. All she wanted was to settle down in a safe, secure home. She was fed up with being homeless and having to move around every couple weeks, especially with a baby to care for. She accused Reg of being an irresponsible provider by not making the proper arrangements when he was offered work. She told him to use his head rather than behave so impulsively and urged him to get a real job so they could afford a home in which to raise their daughter. Reg felt bad, but argued he was doing his best to make a living to support the family. He didn't want his wife and dear Barbara to experience the same heartbreak his mother and he had when he was a youth while his father was on the road as a traveling player.

In addition to having trouble on the homefront, there was trouble in their home country. On April 6, 1917, the United States entered the First World War, joining the Allies in their efforts against the Central Powers. Reg considered joining the war efforts so his brother's death would not have been in vain, but Rene objected and told him to instead get a job. Reg slipped on his boxing gloves and returned to the ring to make some money so they could get back to New York. He was booked for a few boxing matches in Oakland and over the course of two weeks, he won the belt with a sigh of relief he was again able to meet their board bill. Just in time, Reg received a telegram from playwright Edward Peple with an offer to perform a lead role in his upcoming production on Broadway. He jumped at the opportunity and used all the money he earned from boxing to buy train tickets for the family's journey across the country. Upon their return in New York and one day after celebrating Barbara's first birthday, Reg opened with Peple's play as Harry Shirley in *Friend Martha* (1917) at the Booth Theatre on 45th and Broadway. It ran three weeks, then Reg again was out of work.

As WWI was now in full swing, Reg told Rene he felt obligated to fight for their home country and he was going to enlist. Rene thought it would be terrible for him to leave her alone to raise their daughter with the threat of losing his life at war. She fought hard to change her husband's willful mind, but Reg left the apartment and headed to the British Recruiting Mission in New York City. The twenty-five-year-old Englishman enlisted with the British Army Reserve and after saying goodbye to his wife and baby daughter, Reg boarded a train to the Artists Rifles in Halifax, Canada, to learn marksmanship skills with the Army's training corps. He had never handled a gun before, but with a couple of weeks practice he became a skilled marksman. The following month, Reg shipped off to London with the 2nd Artists Rifles for the real thing. There, he used his natural marksmanship and protected the London area, becoming a first-class long-distance sniper while fending off the Germans.

In early spring 1918, Reg was transferred to Throwley, Kent, for air defense duties and exercised his excellent snipe skills while learning to be an observer and aerial gunner with the British Army's Royal Flying Corps. The Royal Flying Corps began as the air arm of the British Army until it merged with the Royal Naval Air Service in 1918 to form the world's first air force, the Royal Air Force (RAF). With his penchant for fighting and prior training with Sir Harry Preston, Reg not only won riflery competitions, but put on his gloves to compete in the military's boxing matches at the base. That May, he won the Royal Air Force's first Brigade Heavyweight Boxing Championship. As he trained to be an aerial gunner at Throwley, Reg began his pilot training course and was promoted to lieutenant while he served in the 112th Squadron of Great Britain's Royal Air Force.

It had been fifteen years since the Wright Brothers took their first flight, and since Reg saw the first "aero planes" fly overhead from Farnborough when he was a schoolboy. Aero planes were just coming into military use and World War I was the first major conflict involving large-scale use of aircraft. Germany had employed Zeppelins for reconnaissance over the North Sea and also for strategic bombing raids over Britain and the Eastern Front. Great Britain had tethered observation balloons that were used extensively for artillery spotting. Pilots and engineers learned from the early flying machines, leading to the development of many specialized aircrafts, including fighters, bombers, and trench strafers. Now, with a major war in force and with the new use of aero planes as fighters, newly designed state-of-the-art aircraft were quickly manufactured in Great Britain.

In 1918, Sopwith Aviation Company designed a new cutting-edge biplane, the Sopwith Snipe. A British single-seater fighter plane, the "Snipe" was considered the ultimate in small rotary-powered fighters of its time and the Allied answer to the wicked Fokker D.VII. It was over nineteen feet long with a wingspan of approximately thirty feet. Its 230 horsepower Bentley rotary engine pushed it to 121 miles per hour with a distance range of about three hours. Armament consisted of two Vickers fixed machine guns. It was the most powerful and advanced of the Sopwith rotary-engine aircraft and it proved to be the most efficient scout of the entire war flown by the British, Canadian, and Australian Air Forces.

The Royal Air Force acquired a series of Sopwith aircraft and recruited pilots to fly them. The RAF grabbed their star pugilist marksman, Lt. Reginald Denny, and trained him to operate their brand-new Sopwith Snipe single-engine piston biplanes. Reg had always fought with his hands; now he'd use weapons in the form of the world's most advanced machinery for battle, amongst the first pilots to fly the cutting-edge fighter plane. He trained as a flight cadet to conduct offensive and defensive missions in an effort to prevent the Germans from invading the Western Front and was then sent to the south coast of Hastings. There he learned to fly the craft on reconnaissance missions over the English Channel using newly developed radio communications, and to maneuver as an aerial gunner while operating the aircraft. He was a natural and quickly caught on to flying the plane in aerial acrobatics up to altitudes of 20,000 feet in the open-air cockpit. Fearless and daring, Reg performed aerial loops and dives that the other pilots were hesitant to do. His commanding officer cautioned him, "Reggie, you're the best gunner in the bunch, but you're going to kill yourself if you continue to fly. Stick to the guns!"

Although risking his life in combat was hardly Reg's favorite pastime, the fighter soared on cloud nine as he mastered the new aerial art of flying. The only effective way to get experience in aerial combat was to practice shooting at live flying targets in mock dogfights. During gunnery practice over the English Channel one evening, Reg and his wingman were testing aerial maneuvers with the other pilots. It was a dark and daring game of chicken until Reg hit his wingman during the friendly fire exercise. Both planes soared to the ground but luckily no harm came to either plane or its pilot as they each made a crash landing. Reg vowed never to endanger the lives of his comrades again. Instead, he flew as a target and dodged them with masterly skill. For practice, he resorted to making drawings of the Snipe with details of its parts and their operation, as well as drawn-out strategic moves. In addition to the drawings, Reg created model planes to mock dogfights rather than risking lives in the real thing.

That October, Reg's squadron was ordered to fly to the northern coast of France as the Germans were making their way to England. While airborne, Reg observed several German Fokker D. VIIs ready to attack a lone Royal Canadian Air Force (RCAF) Snipe. Reg left his squadron and joined the Canadian pilot to help him in battle and counter the attack. He thrust his plane into the action to help the surrounded Snipe and flew in to divert the planes from his ally. Always pushing boundaries, Reg didn't follow the textbook formation and inadvertently diverted some of the Fokkers by flying into them. Reg's Snipe was hit, and he was shot across the stomach. As parachutes weren't allowed for combat fighters during WWI, Reg remained in the plummeting plane and crashed into the English Channel. He made it out of the plane before sinking and swam to safety. A Canadian military rescue boat came to pick him up for transport to the hospital.

The Canadian pilot made it out of the attack alive. Major William George "W.G." Barker was with the No. 201 Squadron of the Royal Canadian Air Force. Although wounded in both legs and one arm, Barker managed to destroy three of his opponents before crash landing. He survived and was awarded the Victoria Cross by King George V. Ace fighter pilots were portrayed as modern knights, but Reg didn't think he deserved any credit. Having failed his mission, he felt ashamed and defeated.

On November 11, 1918, the Armistice was signed marking the end of World War I. Reg had been sent to the RCAF repatriation camp, where he healed from his injuries and awaited orders for release from the RAF. On New Year's Day, a parade was called and the veterans at the camp were told any man with an urgent reason to return to Canada or the USA, and who was willing to sacrifice his first-class passage, could sail the next day on a tropical fruit boat in its final destination to New York. Ordinarily, Reg would not have been given his release until the spring, but his injuries, and his wife and daughter were considered sufficient reasons. Reg agreed to give up his first-class ticket on a passenger ship for travel on a freight vessel back home.

The next day, Reg boarded the United Fruit Company's "Toloa" and began the week-long journey across the Atlantic. The ship was packed to the brim with troops and Reg wondered if he had made the right decision. He was still healing from his injuries and the steamer was overcrowded and filthy. When they encountered a storm halfway across the ocean, the vessel was tousled about on thirty-foot waves and the trip became unbearable. It was like an ancient Viking ship packed with warriors who had just finished a gruesome battle and were still filled with adrenaline. Many of the men were injured and the journey itself was like being at war. Upon arrival at the port of Halifax, a mutiny broke out when the commanding officer tried to force the fatigued war vets to clean up the inhospitable ship before docking. Most of the troops had disembarked and only two or three hundred would continue on to New York. Reg was one of three remaining commissioned officers on board and it was impossible for him to regain any form of discipline. He made his escape and jumped overboard with the rest of the troops, swam onto a small pilot boat, then found his way to the transportation office in Halifax where he was provided rail transportation to New York.

4 WAR VET ON BROADWAY

GONE NEARLY TWO YEARS, the injured war vet couldn't wait to get back to the comfort of his family. When he finally arrived at Grand Central Terminal in New York, Reg tracked down Rene at Henry Miller's Theatre on Broadway. She had secured the lead role as Delphine Falaise in *Mis' Nelly of N'Orleans* (1919) and was getting ready to go on stage. Reg surprised his wife as he entered her dressing room, holding a bouquet of flowers and singing "Over There." He rushed to embrace her, but Rene pushed him away. She was enraged by her husband's audacity to show up when she was about to perform, after being gone for two years with no contact whatsoever. She had a hell of a time surviving as a single mother of a baby with no support from her husband and had been forced to double up on her stage work. Rene insisted Reg leave at once, so he meandered out of her dressing room and went to the apartment to reunite with his three-year-old Barbara, who didn't even recognize him.

When Rene returned to the apartment that night, Reg explained the difficulties he'd had at war, but she was in a highly nervous state and didn't empathize. She told him she couldn't handle his indifferent, impulsive, and irresponsible nature any longer. Reg tried to reason with her, but Rene said she was going to the courthouse in the morning to file for divorce. Instead of putting her estranged war vet husband on the streets, she said she'd allow him to stay at her apartment until he got a job.

A couple days later, Reg was offered a small role in *The Dangerous Age* (1919) at the Blackstone Theatre in Chicago. He hit the tracks to the Windy City and jumped into rehearsal there. During the second week, and on the eve of the play's premiere, Barbara's nurse Annie called Reg. She frantically told him that Rene had a complete nervous breakdown and was taken away by ambulance to a mental hospital. Annie said she took Barbara to live on a farm with some friends until her parents could get their act together. Reg felt bad he had abandoned his wife and daughter when they needed him most. For the first time, he realized how his mother became ill and he felt ashamed for repeating the selfish behavior of his father. Reg got an advance on his salary, returned to New York, and moved Rene to a sanitarium in Astoria to recover. He then returned to Chicago to finish work on the play and made just enough money to pay his hotel bill with train fare back to New York City.

Reg strode toward Broadway with desperate eyes. In just two years, landmarks had changed, people had changed, and most of all, he had changed. Here was the once familiar street, along which he hunted for work, and in which old friends now gazed with unfriendly eyes upon a former soldier. The manager who had said, "There'll be a job waiting, boy," had long since lost his patriotism. "When you come back," one producer had promised, "the finest part in this office is yours." Reg soon realized out of sight was indeed out of mind when that Broadway producer and many others slammed the door in his forgotten face. To fight for his native land, Reg had gaily tossed away his family and a stage career.

For weeks, he roamed the streets of New York with no food, home or shelter in which to take refuge from the rain or other cruel elements. He came face to face with despair, so much so there seemed to be little left worth living. He wanted to end his life. Reg went to make one last visit with Rene at the mental institution in Astoria before he'd perform his final act. She was at the end of her rope as well and demanded Reg snap out of his self-pity. She suggested he contact producer Morris Gest, whom they had met just before Reg went off to war. With nothing to lose, Reg strolled into Gest's office only to have the door shut in his face. Well, that was that. As he headed out of the building, Gest's secretary chased Reg down and gave him a letter. The Russian-Jewish producer had heard of the war vet's difficulties and felt for him. Wishing to spare him humiliation, Gest had enclosed a substantial check with a note of encouragement. He wrote that he'd arranged for Reg to meet with his good friend, fellow Russian-Jewish immigrant turned producer and Broadway theater conglomerate magnate, Lee Shubert.

Shubert called Reg in and signed the WWI vet to a two-year contract for a role in *The Passing Show of 1919* musical revue. The title was ironic, for as soon as rehearsals began, the Actors' Equity Strike was called which forced all actors to pass on any stage work. Being one of the Equity's first members, Reg went to Shubert to tell him he had been ordered to strike, yet, due to his obligations to the producer, he would sacrifice his self-respect and continue rehearsals.

"You will go on strike," Shubert said, "and forget the obligations for the present."

Knowing of his financial difficulties, Shubert loaned Reg money to live on until the strike was over and advanced him eight weeks' salary. Now the stage actor could focus on establishing a home rather than killing himself. With hope, a secure contract, and some money in his pocket, Reg was able to obtain a small apartment where he brought Barbara and released Rene out of the sanitarium to join her family. Reg vowed to Rene that he'd never leave them again, that she would never have to work again, and that she could focus on being a mother to their wonderful daughter. He was truly committed to the welfare of his family.

Reg decided to take another shot at flickers and began the dismal rounds of door knocking at the new film studios in Fort Lee, New Jersey. Needing a handsome leading man for his wife Norma Talmadge, director Joseph Schenck auditioned actors for a movie he was prepping. Schenck had seen Reg on the Broadway boards before the war and had his producer, John Emerson, call him in for his first screen test. Three days later, once the film was developed, Schenck sent for Reg and lost no time breaking the bad news.

"My boy, you had better know it now than later. You'll never do for pictures, never," claimed Schenck. "You don't screen well at all. You have a bad mouth—"

"What's the matter with my mouth?" Reg interrupted.

"Why, it's crooked!" said Schenck, "And you have a bad walk."

"What's the matter with it?" Reg asked, a trifle less belligerently.

"It's more of a waddle than a walk," said Schenck, "and on the screen your whole personality is lost. You're altogether all 'blah!'" Schenck shook his head. "Denny, stick to the stage."

Reg's crooked grin turned down to a frown. He left the film producer's office disheartened, discouraged, and despondent. When he returned home to break the bad news, Rene claimed she had recovered and wanted to perform again. Reg objected and refused to allow her to return to work. The struggle was wearing, and Rene was again fed up. She threatened to take Barbara and leave the man who had stolen her heart, her career, and her dignity.

The next day, Reg's agent sent for him and instructed him to go over to the World Film offices where Thomas Edison's pioneer of cinema, Oscar Apfel, was casting a picture. Much discouraged, Reg meandered over to the World Film Studios at Fort Lee, New Jersey, to audition for the part. When Apfel called the actor into his office to tell him he got the role, Reg warned his prospective employer of what Schenck had told him.

"But I must tell you," he said weakly, "that I screen very badly. I have a crooked mouth, and I waddle, and my whole personality is lost."

"How much salary do you want?" asked Apfel.

"Anything you'll give me," Reg responded.

"That's more important. We haven't much money to spend. You're cheap and I'll take the risk." Apfel grinned at Reg. "You're hired."

Apfel cast Reg for the role of Tom Waring in the dramatic comedy *Bringing Up Betty* (1919) opposite prominent film star Evelyn Greeley. Reg had the opportunity to use his athletic boating and swimming skills learned from Sir Harry Preston when his character entered a yacht race and jumped into the ocean to rescue a drowning damsel in distress. He earned $250 per week, which was half the usual price for leads. This under-cutting scored him the job; leading men were scarce and expensive at the time due to the stage strike. Reg co-starred again with Evelyn Greeley in Apfel's next film, *The Oakdale Affair* (1919). In the adventure drama, Reg played an author posing as a vagabond who gets caught up in a crime of mistaken identity but ultimately wins the girl. Both films were made in Fort Lee where most of the major motion picture companies had set up their original East Coast film studios.

On September 6, members of the Actors' Equity finally came to terms and the stage strike ended. Reg finished work on the Apfel films and gratefully returned to sing before a live audience with the famous Shuberts in order to fulfill his contract. Production of the *Passing Show of 1919* resumed, and Reg played Prince William with the large star-studded musical at Shuberts' Winter Garden Theatre on Broadway. As part of the show, a boxing match was arranged in the gymnasium of the nearby Friars Club. Reg used his fighting skills and traded punches in the ring with fellow *Passing Show* actor Eddie Miller. It was a good fight that earned Reg another belt when he won the championship, this time for the stage.

Reg played in the *Passing Show of 1919* until February when Shubert loaned him out to Arthur Hopkins to perform in Shakespeare's *Richard III* (1920). He was cast in the role of King Edward the Fourth with popular American stage actor John Barrymore who played the villainous lead of Richard. Reg admired Barrymore's extraordinary talent in his first Shakespearean effort and the two became fast friends; however, Barrymore frequently showed up to rehearsals drunk. He raged and belligerently yelled at other actors when they mouthed their lines or took too much time rehearsing. Reg frequently stepped in to calm down the brilliant yet inebriated actor.

On March 6, 1920, the play opened to a full house at the Plymouth Theatre on Broadway. In one of the scenes, actress Tracy Barrow was supposed to threaten to choke the queen. She dragged out her lines in such a way that got Barrymore wild, but it added to his performance and the critics were astounded with the actor's authentic display. The second week, Barrymore became so enraged he grabbed the actress by the neck and strangled her. Reg rushed on stage and forcefully removed Barrymore's hands off the actress's throat for fear he'd choke her to death. The audience thought it was part of the act and gave a standing ovation when the stage stars gallantly took their bows. The next week didn't go so well. During the second act, Barrymore had a complete meltdown on stage, which was not part of his scene, in front of the packed theater. Reg picked up his friend, hurled him over his shoulders, and carried him offstage. Another show was shut down.

Just before his stage breakdown, Barrymore had starred in *Dr. Jekyll and Mr. Hyde* (1920) which was expertly directed by John S. Robertson. Barrymore felt guilty that Reg was now out of work and he arranged for his good friend to meet with his director who was looking for a prince. Reg met with Robertson and after a successful screen test, he was offered the role of Prince Anton in Realart Pictures' WWI drama *A Dark Lantern* (1920) starring opposite screen star Alice Brady and her husband James Crane. Reg almost declined the role as the film was to shoot at Essanay Studios in Chicago and he felt obligated to Lee Shubert; however, once the empathetic producer learned of the actor's film offer, he released him from his Broadway stage contract. After spending two months working at Essanay in Chicago, Reg returned to New York where John Robertson cast him in another Realart Pictures film he was directing, *39 East* (1920). The comedy was based on the Broadway hit starring Constance Binney, who also starred in the film opposite Reg as Napoleon Gibbs Jr.

Due to the success of the Realart films, Reg was contracted by the Famous Players Lasky Company for a few films in succession. He played the role of Keith Larne in the society drama *Paying the Piper* (1921) with Dorothy Dickson and Rod La Rocque, and as "Conscience" in *Experience* (1921) both directed by French-born George Fitzmaurice. Next, Reg played Robert Dawnay with Ethel Clayton and Rockcliffe Fellowes in the romantic drama *The Price of Possession* (1921) directed by Hugh Ford. Reg then returned to work with director John Robertson and took the lead role of Brett Page opposite Elsie Ferguson in Paramount Pictures' *Footlights* (1921). Next, Reg appeared as Charles, Viscount Deeford with his stage co-star George Arliss and wife Florence in the Henry Kolker-directed biographical drama *Disraeli* (1921), then as Dan Appleton in an Alaskan railroad adventure thriller *The Iron Trail* (1921) directed by Roy William Neill which also featured his old neighbor Eulalie Jensen. The plot detailed the competing efforts to build railways into interior Alaska in the early part of the 20th century and the crew went on location to the mountainous region. Reg was getting the knack of acting in front of the camera and making a name for himself on the big screen. Meanwhile, the Apfel and Robertson films had been released with Reg's face becoming familiar to moviegoers across the nation.

As if he wasn't busy enough acting on set, Reg decided to try his hand at writing. He adapted a story from Guy McConnell's *Peaks of Gold* which he called *Tropical Love* (1921). Reg pitched the story to highly successful director Ralph Ince and managed to convince him to direct the film. Ince procured funding from a Puerto Rican company and took the production to the tropical island for filming. Reg played the role of Scen "The Drifter" and Ince hired well-known silent film actress Ruth Clifford for the role of Rosario. When they returned from Puerto Rico and the film was released, it garnered fabulous reviews. The *Oakland Tribune* claimed, "*Tropical Love* is a light comedy romance in which Denny excels." The *Palladium* said, "Ruth Clifford's personality enhances the role of Rosario, the white-skinned girl whose instinct told her she did not belong to the brown woman who called her daughter. A likable hero is Reginald Denny, whose acting is fresh and natural." Reg was pleased with the response and became more confident with his work in film.

Reg appreciated fine art. He had an idea for a new series of stories based around paintings by famous artists which he pitched to Triart Pictures' producer Isaac Wolper. Wolper liked Reg's idea and put up the money to get the films made. Reg wrote the first of the series, *The Beggar Maid* (1921), about the creation of Edward Burne-Jones' painting of the same name. In it, the artist shows that love can thrive between members of different classes by depicting on canvas a picture from Tennyson's poem about the love of King Cophetua for a beggar maid. Herbert Blaché directed the short and cast fifteen-year-old Mary Astor to play the role of Beggar Maid opposite Reg as King Cophetua. Wolper hired a cameraman by the name of Legaren à Hiller, a commercial photographer who specialized in magazine illustration. He was terrific and way ahead of his time which added to the artistic photography of the film Reg had envisioned. Upon completion of *The Beggar Maid*, the short was theatrically distributed by William Wadsworth Hodkinson's company. In 1914, Hodkinson had founded the first U.S. film distributor which merged with Famous Players Lasky Company and named it Paramount Pictures. In 1918, he left Paramount and formed his own distribution company, W.W. Hodkinson.

Reg then wrote his second artist story, *The Angelus* (1921), which was based on the painting by French artist Jean-François Millet. He again starred in the short directed by Herbert Blaché with Mary Astor as female lead and Legaren à Hiller as cinematographer. During production, Hodkinson offered Wolper a contract whereby they would fund the series and make the rest out of Paramount's Famous Players studio in Astoria. When Wolper shared Hodkinson's offer, Reg advised the producer not to accept it.

"You can't have Hiller," Reg told Wolper. "They'll use their own cameraman, and Hiller's your best bet. Stay independent and use the Famous Players release."

Wolper instead sold the series and Reg quit when they wanted to hire another writer to do their own version of the painting stories. As Reg predicted, the studio used another cinematographer and made a small print order. After only a couple more shorts, they shut down production and that was the end of the contract. Shortly after, Reg heard that Isaac Wolper committed suicide.

Prior to taking his life, Wolper had given Reg the magazine *Collier's Weekly* in which sportswriter H.C. Witwer featured boxing stories loosely based on some of his fights he called *The Leather Pushers*. Reg called Witwer and told him he wanted to create a film series based on the pugilist stories and asked for the rights. Witwer agreed but with a percent interest in the films and screen credit. Reg's *Tropical Love* co-star, Ruth Clifford, introduced him to actor-turned-director Harry Pollard. Pollard had megaphoned Clifford in the science-fiction serial *The Invisible Ray* (1920). Reg told Pollard he had obtained his crooked mouth while boxing and shared his idea to make films out of Witwer's stories. He said he'd get the money together if Pollard agreed to make the films with him. Pollard saw the potential and Reg borrowed enough money for the actor and director to make the shorts.

Reg zealously put on his boxing gloves and created the vivid hero part of Kane "Kid Roberts" Halliday in a series of two-reel boxing pictures directed by Pollard. They made the first two, *Round One: Through the Looking Glass* aka *Let's Go* (1921) and *Round Two: With This Ring I Thee Fed!* (1921), which also featured Hayden Stevenson as Kid Roberts' manager. Reg and Pollard soon exhausted their financial resources and couldn't round up additional funds, so they had to halt production after finishing the second episode. They peddled the cans of film around New York hopeful to find a buyer, but all the film agents turned them down on the grounds that no distributor would buy them. Their consensus was that nobody would come to see such a vulgar picture. "Prize fighting? Who would go look at it? Nobody wants prize-fight stories these days."

Broke again and in a last-ditch effort to sell his films, Reg dropped the cans off at the Universal Film Company on his way to an audition for Powers Studio at Fort Lee. In 1910, producer Pat Powers opened Powers Motion Picture Company; two years later he merged with Carl Laemmle's Independent Moving Pictures Company (IMP) and others to form Universal Film Manufacturing Company. As a result of the merger, Powers had served as treasurer of Universal Film Manufacturing Company until he and Laemmle had a battle. Powers left and branched off to form his own studio, which he briefly named Powers Studio. Powers liked Reg and cast him on the spot for a small part in a series of shorts he was producing for the Film Booking Office of America (FBO).

Late one evening the following week, Universal's James Bryson finally got around to looking at the cans of film Reg had left there. After viewing the first reel, Bryson phoned up Carl Laemmle and urged his boss to view the two shorts. The Universal film magnate called out to one of his subordinates. "There's a can of film here that's been peddled all over the town. Let's have a look and find out whether or not it's junk."

After viewing the boxing shorts with his team, the excited studio head began a course of frantic telephoning. "Where is this feller Denny?" he demanded. "Find him, somebody. We gotta have him!"

The next morning, Bryson battered on Reg's door. Reg went to Fort Lee and met with the interesting old producer who was intrigued by the crooked smile he flashed on him. Reg told Laemmle he had already signed with Pat Powers. Laemmle immediately called Powers to advise him that he was putting the boxer to work at Universal. Powers was a sport and let Reg out of his deal, then Laemmle gave Reg and Pollard a deal—eleven thousand five hundred dollars for the negative and one working print for distribution of the series.

Now that they had funding, Reg and Pollard resumed filming the third *Leather Push-ers* episode, *Round Three: Payment Through the Nose* (1922), at Universal's Fort Lee studio. A huge ticker-tape parade was planned in New York City and Universal wanted to use this opportunity to promote the series. While filming the fourth episode, *Round Four: A Fool and His Honey* (1922), Reg helped crew members construct a float in the form of a boxing ring for the parade. Fans cheered when the masked pugilist appeared standing in the middle of the large float pulled by a Cadillac with confetti flying all around. A camera followed the excitement of the curious crowd as Reg proudly flashed his crooked smile and waved his leather gloves like a caped crusader passing onlookers along Broadway. The publicity stunt was a huge success and the series became a nationwide hit.

Pollard and Reg made two more episodes, *Round Five: The Taming of the Shrewd* (1922) with newcomer Norma Shearer as Rose Del Mar, and *Round Six: Whipsawed!* (1922) at Fort Lee; however, they'd forgotten about their lenders who financed the first two episodes and Witwer who they hadn't paid back. Trouble was, they didn't get it in the contract for Universal to assume their loans. Laemmle called Reg and Pollard in and told them the financial issue had to be rectified before his company funded any further episodes of *The Leather Pushers*. In order to clean up their legal problems and continue production of the series, Laemmle shut down Reg's and Pollard's credit and, as a liability measure, forced them into bankruptcy while his company paid off their debtors to take ownership of the series. For payment to the author, Laemmle made a deal with Witwer to publish a book titled *The Leather Pushers* with use of Universal's prints in the book.

While Reg was on a hiatus of sorts, John Barrymore called and asked if he'd be in-terested to work with him on Samuel Goldwyn's production of *Sherlock Holmes* (1922) in which he was starring. Reg took the job and played the role of Prince Alexis in their first film together, which would also be the screen debuts of actors William Powell and Roland Young. After filming in New York, the production would move to London for authentic exterior shots. Carl Laemmle didn't want to lose his new boxing star, so he asked Reg if he'd consider working at Universal City Studios in Los Angeles while they worked out the legal angle of his *Leather Pushers* deal. Reg gratefully accepted Laemmle's offer and wrapped up his work on *Sherlock Holmes*. He packed up his traumatized wife with their five-year-old daughter and boarded the train headed west for a new start in Hollywood.

5 THE RECKLESS AGE

THIS WAS THE DENNY FAMILY'S first trip to Southern California. They were in awe of Tinseltown with its surrounding mountains, towering tropical palm trees, and glorious sunshine. Carl Laemmle treated the family and put them up in a beautiful poolside bungalow at the Beverly Hills Hotel until they found appropriate housing. Reg looked up to the sky and thanked his lucky stars as he stepped foot upon the streets of Universal City Studios and waddled over to Carl Laemmle's office.

Laemmle wanted to try out his newest discovery while the terms of the *Leather Pushers* deal were still being worked, so he cast Reg in a new series about the Northwest Mounted Police directed by his nephew, Nat Ross. Reg got the lead role of Corporal Haldene in the first of the series titled *Never Let Go* (1922); however, he meekly advised the director that he'd never ridden a horse before. Ross asked cowboy actor Hoot Gibson to give the boxer some riding lessons. The two actors got to know each other on Universal's back lot where they galloped together on the equestrian trails in the Hollywood Hills for their getaway until Reg got the hang of riding horseback for his role. He did fine in the first episode but while trying to bulldog a criminal during the second, *Jaws of Steel* (1922), Reg's steed sharply turned one way and he went another. His hard fall resulted in a broken ankle, so Laemmle decided he'd better keep his boxing star in better shape to continue on with his pugilist series. "Uncle Carl" then put Reg to work in a less stunt-driven role with *The Kentucky Derby* (1922) directed by King Baggot. Reg played Donald Gordon, the son of a wealthy racehorse owner, framed for theft. He ends up saving his father's horse from a conspiracy, clears his name and wins the girl in the end. Reg was delighted to work alongside fellow pros Lillian Rich, Walter McGrail, and Gertrude Astor in the film that ended up breaking house records in major theaters on both coasts.

When the contractual terms of his *Leather Pushers* series were finally agreed upon, the studio signed Reg as a player with a five-year exclusive term deal under the Universal Pictures Jewel umbrella. Laemmle had devised a three-tiered film brand system: "Red Feather" films were their low-budgets, "Bluebird" the mainstream releases, and "Jewels" the studio's prestige releases. Jewels were advertised as special engagements with higher theatrical ticket pricing, and Laemmle felt his new star had that draw. The company resumed filming its *Leather Pushers* Jewel series on the Universal City Studios lot beginning with *Round Seven: Young King Cole* (1922). Screenplays were written by a very young Darryl Zanuck with most of the series directed by Harry Pollard. Reg's athletic boxing skills were featured in eleven more episodes: *He Raised Kane* (1922), *The Chickasha Bone Crusher* (1923), *When Kane Met Abel* (1923), *Strike Father, Strike Son!* (1923), *Joan of Newark* (1923), *The Wandering Two* (1923), *The Widower's Mite* (1923), *Don Coyote* (1923), *Something for Nothing* (1923), *Columbia, the Gem, and the Ocean* (1923), and finally *Barnaby's Grudge* (1923).

The training with Harry Preston had paid off and Reg was a natural as the lead of Kid Roberts in the boxing series serial. He played the prizefighter role with such conviction that he took pride in never using a double nor did he wear a mouthpiece while boxing with some of the best pros in the ring. He conducted all of his own stunts and subsequently lost his front teeth while performing many a fight scene, and once was knocked out cold. That didn't stop him and the sequence of the eighteen action-packed episodes which starred the charismatic, handsome fighter was the launch of Reg's journey from stage to stardom on the big screen. He was in the money now and thankfully could afford false teeth to show off his happy, crooked grin. The audiences loved him and so was born the new film star who made boxing films popular.

It was time for the family to get settled in Los Angeles within close proximity to Universal Studios. Carl Laemmle had introduced Reg to real estate developer and owner of the *Los Angeles Times* Harry Chandler. Chandler took Reg up to a homesite in the Hollywood Hills where he was just about to erect the infamous "Hollywoodland" sign to advertise a new development on the land he owned there. Reg loved the views and when he expressed interest in purchasing one of the homes, Chandler disclosed that the community was to be segregated as a "whites-only" residential housing development. Reg didn't understand or appreciate a community with such discriminatory rules, so he declined on Hollywoodland and instead bought a comfortable home just down the hill near Lake Hollywood. The family moved into their first home and Rene was happy that she could finally settle to make a nest for Barbara who was now age seven and attending school. The couple loved to entertain at their new two-story home and would frequently cook the curry dishes they'd learned from their time spent in India. Uncle Carl also assigned a large bungalow on the lot for his new star at Universal City Studios. Rene took great joy in decorating her husband's Spanish-style cottage as the family's home-away-from-home.

The studio then optioned one of Jack London's books as a starring vehicle for their charismatic pugilist with *The Abysmal Brute* (1923). Reg returned to the ring as Pat Glendon, Jr., aka "The Abysmal Brute," and was happy to be playing another hard-fisted he-man role starring alongside beautiful Mabel Julienne Scott under the able direction of Hobart Henley. Rene wanted to play the female lead, but Reg felt it would conflict with his now public persona and instead Henley cast her in a smaller role as Gwendolyn.

As the Brute, Reg played a backwoods prizefighter whose romance with a society girl undergoes a hiccup when she learns of his true vocation. This boy, whose father was also a fighter, had never been anywhere except rural lunch counters and had no sense of etiquette. During a dinner scene at his wealthy fiancée's family home, Reg started to clown the Brute's attempt to ape good table manners. Henley thought Reg was kidding and demanded that he stop.

"You can't do that in a serious film!" exclaimed the director.

"Why not, for God's sake?" asked Reg. "Let's put some comedy in here. It's true to nature, and it'll get some laughs."

After a ten-minute argument on set, Reg persuaded Henley to leave the scene in and they got some light comedy into the action which put the punch in what would have seemed a serious situation. It worked as the audiences absolutely loved it. The Temple Theatre in Toledo, Ohio, reported, "Tremendous business! Crowds immensely pleased!" The critics raved about how Reg was able to bring comedy into a dramatic situation and made it believable without being silly. *The Abysmal Brute* was the first ever pugilist comedy which paved the way for the future of this popular genre as the emergence of "situation comedies."

Universal executives were now convinced they had a money-making star. After the film was released, a beauty cream company placed an ad in a popular movie magazine claiming that Reg used their product as a beautifying face pack to keep up his glowing healthy young skin. His co-stars joked about it and teased him to the point that he sued the cosmetic company for $75,000 on the grounds of false advertising claiming that, as a matter of fact, he only used the old-fashioned beefsteak to preserve what beauty he had.

Universal staff writers Harvey Thew and Byron Morgan drummed up Reg's next action-packed comedy, this time about auto racing. In *Sporting Youth* (1924), Reg played down-and-out chauffeur driver Jimmy Wood who is mistaken for famous racing driver "Splinters" Wood. He takes on Splinters' identity and enters a big race to win the prize money and also the love of a wealthy auto maker's daughter. In preparation for his new role, Reg needed to learn how to drive a racecar. Universal hired professional Indy racecar driver and stuntman Bon MacDougall to teach Reg how to safely speed around the track. For the auto-racing Denny film, Laemmle assigned Reg's *Leather Pushers* partner, Harry Pollard, to megaphone. Pollard wanted his wife, actress Margarita Fischer, to play the female lead of Betty Rockford but Reg didn't think she was suitable for the role. He argued that WAMPAS Baby Star Laura La Plante would be a much better choice. The WAMPAS Baby Stars was a promotional campaign sponsored by the Western Association of Motion Picture Advertisers (WAMPAS) which honored thirteen young actresses each year whom they believed to be on the threshold of movie stardom. Reg made enough of a fuss about his leading lady choice that Laemmle gave him his way and, against their director's wishes, Miss La Plante was cast in the role of Betty Rockford opposite Reg.

In order to get a free crowd of extras, the crew went on location to a race track in the Pebble Beach community of Del Monte during racing season. The night after they got there it really poured and there were two inches of water on the track splattering mud everywhere. After sliding around the muddy curves, Reg went to work on the track with the pros. He again performed all his own stunts and had so much fun racing with MacDougall on the dirt track that he bought the Stutz Torpedo Speedster which he drove in the action-packed comedy. Laura La Plante had so much fun working with Reg that she commented while on location to *Picture Play* magazine about the jokester, "Reggie is such a fine actor that he can burlesque a scene, saying funny words, without losing any of the dramatic effect. I mean, he can act the fool and still make his face behave dramatic, which I can't. In the scene where he was supposed to walk the plank to eternal oblivion, he assumed a tense pose, raised his hands to heaven and as he dived, called back, 'I have but one life to give for Universal Picture Company!' 'Corporation,' corrected Eddie Stein, who is very careful about such matters, being our business boss, and it almost broke up my scene."

When the company returned to Los Angeles, Reg came home to find a brand-new Rolls Royce parked in front of his house. A salesman got out of the luxury car and handed Reg the keys urging him to try it out and keep it for a week. Reg told him he didn't need another car, but the car salesman insisted. "Once your friends see you in that car, a big star like you hasn't got the nerve not to buy it." Reg kept the keys and that weekend he took the car for a spin with fellow actors Ben Hendricks, Jr. and Jack Goodrich. They went to the Los Angeles Harbor of San Pedro and chartered a boat for a day of deep-sea fishing. On the way back home, Reg showed off his new racing skills and rolled the Rolls twice while speeding around the curves of Sunset Boulevard. He and his passengers were rushed via ambulance to the Hollywood Community Hospital with minor injuries. Reg was released the next day and given a reckless driver speeding ticket. The newspapers reported his accident which ended up being an ironic way of publicizing his racy film. Reg subsequently returned the wrecked car to the overly confident auto dealer saying he'd pass on the purchase.

Upon its nationwide release, *Sporting Youth* became another hit for Reg, and it made a new star out of Laura La Plante. Critics unanimously declared the film along the lines of the Wallace Reid auto-racing comedies. Reid was one of Hollywood's major heart-throbs and also a professional racecar driver; he had just died at the young age of thirty-one while undergoing treatment for morphine addiction which he had been using to kill the pain caused by injuries he had sustained in a train wreck. *Photoplay* praised Reg in his performance and compared him with the racing hero. "When Wallace Reid died it seemed that no one could ever fill the place he had left vacant. The screen missed him and missed him badly. Today, it has not forgotten Wally, but it has found in Reginald Denny his worthy successor."

Founding a new reputation as an action hero and leading romantic farceur, Reg was now officially a movie star. The studio got busy drumming up more projects for the "Celluloid Adonis" as the fan magazines now referred to him. Reg's career as a comedian was launched with the release of *Abysmal Brute* and *Sporting Youth*, so Universal decided to capitalize on his newfound talent as farceur yet still exploit his athletic range as a sportsman. They optioned the novel *Love Insurance* by Earl Derr Biggers and adapted it as a film for Reg's next starring vehicle. Laemmle changed the title to *The Reckless Age* (1924) and again assigned Harry Pollard to direct the dramatic comedy.

In *The Reckless Age*, Reg played the role of Dick Minot who's an insurance agent hired by a man to take out a life insurance policy on his wealthy bride. Through a series of comic situations, he challenges the crooked man who hired him and wins the girl in the end. Most of the tame scenes were shot at the Beverly Hills Hotel, but Reg pulled off another speeding car stunt on location just north of Santa Barbara in the small town of Los Olivos. In the scene, he and leading lady Ruth Dwyer were escaping criminals when he raced his car over train tracks just as a locomotive was approaching. They missed each other by a hair and the crew gasped thinking they had lost another Wally Reid. Once the film was released, theatrical exhibitors were filled with enthusiasm. The National Theatre in Stockton, California, reported of *The Reckless Age*, "Finest entertainment we have had in our house this year." The Rialto Theatre in Houston, Texas, claimed, "Crowds filled the lobby and sidewalk awaiting admission."

Universal didn't want their new star to lose his life or get a bad rap, so they took out a $500,000 accidental insurance policy on him and came up with a campaign to counter what the papers were reporting of "Reckless Reg." They drummed up the idea of a "Keep Fit" campaign as example of their athletic star's health and conscious choices. Reg went public in stressing the importance of sensible driving, physical fitness, and a careful diet. He visited the local schools and spoke as a mentor to the kids teaching them to make conscious healthy choices in order to avoid accidents. Reg stressed to the kids, "Health is absolutely essential. Not the kind that means 'I feel fairly well today,' but I mean that bounding, buoyant health that means steady nerves, keen interest and real personality because health, to a large extent, is personality. The time to prepare yourself is when you are young. Build for yourself a foundation, so that as you grow older year by year your physical constitution will never prove a handicap." The athletic actor also demonstrated yogic breathing exercises and movements which the Maharajah had taught him during his stay in India. "You also realize the important part that proper breathing plays in the maintenance of good health. The development of the lungs through breathing exercises is one of the most important factors in athletic training and calm thinking."

Audiences of all ages loved seeing Reg as their hero and the press again went wild with praise. Theaters nationwide exclaimed that *The Reckless Age* was the finest entertainment they had in their houses that year. They loved that in addition to wearing boxing gloves and driving fast cars, Reg always came to the rescue when there was some damsel in distress. He was the perfect crusader cast opposite the silent era's beautiful leading ladies in his action-packed romantic comedies. When asked by the press what kind of parts he liked best to play, Reg responded, "Oh, the kind I am most successful in. Where there is speed and life. The sort of dashing gentleman hero; scenes in a motor, a fast launch, an aero plane, anything with a thrill in it. Yes, I like rescuing pretty girls from the clutches of the villain."

Reg had the chance to show his heroism in his next farcical action comedy, this time in a yacht on the water, in George Barr McCutcheon's *The Fast Worker* (1924) directed by William A. Seiter. Bill Seiter was already an established director who had just finished work on Baby Peggy and Clara Bow pictures. It was the first time that Reg had the opportunity to work with Seiter and the second time he'd work with his *Sporting Youth* co-star Laura La Plante. In *The Fast Worker*, Reg played an architect, Terry Brock, whose friend persuades him to assume his identity by going to Catalina on a vacation with his wife and daughter. Brock falls in love with his friend's sister-in-law, played by La Plante, and when a scandal arises at the resort, a police force, a truck, and a yacht are needed to rescue the architect from the case of mistaken identity. Waves of praise rolled in for Reg's newest farce. The *Detroit Times* claimed *The Fast Worker*, "Different! A laugh a minute!"

Reg welcomed the opportunity to work with Seiter and they had a great rapport. While filming the yacht scenes on location in the Catalina harbor, Reg met William Wrigley Jr. who had just bought the island which he was making into a resort destination. Wrigley took Seiter and Reg out on his yacht for a tour around the island and the actor was hooked. He bought a 50-foot cabin cruiser that was for sale in the harbor and named it the "SS Barbarene" after his beloved daughter and wife. Reg kept the yacht at the Newport Beach Yacht Club and took the family sailing weekends to Catalina where they joined Wrigley's nautical club there as well.

Reg brought in the new year with another racy farce based on Harry Leon Wilson's book of the same name, *Oh, Doctor!* (1925), directed by Harry Pollard. He starred in the role of Rufus Billings, Jr., with his *Beggar Maid* co-star Mary Astor and character actor Otis Harlan in the hilarious comedy. Astor had also relocated to Hollywood where she was making a name for herself by starring with John Barrymore in *Beau Brummel* (1924). In *Oh, Doctor!*, Rufus is a frail hypochondriac who thinks he's going to die soon, so he signs his large inheritance over to some conniving opportunists. When they hire a beautiful nurse, played by Astor, to care for him and who stresses that she prefers strong courageous men, Rufus decides to face his fears and turns from a medicine-soaked weakling into a daredevil. He jumps out of bed and drives a Stutz Torpedo Speedster in an auto race, rides a motorcycle and sprains his knee, almost loses his life trying to paint a flagpole on top of a Los Angeles skyscraper, and lives through it all to expose the criminals and win the girl in the end. Reg once again conducted his own dangerous stunts with racing scenes filmed on location at the newly opened Legion Ascot Speedway in Los Angeles. He got a thrill driving his new racecar on the dirt oval track called the "killer track" because of its treacherous straightaways and dangerously banked turns which would claim the lives of twenty-four drivers during its lifetime. During a scene, Reg pushed his luck to the limit and flipped his speedster, but he made it out alive again unscathed.

Universal was releasing *The Phantom of the Opera* (1925) at the same time and had dedicated all their advertising boards to that film, so the studio's marketing team came up with a clever campaign to get Reg's newest comedy off to a great start. They designed custom billboards shaped like hot-water bottles with 'Oh, Doctor!' in flashy white script lettering against the red bottle that could be seen a block away. The newly opened Piccadilly Theatre in New York City at Broadway and 51st Street led the campaign. One week before the picture opened, the theater's owner, Lee Ochs, hired beautiful New York City models and fitted them in pretty nurse costumes with *Oh, Doctor!* ribbon bands across their waists. They paraded in front of the theater and all along Broadway, each carrying a dainty red heart basket holding envelopes containing candy hearts and handed out "pills" to a steady stream of patient patrons. The envelopes contained the message, "Love Pills for Strong Men with Weak Hearts. Directions: Take two breaths and one pill before each kiss. Compliments of the pretty nurse who prescribes that you see Reginald Denny in Universal's sparkling comedy hit, adapted from Harry Leon Wilson's best-seller, *Oh, Doctor!*" Universal also sold the Stutz Motor Car Company on sending their flashy roadster around the city with an advertisement across the hood that the Stutz was "Driven by Denny in *Oh, Doctor!* at the Piccadilly." The nurses sat atop the chauffer-driven racecar, waving at onlookers as they passed up and down Broadway and 5th during the first week of the run. The lobby of the Piccadilly was adorned with a dummy on a flagpole in front of a painted sky background on one side, while at the other was a standee cut-out of Reg and Mary Astor in front of a bursting thermometer. A big cut-out of Reg diving out of the book *Oh, Doctor!* planted a novel idea.

The film scored on Broadway at the Piccadilly with record-breaking business on the very first day and then through its second week, prompting Ochs to move a previously booked picture out of the way so he could book it for a third week. He said he never saw the critics in a happier frame of mind than after they had seen this production. Louella Parsons in the *New York American* said, "I am always sold on any Denny picture. *Oh, Doctor!* is the best thing that Lee Ochs has booked in the Piccadilly since the theater opened its doors last year."

Nationwide theater exhibitors were thrilled with the audience response and soaring ticket revenues, saying that the film "smashes all house records." The Capitol Theatre in Dallas reported there was a line over a block long waiting for its box office to open. Chicago's Circle Theatre stated that the film "established a new house record that will probably stand for some time to come." In Seattle, crowds stood in the rain for hours while they waited to enter the Columbia Theatre with record business there for an entire week. "Second week bigger than any first week the entire season, despite rain and wind storm. Audiences were wild over it in a continuous uproar!"

The turnout was phenomenal and the critics unanimously named *Oh, Doctor!* one of the best comedies of the year. Harriette Underhill in the *Herald-Tribune* said, "If you think it isn't funny, ask any of the 10,000 persons who crowded in Lee Ochs' theater last night. Everyone ought to see *Oh, Doctor!* for everyone will love it. The picture is perfect entertainment. Hilariously funny." The *Daily Mirror's* Dorothy Herzog said, "Uproarious comedy. A laugh a minute. Guaranteed to keep you simply convulsed with laughter." The *News-Leader* of Richmond, Virginia, praised Reg in his performance: "Mr. Denny's characterization of this young hypochondriac is one of the best things he has ever done. It could so easily have been overdone, which would have ruined it; but he has kept it within the bounds of reason, even though it is extravagantly satirical, and made it one of the most uproariously humorous characterizations seen on the screen since Harold Lloyd in *Safety Last.* He brings out every light and shading of the part, decorating it with his infectious grin, his pleasing personality, and a delicious conception of a shy lover."

The fan mail came in droves. "Dear Mr. Laemmle, Since writing you last, had occasion to see Mary Astor and Reginald Denny in *Oh, Doctor!* I merely wish to say that if there is anything called a panacea for the 'blues,' this picture is it. It is a long time since I had such a hearty and continual series of laughs. Most comedies die down somewhere. The only place this one does is at the FINIS when it is all over. One will have to go a long while, I am afraid, before one will see another wholesome comedy as satisfying as this one. –David E. Hischer, Cold Spring-on-Hudson, NY."

Universal then had Reg starring in *I'll Show You the Town* (1925) based on the novel by Elmer Davis and directed again by Pollard. Co-starring with Reg was 1924's WAMPAS Baby Star Marian Nixon, who was married to prizefighter Joe Benjamin. In *I'll Show You the Town*, Reg played a young college professor, Alec Dupree, whose three well-meaning friends talk him into entertaining three women at dinner on the same evening. One of the women is a wealthy widow interested in saving the almost defunct college, another is the wife of a friend, and the third is a beautiful young girl with whom Alec falls in love. In trying to entertain all three, Dupree involves himself in a net of scandals, misunderstanding, and disgrace from which he finally extricates himself by fast-talking and high-stepping, ending up his evening with the beautiful young girl, played by Nixon.

Universal promoted their newest Denny film with a "See America First" road tour by taking its star to various cities during its release. First stop was in Palo Alto, California, where Reg christened the newly built Stanford Theatre at their grand opening with the premiere of *I'll Show You the Town.* The tour then headed to Salt Lake City where that town welcomed him with cheers. Reg surprised the audience by making a personal appearance at the Capitol Theatre for the film's opening night there and Mayor Charles Clarence Neslen arranged an after-show party for the star at the Newhouse Hotel where he put him up in their Presidential Suite. The following morning, Reg invited the entire road crew to his suite for breakfast and expressed his appreciation to the behind-the-scenes folks. Members of the crew were so impressed that they shared their gratitude to Reg with a statement in *Universal Weekly*: "Let us tell the whole organization and every exhibitor right now what kind of a fellow Reggie is. You may have met a lot of stars in your day, but the See America crew can never be convinced that there is a better and finer fellow than Denny. When a star of the caliber of Denny sends word to the entire crew to come on down to his rooms and enjoy his hospitality, and when the whole bunch walks in, Reg says, 'Hello, Al! How's the trip? Howarya, Fred?' and 'Hello, Doc!' all around. To meet the King and have him treat you the way he did us, it makes you believe in 'we are all the same family' stuff."

Reg returned from the See America First tour feeling uplifted at the overwhelming response he was receiving. The Florence Theater in Pasadena worked with Universal to launch one of the first campaigns of its type. The proposal was to "show the town," Universal City, to its fans. Its owner, T.F. McCoy, sent Carl Laemmle a telegram to share the results of his contest which *Universal Weekly* published. "In the first place, I knew that I had one of the best pictures of 1925-26, for I previewed it weeks ago. I wanted to find some way to get on the front page of the Pasadena papers and so I went out to Universal City and had a talk with Norman Sproul, the business manager. I told him what I wanted to do and received wonderful cooperation from him and from everyone else at Universal City. Passes to Universal City are hard to get and there are thousands of people in Southern California who have never seen the inside of this wonderful city. I asked Mr. Sproul for ten passes good for four persons each. Then I went to the *Pasadena Post* and told them I would like to make a tie-up with the paper whereby the Florence Theatre and the *Post* would give passes to Universal City for the ten best comments on the picture, *I'll Show You the Town.* Needless to say, we got on the front page of the paper and received some wonderful publicity for the Florence Theatre, *I'll Show You the Town,* Universal City and Universal Pictures. When we took the party to Universal City on June 9th, we had a reporter along and received another big story when Reginald Denny personally greeted the winners for photo opportunities at the studio. The *Post* contest was for a criticism of the picture in fifty words or less, the winners to be chosen for their originality and cleverness. Following is the contribution of Mrs. Orin Riley, which was considered the best of all those submitted: 'Lots of Action, Sure-fire PEP, Loads of Laughter, Actor's PEP! Plot's Good, Star's a Whiz, a long, long Way from bein' a Fiz, Forget your Troubles, Dry your Tears, Produce Laughter, Forget your Fears! Forget the Tragic, Play the Clown, See Reginald Denny in *I'll Show You the Town!*'"

Once he presented the film at his theater, McCoy said in *Universal Weekly*, "Consider it the best comedy I have ever seen. Million per cent audience picture. Packed house ate it up. A cleanup picture if there ever was one!"

The owner of Los Angeles' Forum Theatre sent a telegram to Carl Laemmle. "*I'll Show You the Town* not only proved a super-laughing hit of the year but also proved super-box office attraction as number paid admissions both Saturday and Sunday exceeded anything heretofore known at Forum Theatre by more than five hundred people made possible by early attendance. Reginald Denny an absolute knock out. This week also celebrates Forum's First Anniversary. We thank you for giving us such a splendid production and look forward for a record-breaking week. John P. Corning, Forum Theatre."

The studio ate it up all the way to the bank.

Reg got back behind the wheel again in his next racy comedy featuring a road trip, a runaway circus menagerie, and an automobile race that ends with his winning car crossing the finish line in flames. Written by popular sports-romance writers Byron Morgan and Beatrice Van, *California Straight Ahead* (1925) also starred beauty Gertrude Olmstead and comedian Tom Wilson. In this Pollard-directed film, Reg played Tom Hayden who drives a Stutz Bearcat on a road trip across country with a trailer and bungalow in tow. For the bungalow, Universal constructed a huge Pullman car equipped with a dance floor, a radio, a dining section, and all the other comforts of home. It was elaborately fitted as a rolling bungalow, similar to a motor home with electric equipment throughout, and was a decided novelty as seen in the picture. The cast and crew actually went on a road trip to the desert for authenticity of the plot. Long after the last camera had been put away for the night, they camped out on-location while Reg entertained everyone by singing his old operettas to the accompaniment of musicians. The film's closing racecar scenes were filmed at the dangerous Ascot race track where Reg again performed all his own stunts, the last being the Stutz catching fire as he's approaching the finish line.

One of the catchiest marketing campaigns was put on by the Midland and Royal Theatres in Hutchinson, Kansas, for their opening during Valentine's Day week. Sealed envelopes with "For Ladies Only. Your Horoscope. Take One." were distributed to women outside the theaters with a personal note inside: "You are very fond of Reginald Denny, the Universal screen star, and in many ways your life runs parallel to his. On Thurs Fri and Sat Feb 11, 12, 13, you will be fortunate, in that on those days you will have the opportunity to see Reginald Denny in *California Straight Ahead* at the Midland Theatre, and your shrewdness will tell you that this is indeed a winner while the close parallel of your life to Denny's will enable you to interpret that great star's portrayal of 3,000 miles of laughs as few will be privileged and you are insured of a happy week."

The turnout was astounding and exhibitors nationwide raved about their successes claiming the comedy broke house records wherever it was shown. In New York City, the picture opened in a matinee at the Colony Theatre with the longest box-office line in its history. At the time the doors opened for the first show, the line extended up Broadway and well down into 53rd Street where it lasted all afternoon. At the first evening performance there were two lines, one stretching north to 53rd Street, and another south to 52nd Street. Four policemen were required to regulate traffic in the block. It was held over for an additional week there because of the excellent crowds it drew.

At the Forum Theatre in Los Angeles, the film ran over for four weeks due to packed houses. In the United Kingdom, the film premiered at the Rialto Theatre in London and it not only broke all their records but broke with equal enthusiasm in the press who raved over their fellow Brit's personality. In the *Times*, critics boasted about Reg, "It is hailed as another staunch run in Denny's ladder to screen supremacy. With masculine good looks, he directs his indefatigable energies, his impulsive senses of fun into lively channels. His ready grin and his ingratiating geniality are factors quick to promote cheer in the onlookers. He hurls one into laughter irresistibly. His jollity is buoyant and infectious."

The *Los Angeles Times* again compared Reg to the late Wallace Reid claiming, "Denny has that same humanness which made Wally beloved the world over, and he has that same sense of humor which carries over to his audience making it laugh with him as well as at him. *California Straight Ahead* shows these characteristics most clearly. It stamps him as one of the foremost comedians on the screen as well as one of its most likable young chaps. His ability to do all the dare devil stunts that any author can conceive coupled with his infectious smile and boyish earnestness has placed him at the top of the screen ladder up which he has been climbing. Perhaps the best performance from the supporting cast is that of Tom Wilson, the Negro comedian as Tom's devoted but superstitious servant. He really deserves special mention for his facial expressions and clowning, combined with the subtitles, which accompany his every move. It is no exaggeration to say that *California Straight Ahead* is one of the greatest laughter-makers ever produced but added to that there is a good story value, fast-moving action, clever double photography, wonderful scenery, and perhaps the finest motor racing sequences yet screened. Reginald Denny is admittedly without peer or equal. Reginald Denny—well, he is just Reginald Denny!"

While the film received overwhelming positive response from the critics, all was not so rosy on the set. Reg felt the studio was making a monkey out of him. When he first brought comedy into the action drama, Hobart Henley knew how to balance it with *The Abysmal Brute*; however, the studio's executives and Harry Pollard insisted on pushing each situation to the edge with outrageous physical comedy which Reg felt made him into a fool. The broad comedies with all the slapstick and facial expressions were against Reg's true nature and acting style, a contradiction as to how he wanted to be portrayed to the public. He became frustrated with the redundant, silly storylines and while the studio kept pushing for more of the broad comedy, Reg had gotten into the habit of arguing with its writers, scenarists, and director. Pollard really pushed it with *California Straight Ahead* and the ridiculous slapstick antics of the circus folk. There were over-the-top silly scenes with the circus animals, including one with a chimpanzee who kisses a man. Reg felt the studio and Pollard were cheapening his films with slapstick comedy that stereotyped him as a circus clown when told to play along with the absurdities instead of reacting naturally. When Pollard insisted that he stick to acting instead of trying to take his job, Reg threw child-like tantrums. He'd get in Pollard's face and then storm off the set only to return when he cooled off. Although Reg had shared his launch to stardom with Pollard, their on-set arguments only got worse with each new film. Reg finally had it with this last effort and stormed into Laemmle's office demanding they take Pollard off of his films. He was a British prince, not a blithering American buffoon, and he wanted the studio to understand his point of view.

He told Laemmle, "To do farce properly, you take an almost impossible situation, but you play it legitimately. Farce should really be played 'straight.' The farcical situation itself supplies the laughs." Reg went on to convince the studio executives how it should be done. "It might be explained that farce derives its laughs from situations, while comedy is the art of achieving fun through action and talk—for example, throwing pies. Good hokum, I love; low comedy, pies in the face, pratfalls, and so on. But it's got to belong. The timing and everything else has got to be right. Just to take a pratfall, or jump, into a bucket of paint, for no reason—this offends me. It's got to be real. You've got to believe it. You can't burlesque a farcical situation. You can't have an utterly ridiculous situation and pile wise-cracks on top. It just kills the whole thing."

Laemmle was disappointed at the contempt his successful team now felt for each other, but he half-heartedly agreed and listened to Reg. Following the Pollard split, Uncle Carl assigned the more easy-going director Bill Seiter to the next Denny comedy, *Where Was I?* (1925). Also assigned to the film were writers Melville Brown and Edgar Franklin. They wrote a new type of farcical story starring Reg as young businessman, Thomas S. Berford, who's engaged to marry his boss's daughter but is suddenly confronted by a beautiful girl who claims that he's already married to her. He never saw her before, but despite his diaries, records and the testimony of his friends, he's unable to establish an alibi of definite proof of where he was on their supposed wedding day. Reg teamed up again with Marian Nixon and Otis Harlan, as well as Tyrone Power, Sr., and Arthur Lake, who all contributed to the farce. He enjoyed working with Bill Seiter as the director calmed down the written hokum that the scenarists provided. The two teamed together in stellar fashion to do it their own way with less broad comedy, and it worked.

Bill Colling of the *New York Telegraph* boasted, "Reginald Denny busts into town with a farce. Another one. It's called *Where Was I?* and this week it's brightening up the Colony Theatre considerably. Like most farces, the way it is done is more important to its success than the plot. Reginald does it well. He does it very well, aided and abetted by some clever actors."

The exhibitors were again overjoyed with the stellar box-office results of their Denny film. The owner of the Colony Theatre in New York was happy with their audience turnout and wrote to Universal. "I want to tell you that Reginald Denny sure took the cake in *Where Was I?* Reginald Denny is a wonder, I say again, and the best comedian on the screen today."

6

UP AND AWAY

THROUGHOUT THE 1920S, the U.S. economy expanded rapidly and the nation's wealth more than doubled during the period coined as the "Roaring Twenties." Like the racecars in his films, Reg was on fire and making more money than he had ever dreamed. He was no longer the poor, begging, fighting vagabond and was now flying higher than ever due to the success of his film career during this sensational era. For him, it was a festive period of celebration and excess.

"We all had tremendously inflated egos. We felt, unconsciously, that the world couldn't go on without us. There were extravagant parties in those days, too. They were given by the biggest people, and attendance was virtually mandatory. There was a party all the time. Frequently, you couldn't remember when or where the original gathering began. You started with twelve people at somebody's house. After a few rounds of champagne, everybody drifted somewhere else and collected more people. They used to last as long as five days or a week. The guests would collapse, one by one. And only when they were all exhausted, did the party end."

Also known as the Golden Age of Flight, this was the epoch that launched modern technology at the same time civil aviation was getting off the ground. While conducting all of his racing stunts in *Sporting Youth, Oh, Doctor!*, and *California Straight Ahead*, Reg had befriended professional racecar driver Bon MacDougall. In addition to racing his Miller roadster in the Indianapolis 500, MacDougall also raced airplanes and was starting a flying club with members of the Hollywood community. When he found out that Reg was a WWI air ace, MacDougall took the actor out for a flight in his Curtiss JN-4D "Jenny" biplane. Once MacDougall handed the controls over to Reg, the magic returned. He was thrilled to get back in the cockpit and soar once again through the skies without a bunch of Germans at his tail. Reg was back in the saddle and when he landed the Jenny, he had to have it. He bought the racy biplane from MacDougall and used the training he received with the Royal Air Force to resume his flight path in Hollywood. He immediately had Universal's art team paint his personal insignia on the plane—an ambulance with an angel flying overhead and the inscription "Reginald Denny" below. When Reg surprised Rene with a flight in his new open-air biplane, she was exhilarated. It brought life into their souls and Barbara, who was now ten, was thrilled each time she took to the sky with Daddy.

MacDougall invited Reg to join him for a joy ride with fellow flyers who were members of the aviator club he was forming called "The Black Cats." The Black Cats were one of the first teams of barnstorming daredevils who conducted aerial acrobatics in Southern California and were popular among the Hollywood community. The group was made up of WWI pilots, motion picture stuntmen, and automobile racers who wanted to corner the market on all movie stunt work that involved airplanes, automobiles, and motorcycles. For club membership, they had to be willing to do any stunt in an automobile, airplane, and motorcycle as well as take a 2,000-foot delayed parachute jump. One of the other requirements to belong to the Black Cat club was that there had to be thirteen letters in the member's name.

Reg naturally met all the qualifications with thirteen letters in his given stage name. Being impressed with his flying ability, MacDougall asked the movie star to be an honorary member of his club and dubbed him as their Thirteenth Black Cat. Reg was handed the uniform—a black sweater with a cat and the number "13" patch on the front with his name on the back. There were two sets of white claws on his badge which indicated that he was felled twice in the war. Reg kept his Jenny at Clover Field, now Santa Monica Airport, but the Cats' home base was the Burdett Airport located at Western Avenue and 102nd Street in Los Angeles. They flew various models of biplanes, mostly Jennys and Curtis JN-4 "Canucks." The exclusive club emblem also painted on their biplanes featured both a black cat and the number thirteen to defy the curse of bad luck. Each cat was life-sized and lifelike to its last whisker.

Now that the team was complete, the roster featured Bon MacDougall, racecar driver and straight pilot; Sam E. Greenwald, aerial photographer and co-founder of the club; Spider Matlock, all around daredevil and stuntman; Ivan "Bugs" Unger, stuntman; Arthur C. Goebel, WWI veteran and stunt pilot; Herd McClellan, oldest parachute jumper in the world; Albert Johnson, stuntman; Paul Richter, Jr., straight pilot and future co-founder of TWA; Wild Billy Lind, racecar driver; Fronty Nichols, stuntman; Jack Frye, straight pilot; Gladys Ingle, stuntwoman; and Reginald Denny, WWI veteran, racecar driver, and motion picture star.

The Black Cats' maiden voyage launched on the lucky day of Friday the Thirteenth as they swarmed over the streets of Hollywood. When the buzz of airplane motors was heard, and came nearer and louder, pedestrians looked up to see the fleet of thirteen planes dipping earthward. Many ran for cover thinking the city was under attack on the unlucky day. Reg and Art Goebel flew in formation above the crowds who were captivated by the roaring biplanes as they came down just fifty feet above the ground then straight up with hammerhead maneuvers.

These cats took barnstorming to new heights and the feats they performed were outrageous. A pilot operated the plane in the open-air cockpit while stuntmen and famous stuntwoman Gladys Ingle would walk about the entire craft, including on its wings and fuselage, while the airplane was in flight. While in solo flight, the pilot would perform his own stunts by doing rolls looping around upside down and then fly within inches of another airplane so the wing walkers could switch planes midair. It was not for the meek or weak of stomach, nor for anyone who had a fear of heights, or wanted to stay alive. In addition to wing-walking, they would do such daring stunts as playing cards atop a card table fastened to the wings of the plane.

The team of notorious flyers made headlines when they performed one of their daring acts at the Los Angeles Coliseum in front of 79,000 spectators. During half-time at the USC-Stanford football game, one Jenny came in and swooped right over the stadium. MacDougall was flying the biplane with Fronty Nichols standing atop the left upper wing and Spider Matlock on the right wing. Each held a football painted in the school's team colors which they were to toss at the playing field. As they buzzed the field, the plane's radiator burst and spewed scalding water all over the windshield and on MacDougall's flight goggles. He raised his fist to signal distress, and the two wing-walkers made a hasty retreat to the cockpit just as they flew over the crowd. MacDougall made an emergency landing on a vacant lot a few blocks away from the Coliseum, defeating death one more time.

Reg felt more comfortable inside the cockpit. After one scary stunt standing atop the plane while in flight, he climbed down to the landing gear holding on for dear life until the craft landed. He thereafter chose to navigate the plane rather than lose his life as a wing-walker.

Along with all the fun he was having also came physical, mental, and emotional stresses. Reg needed a type of sojourn, a real getaway to chill out, decompress and spend time with his wife and daughter. Hoot Gibson had told him about an area where he had bought a rustic cabin in the nearby San Bernardino mountains 7,000 feet above sea level that made you feel a million miles away from Hollywood. Reg flew his Jenny up to Lake Arrowhead and met Hoot at his cabin in Running Springs on the cliffs called "Rim o' the World." It was quite remote, but Reg loved it. There was an old log and stone cabin down the road from Hoot's sitting on the twenty-acre lot with a seasonal creek running through it, and it was for sale. Reg imagined what he could turn it into, so he bought it on the spot and hired Hoot's construction team to transform the old cabin on his land into a beautiful haven mountain lodge retreat. With the crew, he built a stable with a huge paddock for horses that he and Hoot rescued from the studio's riding stables. Reg's land was surrounded by Hoot, director George Hill, and fellow Brit Ronald Colman as neighbors. The press found out about the stars' refuge and, after a fan followed them up the mountain to their cabins, Reg and Colman hired their own private policeman to look after their respective estates.

Reg was appreciative that he had been given the gift of his stardom to be able to live such a blessed life after all the heartbreak and hard knocks. The family spent their free weekends at the cabin where they enjoyed cozy wonderful uninterrupted times together. Reg loved the mountains where he could get away from the rat race of Hollywood. He was now far away up in the open air to spend every available hour walking the pristine trails along the creek, riding horses, hunting, shooting, and fishing.

"I can breathe freely up in the mountains—it's grand. Some folks who aren't self-sufficient might find it lonely up in the hills. But, as for me, the sight of the sun coming up over the tree-tops in the morning, like a red ball of molten fire, the brisk, nippy quality in the air and the sweet smell of the growing things all around, is like heaven. Our view on a clear day reaches to 140 miles. We can see Mexico and a great half-moon of the Pacific Slope. There is the best of shooting and fishing. The climate is near perfect. Its invigoration is marvelous. We have our own water, lighting, and power plant, and our own English society, plenty of it."

Reg flew his Jenny up to the cabin and proposed to construct a landing field on his acreage in the mountains so he could have his own private airport there and fly to his retreat when he wanted. He planned to build a hangar large enough to house five planes and began negotiations with a local San Bernardino oil company to supply gasoline for the proposed airplane field. Reg claimed that the airfield, his own private airport, would serve as an emergency landing field for aviators flying over the San Bernardino mountains and for planes en route to Big Bear Lake, as well as for firefighters. He was creating the world in which he wanted to live, and his dreams were all finally coming true. Reg had found his family and his home in the sky.

When he came back down the mountain to reality, Reg was called in for a meeting with Uncle Carl. *Photoplay* had featured an article about the Thirteen Black Cats with Reg as their honorary member. In their March 1926 issue, the magazine made a satirical remark about the daredevil actor saying, "… Under Black Cat rulings Denny is allowed only six more falls and he can fly no more, for Black Cats have but nine lives you know." Universal executives were concerned that their top comedy star shouldn't be engaged in such life-threatening activities with the barnstorming daredevils, so Laemmle asked him to not participate with the club any longer. He said that it wasn't good publicity nor fitting for their top comedy star to be conducting such outrageous stunts. He reminded Reg that Universal had an expensive $500,000 accidental insurance policy on him. The legal team then created a clause in his contract which prohibited their ace comedy star from conducting stunt flying until his contract ended in 1928. Reg, of course, acquiesced and after flying with the Black Cats for six months, he regretfully advised MacDougall that he had to take a break from participating with the club until the end of his contract with the studio. Reg continued to fly his Jenny for transportation to and from the cabin, and stayed away from doing such dangerous stunts as the cat left with only six more lives.

7   UNIVERSAL APPEAL

NOT ONLY HAD REG BEEN DUBBED as the "Celluloid Adonis" by the press, he was now being hailed as "The Farce King" and the "King of Comedy." In such roles, he became one of the brightest stars in the brightest eras of silent films. His unique style popularized natural light comedy on the screen, bringing a welcome relief from slapstick while he continuously worked as Universal's leading farce king earning the highest salary for a comedian second to Charlie Chaplin. Reg had made it to the top echelon of movie star status and after the continued success of their Denny films, Universal City Studios added Reg's Jewel pictures to their prominent "White List" with an increase in his Super Denny films from three per year to five.

As a result of the record-breaking success of the Denny comedies, Carl Laemmle proudly made an announcement in the studio's *Universal Weekly* magazine: "This year started off with 'Laugh Month,' but that isn't all. I believe that 1926 is to be 'Laugh Year.' The trend is toward comedy and every picture has always had its 'comedy relief,' but this is to be increased and accentuated so that a more even balance will be struck between the two forms. We are going to put comedy even in *Romeo and Juliet,* and *Uncle Tom's Cabin* will be full of laughs. This trend toward comedy, is of course, in response to a public demand, and I believe that this demand grows out of the ever-increasing tenseness of modern life. Competition in business and the professions grows keener; we live each day, it seems, at a higher pitch and more rapid pace. When we seek amusement we want to relax, to forget the cares and responsibilities of the day. In other words, we want to laugh. When a tendency gets under way, someone always goes too far, and it may be that some will go too far in this direction. Serious drama and slapstick comedy do not, as a rule, mix very well. That is a thing we must guard against, because as there are different kinds of comedy, so are there different places where each is appropriate. Reginald Denny is a comedian, but he is a 'seven-reel comedian,' and the laugh tricks of the two-reels are not for him. In *Gulliver's Travels,* which we will make on a large scale as a fantasy, the comedy element will be prominent, but it will be a fantastic comedy, of course. These differences are subtle, but they must be kept constantly in mind by our writers, directors and actors. The out-and-out comedies are in more demand, also, that is, the short length comedies which have no purpose outside of getting laughs. Some very fine and expensive talent is engaged in the making of these. Which raises the question again, whether there is any higher vocation than that of making people laugh. When people laugh, they are, as a rule, happy; they have put aside their cares and inhibitions. So, the comedian is one of the truest friends of humanity, and the fact that 1926 is to be full of laughter is a very fine augury for all of us."

To launch its Laugh Year, Universal started off with a new string of Seiter-Denny comedies beginning with *What Happened to Jones* (1926). Adapted by Melville Brown from the famous George Broadhurst stage farce, it starred Reg with his now familiar team of Marian Nixon, Otis Harlan, and Ben Hendricks, Jr. in supporting leads. The comedy begins when Tom Jones, played by Reg, is stampeded into a poker party on the night before his wedding date. The party is raided by the police and to avoid their arrest, the poker players battle the cops and escape. Jones and Ebenezer Goodly, played by Harlan, go down a fire escape and enter the open window of a reducing parlor where many lightly clad stout women are roaming the halls. The fugitives dodge from one section to another, finally hiding themselves in electric light bath cabinets with protruding heads covered with towels. They pass for women as the police search the place, but when an attendant turns on more heat, Jones disrobes inside the cabinet to avoid suffocation. Jones and Goodly nakedly escape to the dressing rooms where they dress themselves in women's clothing and then exit the parlor. It's one comical scenario after another on the city streets until Jones, eventually disguised as a bishop, reaches the church where he is to marry his waiting fiancée, played by Nixon. The crew had a blast making the hilarious comedy. Reg was pleased to now be working steadily with easy-going Bill Seiter. Seiter concurred with Reg in that he felt the slapstick comedy didn't fit the British stage actor's personality, so he didn't push for the hokum. The studio execs wanted Reg to play the Jones character with over-the-top broad comedy, but the actor and director agreed they were going to do it their way and have none of the clowning action. The story was silly enough and Reg played it naturally where it was believable.

Once the crew finished work on the film, Reg brought Rene and Barbara up to their mountain retreat where they spent a beautiful Christmas and New Year celebration in the snowy wonderland. When they returned to Hollywood, Reg took pals Ben Hendricks Jr. and "Hub" Lloyd out on the *Barbarene* for a day of marlin fishing from the port of San Diego. They were headed toward the fishing village of Ensenada when a violent storm blew in taking the craft out to sea. Reg, Hendricks, and Lloyd feared the yacht would capsize in the twenty-foot waves and they worked hard to gain whatever control they could. Back home, Rene called the police when her husband didn't return home the next morning nor call. When he didn't show up on set the following day, the studio was not so concerned about *What Happened to Jones*, but what happened to Reg. Laemmle hired two pilots to fly search planes from Santa Monica's Clover Field over the Pacific and the U.S. Coast Guard sent out military boats from San Diego in an oceanic rescue effort to find Reg and his lost companions. After three days without communication, Reg finally navigated his way to the San Diego harbor. He called Rene and Laemmle to let everyone know that they were alive. When he returned home, Rene was upset that Reg had been irresponsible for not checking the weather before he set out to sea. She cried to Reg that the press had broadcast the news all around town that the movie star was dead, and Barbara thought her daddy was gone for good. The studio wasn't so happy about the scare of their star's reckless behavior either. The theatrical exhibitors were happy, though, and again reported record-breaking audiences for their newest Denny release. *What Happened to Jones* was hailed as a "Laugh-Riot" at the Colony Theatre in New York. Due to the overwhelming attendance there, the picture was held over for a second week. The critics said that even they did not realize how tremendously popular Reg was until they tried to force their way into the Colony on opening night. They claimed that it was one of the funniest pictures ever seen on Broadway.

Los Angeles Times columnist Grace Kingsley attended the Los Angeles premiere at the Metropolitan Theater and wrote a complimentary review: "The greatest comedy success of the current season is Reginald Denny in *What Happened to Jones*. Guffaws, not giggles, accompany its showing this week at the Metropolitan. This is the first Denny (Universal) picture to ever play this house and the drawing power of this star asserted itself from the opening day. If you don't laugh until you cry at the sight of Reginald Denny and Otis Harlan dashing about the ladies' Turkish bath with the police after them, and finally taking refuge in the steam cabinets with their heads popping out at the top, while fearful and rueful looks adorn their faces, you will be different from the gang including myself which yesterday simply howled with laughter all through the comedy's unrolling. If the other comedians don't watch out, Denny is going to tear the laurels from all their brows. His comedy gifts are being cultivated, but especially he has a tremendously likable personality. That wide, crooked good-humored grin of his is a fortune in itself."

Guy Price in the *Herald* wrote, "What happened to Jones? Everything short of murder and an earthquake—and even then, *What Happened to Jones* is causing a laugh-quake at the Metropolitan this week, and the way Reginald Denny treats gloom approaches nothing but murder. What didn't happen to him would be hardly worth mentioning."

The *Kansas City Times* reported, "Reginald Denny in *What Happened to Jones*, showing at the Liberty Theatre this week, was greeted with gales of merriment from crowded houses over the weekend. This picture indicates why Universal Pictures Corporation is holding the comedy star against the attractive offers of Paramount and other rival producers. Denny has created an unusual following and each succeeding picture seems to be an improvement over its predecessor."

The Denny-Seiter team then plunged into their next motion picture, *Skinner's Dress Suit* (1926). In a remake of Essanay's 1917 romantic comedy, Reg played the lead role of Skinner and starred with his favorite leading lady, Laura La Plante, as his wife Honey. The cast also included their familiar gang of Ben Hendricks Jr., E.J. Ratcliffe, Arthur Lake, Hedda Hopper, and Lionel Braham. In the film, underpaid Skinner lies to his wife and tells her that he got a raise. Honey excitedly buys her husband a dress suit and, once he puts it on, he's faced with a multitude of problems until he loses his job. Before he can tell Honey the bad news, she whisks him off to a society dance at a hotel where one of his most important clients is staying. By the end of the evening, Skinner has closed a half-a-million-dollar deal and wins a partnership in his old company. There's a scene at the party where Skinner and Honey are teaching the dignified aristocrats a new dance step in the ballroom. It was during this scene that Reg sprang a surprise right on set and made up his own dance which he called "The Savannah Shuffle." He told his "students" that it was a combination of the Charleston and the old blues Gaby Glide, interspersed with a waddling walk. Everyone had a ball learning the steps and, during the gay party, Bill Seiter proposed to Ms. La Plante to make it a real celebration.

While the cast was dancing away, Will H. Hays came for a visit to the studio for a routine tour inspection. From 1918 to 1921, Hays was chairman of the Republican National Committee and the first chairman of the Motion Picture Producers and Distributors of America (MPPDA), now the Motion Pictures Association of America (MPAA). He became the namesake for the Motion Picture Production Code, informally referred to as the "Hays Code," which spelled out a set of moral guidelines for the self-censorship of content in Hollywood cinema. Being the studio's top star and ambassador, Reg played guide and gave the "Czar of Movies" a personal tour of Universal City Studios. Reg also taught Hays how to do the "Savannah Shuffle," showing him that *Skinner's Dress Suit* was good, clean, family fun.

In one of their advertising campaigns, Universal teamed with a couple of merchandise companies for promotion of the film. Parker Pen featured an ad with a photo of Reg in his dress suit holding the pen with the caption, "I might just as well try to do without my make-up box as to be without my Parker Duofold Pen." One of the largest watch manufacturers in the United States, Helbein-Stone Company, created four new model Helbros watches which they called the "Reginald Denny" model, the "Denny Jr.," the "Laura La Plante," and the "Laura Jr." The watch company and the studio teamed together with their merchandising promotion by featuring full-page ads with photographs of both Reg and La Plante admiring their new watches. Just before the Christmas holidays, Universal featured a campaign in the popular magazines *Liberty*, *Vogue*, *Vanity Fair*, *Photoplay*, *Sunset*, *Harper's Bazaar*, and *College Humor* with coupons for autographed pictures to be sent with each watch as gifts.

After release of the picture, the press and exhibitors once again raved. Mae Tinee of the *Chicago Tribune* wrote, "Optiences at the Oriental Chicago are having hysterics over *Skinner's Dress Suit*. Haven't seen so much joy unrestrained in a movie theater for a long time. Well, it IS a funny picture. And it's human and folksy and lovable besides. It is so real that the interests of that young married couple, the Skinners, are acutely yours throughout the film. …[Reginald Denny] has never had a better role than that of Skinner and never a better actress or more appealing vis-à-vis than Laura La Plante playing opposite him. …Everything about *Skinner's Dress Suit* hits on all cylinders." The *San Francisco News* said, "Reginald Denny is decidedly in his element as Skinner. He gets out every ounce of fun there is in a role of the harassed young husband and the situations which he finds himself. Laura La Plante is wholly delightful as Honey. As Charlestoners the pair are medal winners."

Reg's "Savannah Shuffle" became the new craze. *Photoplay* featured a story with instructions on how to do the dance with, "Denny and La Plante Show You How to Do the 'Savannah Shuffle.' Now all Hollywood is doing the Savannah Shuffle!" Reg and Laura La Plante had now taken the silent film throne as the "King and Queen of Comedy."

After all the fun making *Skinner's Dress Suit*, Reg then starred again with his familiar team of Bill Seiter, leading lady Marian Nixon, and pal Ben Hendricks, Jr. in a rollicking picture made from a story by John Hunter Booth titled *Rolling Home* (1926). Reg played a promoter, Nat Alden, who's had bad luck on a deal and his boss fires him. When he packs up his office and leaves, Alden runs into an old Army buddy, Mason, who now works for his ex-boss as a chauffeur. Alden talks Mason into driving him home in his ex-boss's Rolls

Royce and when he arrives in his hometown, all sorts of farcical situations bring him to real wealth and love.

To promote the film and their Super Denny pictures, Universal arranged an appropriately named "Rolling Home" road tour as an exploitation campaign to bring its star in close touch with his fans in key cities across the country. Reg packed up and rolled off the lot from Universal City to New York City on a colorful three-week road tour. His first stop-over was in Kansas City, Missouri, where Reg had been especially invited by its mayor, Albert Beach. The principal event was his part in the opening of the new Million Dollar Madrid Theatre with the premiere of *Rolling Home*. Reg's next stop was St. Louis where Mayor Victor J. Miller welcomed him to the City Hall at a luncheon with prominent civic officials, then a cocktail reception and dinner at the Municipal Opera House. In Cincinnati, the next stop, Reg was welcomed by Mayor Murray Seasongood with another honorable event, then as special guest of the Kentucky Jockey Club at the Latonia Derby where he was presented to the crowd of sixty-thousand people. The Denny Days in Indianapolis and Pittsburgh were occupied with similar activities hosted by the mayors of those towns.

When he finally made it to New York, memories of his Broadway struggles tugged at the heartstrings. This would be his first trip back since he left for Hollywood four years prior and Reg stipulated in his tour across the continent that he should have but one day in New York to himself with three personal objectives. The very first was to make a visit to the offices of Morris Gest and Lee Shubert. Reg strolled into each with an envelope containing a handwritten thank you note accompanied by a substantial check in repayment of the loans for which the two had given him when he was down and out. The second was to buy a new Elco yacht, larger than the *Barbarene* in case he got lost at stormy seas again. The last was to visit Mrs. Barnes at the old boarding house on 55th Street in which he lived during the lean and hungry days when he first performed on Broadway. Unfortunately, when Reg arrived on 55th Street, he found that all the houses had been torn down to make way for more pretentious buildings and a tailor establishment. No one seemed to know where Mrs. Barnes could be found, which was a bitter disappointment to Reg as he had planned a very elaborate surprise for her.

That night, huge crowds welcomed Reg on Broadway with cheers when he made a personal appearance at the Colony Theatre for a special showing of *Rolling Home*. The popularity of the picture and its high amusement value was judged from the fact that one of the patrons present that night, a woman, became hysterical with laughter and had to be carried out. The following day, a Denny luncheon was held in one of New York's most popular grill rooms at the new Hotel Buckingham with more than one hundred guests. The critics and motion picture editors of practically every New York daily were present as well as the editors and special writers of the publications dealing with the screen world.

Picture Show magazine's Margaret Chute traveled all the way from London to attend the luncheon with high hopes to meet the Universal star for an interview. She wrote about her first interaction with him in her magazine article: "A swaying mob of excited people had been enquiring in agitated tones, 'Has he arrived? Where is he? Will he turn up, after all, d'you think? Have you seen him yet?' Above the babel a stentorian voice shouted exultantly, 'Here he is!' and immediately dozens of voices cried joyfully, in chorus, 'There's

Reg! Good old Reg! Here he is! Howdy Reg!' Down the stairs a tall, athletic figure, in a well-cut blue serge suit, came hurtling at least three steps in a stride, his cheery face one broad, glad grin. 'Hullo, Everybody!' remarked Reginald Denny, in his nice English voice. 'Glad to see you!' Into the melee somebody dragged me, mentioned my name, said I'd arrived from London, and I found myself shaking hands with Mr. Denny a bit chokily, on my side, for it was good to hear an English voice. Under cover of the general clamor I managed to whisper, 'I've got an introduction to you from Maisie Gay; she sent her love, and Arthur Margetson, and—' 'Dear Maisie! How is she? And Margetson? This is fine!' remarked the hero of the day. Then, before we could utter another intelligible sound, he was pounced upon by the Powers-That-Be, in the Universal Films, and escorted firmly to the big luncheon room where a perfectly palatial lunch was panting to be served, all in Reg Denny's honor. As he vanished through the crowd, he managed to ejaculate, 'See you afterwards,' and I went off to my place, quite content. There he sat, in the seat of honor at the luncheon given for him, surrounded by film and newspaper celebrities, and with Will Hays, Czar of all the Movies, smiling happily on his right. It was my first experience of a big film luncheon, and I was thrilled to the bone! Speeches followed an excellent meal, and when Reginald Denny stood up, with cheers thundering to the roof, he proceeded to make a delightfully modest, humorous speech. It was a typically British speech, straight from the shoulder, candid, and without any frills. Luncheon ended with another wild mob surrounding Mr. Denny, while a tactful publicity manager whispered to him that appointments had been made for various important journalists to interview him at his hotel, from 3:00 to 5:30, at intervals of twenty minutes. 'Great Scott!' gasped the star. 'And do I have to think of something different to tell each one? I shall never survive it!' Managing to catch Mr. Denny more or less undisturbed for three seconds, I stated hurriedly that I was on my way to Hollywood. 'Fine!' said he. 'We'll show you what filmland's really like. Look here, when you know the date you are due in Los Angeles, wire me—let me put down my address. Anybody got a pencil? And if I'm back by that time, I'll be at the station to meet you. That's a bet!' We all dived up into the bright sunshine of Fifth Avenue to find crowds planted firmly on the pavement, with cameras both moving and still lined up ready for action. Denny tried to slip away, but somebody grabbed him and then I was told to conduct an imaginary interview with the star, out on the pavement, in broad daylight, with cameras grinding and clicking, and policemen trying to move on the gaping crowd."

Helen Rockwell of *Picture Play* featured a story in the magazine about Reg after he met with press agents for tea at the Hotel Astor. At the tea, Reg casually discussed his climb to fame with his lean days in New York and expressed how grateful he was to Morris Gest and Lee Shubert. He also shared the insulting advice which he'd been given by both his father and Joseph Schenck. Rockwell closed her story about the *Rolling Home* star on a witty note: "And speaking of the Schenckian judgment, I am reminded of the remarks of two little flappers of my neighborhood who have huge scrapbooks filled with pictures of their favorite actors. 'And here's Reginald Denny,' they gurgle. 'Hasn't he the most adorable crooked mouth!' Let Mr. Schenck shrivel up over that one!"

Reg and the road crew left New York and then traveled to Pennsylvania where he spent the day at Philadelphia's Sesqui-Centennial for the city's first world fair commemorating the 150th Anniversary of the signing of the Declaration of Independence. He was personally welcomed by Philadelphia's mayor, W. Freeland Kendrick, and shown the historic document with photo ops of the Brit with the American freedom declaration. Reg then traveled to Washington, DC, where he spent a day at the national Capitol with Universal chief Carl Laemmle to meet with one of the movie star's fans, President Calvin Coolidge.

Similar stops were made in Cleveland, Detroit, Chicago, Minneapolis, and Milwaukee as the crew made their return westward. Frank Vreeland reported in the *New York Telegram*, "As Denny stepped off the train in Milwaukee and was being greeted by a group of newspaper reporters, there was a sudden shout from the baggage crew, uploading a cargo of trunks. 'Hey, there, Regy-nald!' Reg turned from his interviewers and shouted back, 'Hey, fellows! How are you?!' The blue overcalled baggage smashers agreed that he is 'a regular guy' even if his name is Reginald. That appears to be the verdict of everyone who has ever met Denny. He's 'a regular guy.' On his tour across the continent, Reg made friends wherever he stopped. They all surmised that he must have discovered some Coue method which enables him to get better and better."

Tamar Lane, editor of the *Film Mercury*, said of Reg, "If I were a producer, I would rather have Denny than any other actor in the silent drama. Denny can play drama, and he can play comedy. He is one of the best, if not actually the best, light comedian and farceur that the screen has ever known. In addition, he appeals equally to theater-goers of both sexes, something very rare in any kind of celebrity, and a factor which always puts a player up among the biggest box office attractions."

Nationwide press releases followed claiming that Reg was the best light comedian the screen had ever known, proving that Reg's personal appearances across the country had a phenomenal impact. "His appeal is universal. Men, women, children," wrote Dorothy Spensley in *Photoplay*.

British columnist Margaret Chute got the surprise of her life when she made her trip out west to find that Reg had kept the promise he made to her while in New York. As she shared in *Picture Show* magazine: "… About fifteen days later, when I started on my four and a half days' journey across America, I wired to Reginald Denny giving the date and time of my arrival in Los Angeles, which happened to be 2 o'clock on a certain Wednesday afternoon. I had not the slightest idea if he had got back to Hollywood or not, but he had told me to let him know, so I obeyed. It was impossible for me to hear from him, so when the Santa Fe Limited drew into Los Angeles on a gloriously sunny day, I felt rather far from home. Looking out of the window, the first thing I saw was a bunch of movie cameras. The second thing was a tall figure, in white golfing clothes, hatless, with the sun shining on fair hair and lighting up a face that was one big smile of welcome. True to his promise, Reginald Denny was at the station to meet me! I thought it was the most sporting thing imaginable; and only later did I learn that he had broken up a very precious fishing holiday, so that I might find someone from England waiting when the train came in. Outside the station stood the long, dark-blue limousine that is driven alternately by Reginald or Irene Denny. We climbed in, and then for over two hours Mr. Denny drove me round Hollywood. We raced along—he always drives fast, for speed is his great craze—but somehow we did not seem to be hurrying, so admirable is his driving ability. He pointed out studios, private houses, important restaurants, and shops. And then he drove me out towards the sea, to show me the fine houses in Beverly Hills, and the big piece of land he has purchased recently on the side of a young mountain, with a view across to the ocean. In that heavenly spot the Dennys are going to build a new house, and next time I go to Hollywood I hope to see them there. While my visit to Hollywood lasted, this year, I saw a good deal of Mr. Denny and his fascinating wife; and it does not take long to discover how popular they are. Their chief charm, I think, is the fact that they both possess a huge sense of humor; and that both of them are sportsmen in every sense of the word."

Reg's popularity was now off the charts and he was literally the talk of the town. His pictures took another step upwards in screen importance when Carl Laemmle announced in *Universal Weekly* the next Denny starrer, *Take It from Me* (1926), to be the launch of the studio's "Reginald Denny Productions." Reginald Denny Productions were then regarded by Universal as in a class by themselves as separate releases and ranked in importance ahead of the other Universal Jewel productions. Directed by Bill Seiter, *Take It from Me* was adapted from the popular musical comedy by Will B. Johnstone and Will Anderson. In it, Reg starred as wealthy Tom Eggett who has one of those gold-digging fiancées, played by Blanche Mehaffey. However, when said dough has been deposited on a horse with a jockey who wore his winter underwear and lost the race by weight only, then the farce begins to gain speed, both in action and giggles. For the film's release, Carl Laemmle formally dedicated the ninth of October as official "National Denny Day." At a special ceremony at Universal City Studios, Uncle Carl made an official announcement: "October 9th will be 'National Denny Day,' in honor of Reginald Denny, whose first big production for the 1926-27 season will reach the screen on that date. It is *Take It from Me* and is the first of the six Reginald Denny Productions scheduled for the coming months." The week of October 9, consequently, was hailed as "National Denny Week" and *Take It from Me* marked the beginning of a new series of the studio's Super Denny pictures. More than five-hundred big theaters played *Take It from Me* beginning on October 9 and booked it for the entire week while many hundreds of other theaters played other Denny successes during the ensuing weeks. The film's premiere was held at Los Angeles' Uptown Theatre with a big party afterwards celebrating Reg and Seiter's success.

The film was a hit. "The Day of Denny Is Here," according to the readers of the *Saturday Evening Post, Liberty,* and *Photoplay.* The columnists personally wrote to Carl Laemmle about Reg's pictures and how they all turned out on National Denny Day to honor their favorite comedian claiming that "there's not a bigger go-getter box-office star in the business," adding that "Denny is by far the most popular comedy-drama artist in pictures today and even his popularity continues to mount higher with his every new picture."

The *Los Angeles Record* raved, "*Take It from Me*—it's just one grand and glorious fancy-free funny farce! Reggie Denny is just one of those movie heroes who has a nice little fortune left to his easy grasp by a thoughtful, but, departed uncle—then there was that tricky will which provides—and oh, how it provides—that he do so-and-so to win the remaining mass of money and, of course, the girl!" Eleanor Barnes in the *Los Angeles News* wrote, "Denny excels himself in this picture, which has a real plot, replete with love interest and is worked out in that interesting way that William Seiter productions generally are. Denny and Seiter are getting to be like the Siamese twins of picturedom, but the happy combination seems to make the box office manager smile, as well as the public, so everybody should be satisfied."

As *What Happened to Jones, Skinner's Dress Suit, Rolling Home*, and *Take It from Me* were turned out by the Denny-Seiter comedy team, they topped each preceding picture by an even greater success. Bill Seiter was again responsible for the excellent direction and was now being praised as one of the few director-artists in the business due to his work with Reg.

Next of the Super Denny pictures directed by Seiter was *The Cheerful Fraud* (1927). Adapted for the screen by Harvey Thew and based on the popular humorous novel *Following Ann* by the well-known English novelist K.R.G. Browne, the story seemed especially tailored for Reg. The cast included Gertrude Olmstead as his leading lady, with Otis Harlan, Gertrude Astor, Emily Fitzroy, and Charles Gerrard in supporting roles. In the pugilist racecar crime farce based in England, Reg now had the opportunity to play one of his own countrymen. To create an authentic British atmosphere, Bill Seiter had a big English country house constructed on the Universal Lot just for this picture. Reg worked with the crew on assembling the sets and props which would be entirely in harmony with the locale of the story. Because Reg helped the union staff build the estate, they expressed their gratitude by gifting him with a crafted bear rug-shaped plaque which he hung in his office.

In *The Cheerful Fraud*, Reg played a wealthy young pugilist, Sir Michael Fairlie, who pursues the affection of a woman who's playing hard to get, portrayed by beautiful Gertrude Olmstead. To get closer to the girl, Fairlie takes the fraudulent job as her family's butler. Complications ensue when he's forced to be in two places at once without exposing his harmless deception. During a fight scene, there was no play-acting as Charles Gerrard sadly testified while Reg once again conducted his own stunts and gave his co-star a black eye. While on set, a famous Hungarian boxer and policeman, Ted "Kid" Lewis, came for a visit to Hollywood to personally meet Reg. The studio photographer took photo ops of the two world boxers on the set as if they were in a match in England.

During the film's production, Carl Laemmle was in London and he became seriously ill with a severe attack of grip. The studio chief was hospitalized for a month while his son, Carl Laemmle Jr., took over the reins. Uncle Carl finally recuperated enough to return home in time to make it to *The Cheerful Fraud* premiere, which he attended with Reg at the Uptown Theatre on New Year's Eve. The reception accorded the picture was the best tonic in the world for Laemmle Sr. who left the theater wreathed in smiles and stated to the press, "The popularity of *The Cheerful Fraud* may be taken as an earnest of the high quality of the other Reginald Denny Productions yet to come along this season."

Exhibitors were anxious for the film's release and Universal reported that the demand for bookings on this production exceeded anything ever met with before in the history of the organization. The film was to be released on January 16, 1927; however, it was shown during Christmas week in a small number of key cities, with the biggest premiere presentation at the Paramount Theatre on Broadway in New York City. *The Cheerful Fraud* was the first outside production to be booked into the rival studio's new house and was shown there during the week of December 25, 1926.

On January 10, Paramount Theatre's director of buying and booking sent Universal executives a letter featured in *Universal Weekly*: "At the time we negotiated for the exhibition of Reginald Denny in *Cheerful Fraud* for the Paramount Theatre, New York, I felt confident that the picture would give satisfaction at the box office for two reasons. First, because of its entertainment value and second, because of the popularity of the star. However, the results we did obtain so far exceeded our expectations that we have decided to pay you an additional $2,000 and enclosed herewith please find a check for that amount. With best wishes, I am Sincerely Sam Dembow, Jr. Director of Buying and Booking, Paramount Theatre." At the same time word came from an exhibitor in Los Angeles that *The Cheerful Fraud* broke all house records on its opening day at the Uptown Theatre and played to the biggest business ever done by that house in one day.

The press once again published fantastic reviews. Roscoe M'Gowen in the *New York Daily News* wrote, "Do you like farce? Do you like Reginald Denny? If so, you ought to have a good time at the Paramount this week. Probably he has never cavorted and grimaced through a fluffier bit of tomfoolery than *The Cheerful Fraud*. Ably aided by the roly-poly bundle of winsome male futility, Otis Harlan, and by the highly competent Gertrude Astor, Mr. Denny is, above all things, cheerful. Denny already is regarded on all sides as the best ace farceur on the screen. In this latest production he eclipses all of his former efforts. It is Denny at his Denniest." The film won a place on Mae Tinee's list of the six best photoplays in the January 1927 issue of the *Chicago Tribune*. "*The Cheerful Fraud* featured Reginald Denny in a gay piece that has been delighting the Denny fans. Another comedy—and another pretty clean one, featuring a man who, like Harold Lloyd, can be relied on not to sling dirt on the silver sheet."

Once again, the Seiter-Denny team made motion picture headlines. During production of the film, Bill Seiter and Laura La Plante got married with Reg as best man and Rene as Laura's bridesmaid. The sense of enjoyment spread on to the screen and was reflected in the playing of the cast which had become the happy family Reg had so desired.

8 FAST AND FURIOUS

REG ENJOYED THE MOMENTUM of his successes and he had been keeping up with the non-stop pace; however, his flight from rags to riches came at a cost. The actor was now overworked while he overplayed in his spare time. Not only was Reg physically conducting his own daring and strenuous stunts, the comedy required of him was just as physically demanding in order to keep audiences cracking up. He begged Carl Laemmle to make the switch and put him in dramatic roles that were more fitting for his nature. Laemmle finally gave him his way and cast Reg as a World War I veteran in Universal's drama *The Whole Town's Talking* (1926). The film was to be directed by another of Uncle Carl's nephews, Edward Laemmle, and it offered Reg the perfect opportunity to play a role more suited for him. Edward Laemmle and the studio executives, however, felt differently; they feared Reg couldn't play a dramatic role and more importantly that it would confuse audiences for a comedian to play a straight character. They instead cast Edward Everett Horton for the role of Chester Binney and decided to keep Reg in the over-the-top comedy roles that were earning the studio so much money.

It suddenly dawned on Reg he had created the farce in serious dramas, but now the studio couldn't see him as anything but a comedian as they pushed to make each film funnier than the last. Old man Laemmle felt bad that his executives hadn't cast Reg in the WWI drama in which he so badly wanted to star, so he made an exception in his contract and agreed to let him fly his Jenny in scenes for their WWI aviation film *The Lone Eagle* (1927). Universal wanted to capitalize on Charles Lindbergh's successful solo flight across the Atlantic, so they decided to make their own story of a wartime "lone eagle" in their appropriately named film directed by Emory Johnson. For the aerial sequences, Johnson used a mix of stock wartime footage and actual piloted planes. The real flying scenes were shot at Santa Monica's Clover Field where Reg kept his Jenny. He was happy to be given the opportunity to fly his biplane in this film instead of acting as a monkey in another. Along with Art Goebel, Reg and his Black Cats partners flew over the Pacific Ocean in mock dogfights for use in realistic aerial scenes. Reg loved flying once again with Goebel and being able to use his aerial acrobatic skills caught on film. In addition to flying his plane in *The Lone Eagle*, Reg also used his carving skills and assisted Universal's union crew to create miniature scale models of the warplanes, which they used to simulate the real thing when the real thing was too dangerous.

Since the studio wouldn't write an adventure drama for their comedy star, Reg returned to the pen and decided to write an action-racing story for himself. In *Slow Down*, he wrote about a speed fiend named Tom Brown who's bedridden as the result of a careless motor accident. As a result of his racy lifestyle, Brown has a nervous breakdown and isolates himself, but is then unexpectedly called upon to take part in a dangerous race to win the love of a woman. When Reg pitched his story to Laemmle, the studio head loved it and gave him the greenlight. What he didn't realize was the story reflected where Reg was in his own life, which would turn out to be another prophetic turn of the page.

Reg wanted Bill Seiter to direct his dramatic action film, but the studio had other plans. They didn't like that the actor and director disregarded their scenarios as written and instead did it their own way. They were concerned that Reg was overthinking everything, abusing his star power, and had become too demanding, thus wasting time on set and wasting their money. Laemmle tried to accommodate his favorite star in every way possible, but he was being advised by his executives otherwise. It was a fight all the way with Universal's writers and studio executives fearing that Reg was becoming too powerful, and that he and Seiter were forming their own production. The studio instead assigned their ace comedy writer, Melville Brown, to megaphone Reg's *Slow Down*. Mel had written numerous scenarios for Reg's successful Seiter-directed films and he was subsequently promoted to the directorial staff at Universal City. He cost the studio a lot less money than Seiter, thus helping with their production budget; however, Reg was not happy about yet another change against his wishes.

Filming of *Slow Down* began that November on location at the Del Monte race track in Pebble Beach. In order to make the racing scenes as real as possible and to save money, a real car race was again incorporated into the film. On the race track were a dozen internationally known auto racing drivers who operated the various entries in the thrilling auto race which marks the climax of the picture. Writer Paul Gulick was in Monterey on location and he witnessed Reg making a couple of loops around the Monterey track. In *Universal Weekly*, he featured a story about Reg's driving. "I had the pleasure of spending several days at Monterey with Denny and seeing the way in which Melville W. Brown, the kid director, achieved effects with him. I watched Reg race in a little low-down Miller Special that they said could do up to 150 miles, but it looked like 200. When Reg pulled up to me, he asked me to take a turn with him. I turned from him so fast that the whole company laughed. Reg is touted as a speed demon and no amount of caution and not even the laws of gravitation or centrifugal force cause him any concern."

It rained heavily the next shooting day. Instead of holding off on filming, Mel Brown had the crew continue the automobile scenes on the slippery muddy roads in order to meet the shooting schedule and to save money. In a scene they were filming that day, Reg's touring car is passing a big limousine on a road that's supposed to represent an unimproved stretch of turnpike in Maine. When Reg's roadster accidently splashed the limousine's chauffer with a gob of mud right smack in the eye, Mel Brown right then and there ran off three extra comedy scenes, which were not scripted. Most directors would have called "Cut!" at the splash and reshot the scene according to script, but not this new director. Mel turned Reg's action-drama into a comedy; thus, another temper tantrum on set.

The next day while filming additional motor racing scenes, there was a gnarly shot for the film's opening sequence. Reg's new leading lady in the film, Barbara Worth, said she could drive a racecar and asked Mel if she could take a shot at the roadster for the scene. Against Reg's refusal, the director agreed to let her. As Worth was speeding around a sharp curve with Reg in the passenger seat, she didn't slow down and took a turn too quickly then crashed into a brick wall. Reg was thrown out of his speeding car and also hit the wall. His car was wrecked, and the crew thought he was dead. An ambulance was on set and they rushed Reg to the hospital with a fractured skull, a broken arm, a broken pelvis, and a broken ankle. He was then flown back to Los Angeles where he could recuperate near his wife and daughter who were again worried sick.

Once he could speak, Reg expressed to Laemmle how upset he was that the studio had delegated a beginner director for such an action-packed, risky film. He blamed them for hiring Mel Brown who turned his adventure-drama into a comedy, and he let an actress drive a racecar without first testing her skills with one of the pro-racers. It was too much of a stunt film for a starlet who was just starting out and did not have the car-racing experience that she claimed. Laemmle apologized and said he'd speak with his green director. As a joke, Reg suggested that they change the title of his film from *Slow Down* to *Fast and Furious*, which the studio head took to heart and made the formal change.

A couple weeks later, Reg was released from the hospital and soon returned back to work on the Universal lot for completion of the film's non-action interior shots. He was still healing from his broken bones when he started feeling nauseous and getting sharp pains in his stomach. He kept on working all the same. Just as the crew was wrapping up one of the last scenes, Reg suddenly had a severe appendicitis attack and was rushed to the Sylvan Lodge Hospital in Los Angeles where he was taken into the operating room in time, before the rupture killed him.

Hospitalized and again confined to his bed, Reg was surrounded by the medical staff as well as well-wishing patients who were big fans. One of the patients there had a lung condition and expressed to the theatrical star that she couldn't go to his movies any longer due to the "stale air" she had been breathing from being in the crowded theater. More patients chimed in about such air pollution without proper ventilation in confined spaces. Reg listened, then he used his star power and began a literary campaign with a nationwide movement for better ventilation systems in theaters, schools, and public buildings. The film star took out an ad in *Variety*, as well as other top newspapers, with a public statement to obtain the enactment of a national pure air law, urging Congress to pass a bill for health so it was mandatory for enclosed public environments to have air conditioning. He also wrote to theatrical exhibitors nationwide urging them all to get air conditioning in their theaters. Reg stressed that all theaters be equipped with air conditioning for the comfort and health of their patrons. "In theaters and other auditoriums where groups of people gather, there is such a thing as crowd poisoning unless the place is scientifically ventilated. Although the big theaters have been leaders in air conditioning, there are still many of the smaller type theaters where the air is very poor. The important thing to remember is that the effect of a good picture is spoiled by poor air conditions. Tests have shown that air decidedly affects a person's capability for enjoyment or mental effort."

In response to Reg's campaign, the president of the leading air conditioning company, Electrozone, wrote him a letter: "Dear Mr. Denny: In a copy of the *New York Daily News*, Friday March 25th, we note that you are enthusiastic in your efforts for pure air ventilation in theaters and places of public gathering. We wish to say that we are heartily in accord with your ideas and will be glad to cooperate with you in every way possible to bring about this very desirable innovation in all sections of the country. There are a number of theaters in the West who are using ozone ventilating systems, and we are having a hard pull in the East to get the Architects, who seem to know nothing about ozone ventilation, as you, who are engaged in entertaining the American public continuously, that realize the absolute necessity of pure air in theaters and public buildings. We have some very interesting scientific documents which, no doubt, will be of great value to you in your campaign for better air conditions in theaters, and we will be very glad, if you express a desire, to send you any and all information that we have been able to gather over a period of ten years of research work in the laboratories of the General Electric Co., and our own efforts in this line. We will be very much pleased to get any information that you may have gleaned along the lines of impure air and shall certainly use every effort that we have at our disposal to carry on this very much needed reform. If there is anything that you would desire in the way of information, etc. from us, kindly let us hear from you and we will reply very promptly. The writer has the honor of having one of the first operations performed in the city of Chicago for appendicitis (if you call this an honor) and is therefore one of the oldest members of the 'Appendix Minus Club,' and I certainly wish you the best of health, recovery, and success in your own business and in the good work that you have pledged to aid. Hoping that we may have the pleasure of hearing from you, we remain Yours very truly, E.X. Jones, Electrozone Corporation of New York."

Hundreds of theater owners as well as members of Congress also replied to Reg and thanked him for the suggestion. Everyone wholeheartedly agreed and, as pure air was now a priority to them, changes would be made quickly so all of his fans could enjoy Super Denny films with a breath of fresh air.

When Reg was again released from the hospital, the crew finally wrapped production on *Fast and Furious*. Another delay occurred when the highly flammable nitrate film caught on fire in the cutting room at Universal while Mel Brown was working with the editor. Mel and his editor quickly removed the reels and ran out while the studio's firefighters put out the dangerous blaze which almost destroyed the entire film. Reg was relieved to learn most of the film was salvaged as that was the original and only copy of the picture from its cameraman; his hard work and injuries would've been in vain if lost in the flames. All this had him reflecting on his own fast and furious life, that it could all be taken away in a flash. He had pushed his luck to the point of near death, racing on dangerous tracks and the highways of Southern California, yachting in the Pacific to near death, flying airplanes with a bunch of daredevils, and working more than any other actor in town. It seemed he had truly been defying the odds as a cat with nine lives.

Meanwhile, Rene was ready for another nervous breakdown. While she had gratefully supported Reg's quick rise to fame, she was again living as a single mother to raise their now ten-year-old Barbara on her own while he reveled in the spotlight and behaved in a reckless manner. Although her husband was being a good provider, she felt he was being careless by taking part in such life-threatening activities, as well as his now publicized meltdowns on set. Her role had transformed from a loving, supportive wife into that of a worried and scolding mother. She insisted that Reg take a real break from his hectic schedule to recuperate from Hollywood and for the family to heal together. Reg decided she was right, and he told Laemmle he'd be taking a couple weeks to recuperate from his many injuries. Uncle Carl agreed and told his comedy star they'd put off production of his next film until he was ready.

That spring, the family left their home in Hollywood and headed up to their peaceful cabin in the mountains. One morning, Reg and Barbara took a walk on the path near his new landing field. There, they noticed an injured female hawk on the mountainside. Reg took off his jacket and with it he carefully picked up the raptor bird to bring her back to the cabin. He and Barbara built a coop for the hawk and nicknamed her "Georgie," short for Georgina. Reg spent hours with Georgie as he carefully mended her broken wing to health while mending his own broken wings. He and Barbara together bonded with the hawk as they acclimated her to independence. When it was finally time for her to take flight, Reg smiled as he and Barbara released Georgie to the skies to once again be free.

After spending two weeks at the cabin, Reg knew he had to get back to the studio for his next film. Carl Laemmle called him in for a meeting and again apologized for putting his favorite actor's life in jeopardy while also wrecking his racecar. He told Reg that he'd be reimbursed for the losses and expressed appreciation for all of his hard work over the years. Laemmle then said he was happy to share that the studio was dedicating more money to their Super Denny pictures, and that production costs for his pictures had been materially increased over the cost of his past and current releases. This increase, he said, would go into story value, directorial supervision, gag-men, better sets, and stronger casts. He then told Reg that Bill Seiter would be directing his next film titled *Out All Night* written by Gladys Lehman. Reg thanked Uncle Carl and expressed his gratitude for the care he took to ensure his health and happiness.

After his meeting with Laemmle, Reg immediately picked up work on the less action-packed film *Out All Night* (1927). A lot of folks were waiting for commencement of Reg's next film, and of all the people in the world most anxious for his recovery were Bill Seiter and Laura La Plante. They had gotten married during the fall of the previous year but had delayed their honeymoon twice until their respective films had finished production. Reg was happy to be reunited with his familiar winning team of Bill Seiter, Marian Nixon, and Ben Hendricks, Jr. in the story about young playboy, John Graham, and an actress, Molly O'Day, who are secretly married and take a cruise on an ocean liner. Through a series of mishaps and mistaken identity, Graham poses as the ship's surgeon and as a scrubwoman in his frantic efforts to get to his secret bride on the cruise. The cast all had a great time working together, but Reg was still not fully recovered and had to take several breaks while on set during filming.

Just after completing *Out All Night* and prior to the release of *Fast and Furious*, Universal announced the first nationwide star tie-up with the Kellogg Company of Battle Creek, Michigan, who advertised their famous breakfast food, PEP Bran Flakes, together with Universal's popular star. The joint marketing effort was broadcast on more than two hundred billboards with life-size color art of Reg in his racecar with the cereal box and

"Reginald Denny Peps Up with PEP!" In addition to the billboard ads, the campaign was featured in newspapers and magazines distributed throughout the U.S. and Canada to reach more than fifty-million people during the summer of 1927. The Kellogg team announced in *Universal Weekly*, "In the selection of a star who represented action, speed and real pep, the choice naturally fell to Reginald Denny in his high-speed drama, *Fast And Furious*. Another natural because of Denny's upcoming hurry-up comedy-drama, *Out All Night*, with the uplifting effect of Kellogg's PEP in the morning."

The day after completing work on *Out All Night*, Reg and Rene attended the premiere of *Fast and Furious* where they finally saw the action that led to his injuries. The first thing thrown on the screen as the picture opened was a view of a winding road rapidly disappearing underfoot as a speeding car eats it up. A familiar diamond-shaped road sign looms up beside the road and zooms in to a close-up with the film's title. When the names of the cast fade out, the speedy motor journey resumes. The passengers, the audience, were unable to see the driver, or even the hood of the car they were riding in, but they were able to see the speed at which they were traveling. The speedometer was glimpsed in intervals hovering between 60 and 70 mph. Other cars on the road were avoided in zig-zag fashion by the narrowest squeaks, and occasional glances backward revealing a trail of wreckage. The sequence ends when a telephone pole cannot be avoided where wires, poles, and wreckage filled the screen in a chaotic whirl. The audience screamed as if they were reacting to the accident, which made its viewers feel as though they were actually in the car itself. This type of "virtual reality" opening sequence had never been done before, as though patrons were driving the car in a sort of ride similar to the attractions now at Universal's theme park.

The action-packed film was a huge box-office success and started off in super style. Earl Cunningham of the Colonial Theatre in Indianapolis wrote to Universal, "World premiere of Reginald Denny in *Fast and Furious* opened here Sunday establishing a new house record. Great picture in every way and will make money anywhere any time. Congratulations to Universal on this bang-up automobile racing story and picture." The press raved about it, especially impressed with the opening scene in which Reg acquired his broken bones. Harold N. Hubbard in the *Hollywood Citizen* said, "With a clever opening sequence that will seldom be equaled in its ability to catch and hold the interest of an audience, *Fast and Furious*, new Reginald Denny picture which opened last night at the West Coast Uptown Theatre, lives up to its title throughout. Even the laughs come 'fast and furious.'"

From the *Los Angeles Times* came, "When the year's last foot of celluloid has clicked its perforated way through the projection machines and the big mogul critics—in penitence for some of the unkind things they have said in the past—step manfully forward with their annual bouquets for the best this and the best that, it is suggested that they reserve a place in their list for *Fast and Furious*, a Universal picture at the Uptown, as the one with the cleverest opening sequence in a blue moon. It is well done. Whether the treatment is called subjective or something else, it most certainly tells its story in motion pictures, with a steady build up to the crash. The likable Reginald Denny proves as likable as ever in *Fast and Furious*."

Gregory Goss in the *Los Angeles Examiner* wrote, "*Fast and Furious* is the pace set by Reginald Denny in the picture of that title now at the Uptown. Racing cars and paved highways do their part in establishing a momentum with only romance to act as a brake.

Denny himself wrote the story, so naturally the leading role is tailored to fit his ener-getic and engaging personality. He encounters a series of incidents slightly reminiscent of Douglas MacLean's efforts to ride *The Hottentot*."

Mae Tinee in *The Chicago Tribune* wrote, "In this picture the hero loses his nerve. No wonder. One moment he is a happy carefree soul, speeding along a country road at a minimum speed of ninety miles per hour. The next, though apparently quite all right to the human eye, he is inside a total wreck whose cracks and fractures and dislocations are displayed to your fascinated eyes not so much later by means of X-ray."

The press didn't realize how true to life it all really was. Mel Brown had used all the footage of Reg's real-time crashes and the studio capitalized on his injuries. He was re-imbursed for the roadster, but instead of buying a new racecar Reg decided he'd keep his original film title for himself and literally "slow down." He had received too many speed-ing tickets while racing to and from the mountains anyway and, as a result, his driver's license had been suspended.

After five years of working non-stop meeting the physical demands of his films while he fulfilled his Universal contract above and beyond the terms, Reg was injured and ex-periencing exhaustion. It was time for an escape from the studio, the press, his fans, and America. The mountain cabin had proven to be too easily accessible for Reg to be drawn to the studio and for others to come up. Reg's sister Nora was worried for her brother and insisted that he come stay with her for a peaceful sojourn away from hectic Hollywood. It had been over ten years since Reg and Rene had been to their homeland together and they longed to return to England so Barbara could get to know her relatives. Reg had another meeting with Carl Laemmle. When Laemmle asked how he was healing, he told his boss he needed a break if he was to remain their top comedic action star. Reg stressed how grateful he was for what the studio chief had done for him, but he hadn't had a real vacation after working five years straight with numerous stunt injuries and surgeries. Carl Laemmle empathetically agreed and said he'd put the next Super Denny picture on hold. He offered the star six weeks of uninterrupted vacation. It was time to go home.

Reginald Leigh Dugmore (1893). Courtesy of Reginald Denny Collection

Master Reginald Denny as Prince Charles Ferdinand in *A Royal Family* (1899). Courtesy of Reginald Denny Collection with photo credit to Alfred Ellis & Walery.

Georgina Pike Dugmore (1899). Courtesy of Reginald Denny Collection

W.H. Denny as Jester during Shakespeare Australian tour (1902). Courtesy of Reginald Denny Collection with photo credit to Talma Australia

Reg as Harry Shirley with Oza Waldrop in *Friend Martha* (1917) at the Booth Theatre on Broadway. Courtesy of Reginald Denny Collection with photo credit to White Studio.

Lt. Reginald Denny of the Royal Air Force (1918). Courtesy of Reginald Denny Collection with photo credit to Bushnell.

Seated center at RCAF repatriation camp waiting to go home post-WWI (1918).
Courtesy of Chronicle/Alamy Stock Photo.

As Prince Anton with Alice Brady, Roni Pursell, and James Crane in *A Dark Lantern* (1920).
Courtesy of Reginald Denny Collection and Marc Wanamaker/Bison Archives.

Headshot used in *The Price of Possession* (1920). Courtesy of Reginald Denny Collection.

As Robert Dawney with Ethel Clayton in *The Price of Possession* (1920).
Courtesy of Marc Wanamaker/Bison Archives.

As Brett Page with Elsie Ferguson in *Footlights* (1921).
Courtesy of Marc Wanamaker/Bison Archives.

As Scen the Drifter with Huntley Gordon, Ruth Clifford, and Ernest Hilliard in *Tropical Love* (1921). Courtesy of Marc Wanamaker/Bison Archives.

The Leather Pushers lobby card as Kane "Kid Roberts" Halliday in *Round One: Through The Looking Glass* (1921). Courtesy of Reginald Denny Collection.

Lobby card for *Round Two: With This Ring I Thee Fed!* (1921).
Courtesy of Reginald Denny Collection.

Lobby card for *Round Three: Payment Through The Nose* (1922).
Courtesy of Reginald Denny Collection.

Lobby card for *Round Four: A Fool and His Honey* (1922).
Courtesy of Reginald Denny Collection.

Lobby card for *Round Five: The Taming of the Shrewd* (1922).
Courtesy of Reginald Denny Collection.

Lobby card for *Round Six: Whipsawed!* (1922).
Courtesy of Reginald Denny Collection.

Lobby card for *Young King Cole* (1922). Courtesy of Reginald Denny Collection.

Lobby card for *He Raised Kane* (1922). Courtesy of Reginald Denny Collection.

Lobby card for *The Chickasha Bone Crusher* (1923). Courtesy of Reginald Denny Collection.

Lobby card for *When Kane Met Abel* (1923). Courtesy of Reginald Denny Collection.

Lobby card for *Strike Father, Strike Son* (1923). Courtesy of Reginald Denny Collection.

Lobby card for *Joan of Newark* (1923). Courtesy of Reginald Denny Collection.

Lobby card for *The Wandering Two* (1923). Courtesy of Reginald Denny Collection.

Lobby card for *The Widower's Mite* (1923). Courtesy of Reginald Denny Collection.

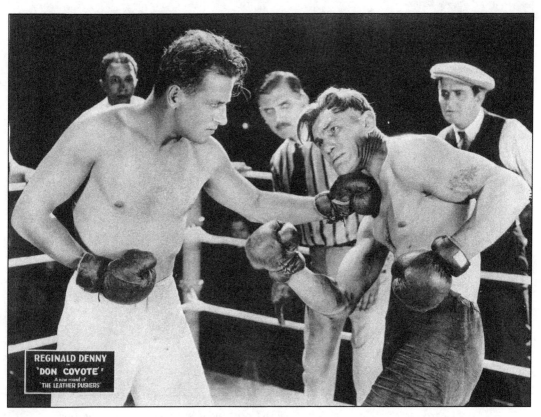

Lobby card for *Don Coyote* (1923). Courtesy of Reginald Denny Collection.

Lobby card for *Something For Nothing* (1923). Courtesy of Reginald Denny Collection.

Oceanfront boxing ring in *Columbia, The Gem, and The Ocean* (1923).
Courtesy of Reginald Denny Collection.

Lobby card for *The Abysmal Brute* as Pat Glendon, Jr. at dinner with Mabel Julienne Scott (1923). Courtesy of Reginald Denny collection.

The Brute wins the belt and the girl in *The Abysmal Brute* (1923).
Courtesy of Reginald Denny Collection.

As Jimmy Wood with Laura La Plante in *Sporting Youth* (1924).
Courtesy of Marc Wanamaker/Bison Archives.

Walking the plank in *Sporting Youth* lobby card (1924).
Courtesy of Marc Wanamaker/Bison Archives.

As Dick Minot with Ruth Dwyer and their "Taxy" driver in *The Reckless Age* (1924).
Courtesy of Marc Wanamaker/Bison Archives.

On location at Catalina Island with actors Lee Moran and T.D. Crittenden, director Bill Seiter, assistant director Nate Watt, 2nd assistant director Louis Milestone, cameramen Ben F. Reynolds, and Bert Six with crew of *The Fast Worker* (1924). Courtesy of Reginald Denny Collection and Marc Wanamaker/Bison Archives.

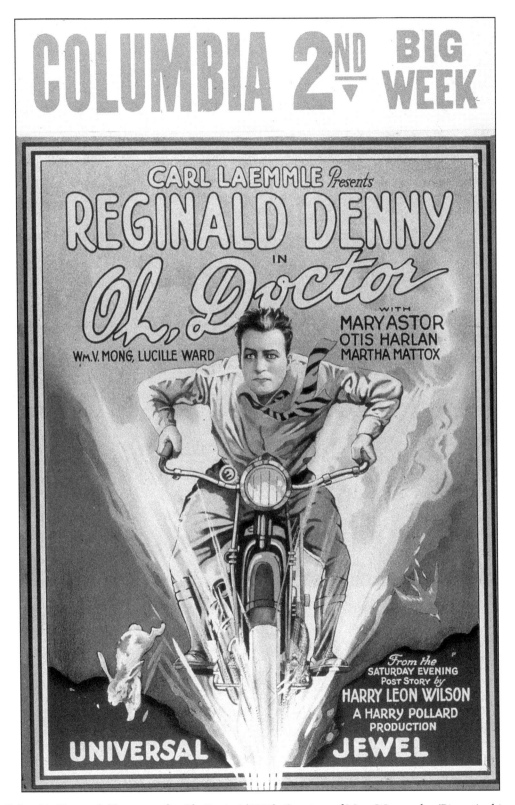

Columbia Theatre lobby poster for *Oh, Doctor!* (1925). Courtesy of Marc Wanamaker/Bison Archives.

As Alec Dupree in *I'll Show You The Town* (1925). Courtesy of Reginald Denny Collection.

With Marian Nixon in *I'll Show You The Town* (1925). Courtesy of Reginald Denny Collection.

As Thomas S. Berford with Lee Moran and Marian Nixon in *Where Was I?* (1925). Courtesy of Reginald Denny Collection.

Captain Reginald Denny of the *SS Barbarene* (1925). Courtesy of Reginald Denny Collection.

Spear fishing in the Pacific (1925). Courtesy of Reginald Denny collection.

After a day of fishing off Catalina Island (1925). Courtesy of Reginald Denny collection.

Eyes to the sky (1925). Courtesy of Reginald Denny collection.

With his Jenny (1925). Courtesy of Reginald Denny collection.

A day of flight with Rene, Barbara, and his Jenny (1925).
Courtesy of Reginald Denny collection.

In his Jenny with fellow aviator and a few screws loose (1925).
Courtesy of Reginald Denny collection.

Dubbed as a Black Cat by Bon MacDougall with Sam Greenwald, Herb McClellan, Spider Matlock, Al Johnson, Fronty Nichols, Paul Richter, and Art Goebel at Burdett Airport (1926). Courtesy of Marc Wanamaker/Bison Archives.

The Thirteenth Black Cat (1926). Courtesy of Reginald Denny Collection.

With Edsel Ford's Stout Metal Airplane Company executives (1926).
Courtesy of Reginald Denny collection.

As Tom Jones with Emily Fitzroy and Otis Harlan in *What Happened To Jones* (1925).
Courtesy of Reginald Denny Collection.

In drag with Otis Harlan in *What Happened To Jones* (1925).
Courtesy of Reginald Denny Collection.

Universal's WAMPAS promotion featuring Virginia Valli, Laura La Plante, Mary Philbin, Margaret Quimby, Jean Hersholt, Hoot Gibson, Norman Ferry, Jack Hoxie, Arthur Lake, Charles Puffy, William Desmond, and other Universal stars with Betsy Lee standing on bench behind Reg (1926). Courtesy of Marc Wanamaker/Bison Archives.

At home with Rene, Barbara, and their German Shepherd (1926).
Courtesy of Marc Wanamaker/Bison Archives.

As Skinner with Laura La Plante as Honey in *Skinner's Dress Suit* (1926).
Courtesy of Reginald Denny Collection.

Skinner and Honey teaching students the "Savannah Shuffle" in *Skinner's Dress Suit* (1926).
Courtesy of Reginald Denny Collection.

Grinning at lobby poster of Skinner. Courtesy of Reginald Denny Collection.

With Mayor Murray Seasongood and his team in Cincinnati during Rolling Home Tour (1926).
Courtesy of Reginald Denny Collection.

With Carl Laemmle on Capitol Hill in Washington DC during Rolling Home Tour (1926).
Courtesy of Marc Wanamaker/Bison Archives.

With Carl Laemmle on front steps of The White House (1926).
Courtesy of the Library of Congress.

Boarding train while rolling home during Rolling Home Tour (1926).
Courtesy of Marc Wanamaker/Bison Archives.

Portrait photo sketch by M. I. Boris (1926). Courtesy of Reginald Denny
collection with photo credit to M.I. Boris.

Portrait sketch by M. I. Boris with an autographed note to Betsy Lee (1926).
Courtesy of Reginald Denny collection with photo credit to M.I. Boris.

As Tom Eggers in *Take It From Me* (1926). Courtesy of Reginald Denny collection.

Universal publicity portrait by Freulich (1926). Courtesy of Reginald Denny collection with photo credit to Roman Freulich.

With World Welterweight Champion Ted "Kid" Lewis on Universal set (1926).
Courtesy of Marc Wanamaker/Bison Archives.

With Bill Seiter and boxing dummy on Universal set of *The Cheerful Fraud* (1926).
Courtesy of Reginald Denny Collection.

As Best Man at Bill Seiter's and Laura La Plante's wedding (1926).
Courtesy of Reginald Denny Collection.

Driving racecar for virtual reality opening sequence for *Fast and Furious* (1926).
Courtesy of Marc Wanamaker/Bison Archives.

As Tom Brown with Armand Kaliz in *Fast and Furious* (1927).
Courtesy of Reginald Denny Collection.

As John Graham in *Out All Night* (1927). Courtesy of Reginald Denny Collection.

9

MOTHERLAND

REG, RENE, AND BARBARA FLEW TO NEW YORK and then boarded Cunard's *RMS Berengaria* for their long overdue trip to England. The family sailed across the Atlantic on the luxury ocean liner headed for Southampton where they were to take a train onto Richmond for a peaceful visit with Reg's sister. Nora had married a wealthy railroad and tobacco magnate, Stockwell "Tiny" Reynolds Diaz-Albertini, who owned a castle estate called White Lodge outside of London on the Thames, where the family was to stay. The farce-comedy ace thought that he and his family could slip out of Hollywood and ship from New York with no publicity, and thus spend their time in England quietly. Reg was surprised when the ship pulled up to the port where he was greeted by thousands of smiling fans with a swarm of newspaper reporters and cameramen awaiting his arrival.

While the family was still aboard the ship, press agents hoarded around them. In response to their barrage of questions, Reg gallantly made an announcement: "I am over here on holiday and I particularly want to avoid any film fan hero-worship, or rubbish of that kind. I should hate any fuss or bother made during my visit to this country, and I have begged my company to see that while I am over here I am left unmolested."

The family made it through the large crowd and took the train from Southampton to London where they were again greeted by thousands of cheering fans. Reg's heart melted as his welcome in England was one of the warmest ever accorded to a returning Englishman in brotherly adoration. It far exceeded in spontaneity and real friendliness that ever given to any film star and it brought tears to his eyes. It set in with Reg that he was refreshingly back home. "Coming up in the train from Southampton, where I arrived in the *Berengaria*, I kept looking out and admiring those wonderful fresh fields. It had been raining a little, and the trees and hedges glistened in the sun, while the clouds of the passing storm on the horizon formed a remarkable background. After the Hollywood atmosphere it is good to come back to the old country, to the leafy lanes and country simplicity."

He was a smiling, modest hero when he faced a battalion of quizzing pressmen and graciously responded to their questions. "Eight years is a mighty long time for one to be away from one's native land, and I have not been here more than twenty-four hours before a large number of people asked me, 'Has England changed during your absence?' But I have already found an answer to the question and the answer is, 'No.' I find England as beautifully green as ever, and London—oh boy! It's great to be back in London. And even if the architecture of Regent-street is a bit altered and Piccadilly is up—why, Regent-street is just the same after all, and I can't remember Piccadilly being anything but up. Yes, London remains the greatest city in the world, but what attracts me most is the English countryside."

When asked about his success in Hollywood, Reg gave a brief and humble history of his hardships, stating that hero-worship of Hollywood film stars was overrated. "It is feted too much in America, but then they like it. You cannot appreciate fully the charm of English people, even as an Englishman, until a long exile has forced it upon you. It is wonderful to be home. For myself, nothing, I hope, will ever rob me of my English characteristics, not even the awful glare and glamour which must inevitably surround a man who is unfortunate enough to become a film star." He downplayed any success he had in life, including his boxing abilities and his war service. "Just the very first thing I want to do on this visit to England, which is my first visit to my native country since 1919, is to correct two wrong stories that are floating around. The first is that I was at one time heavy-weight champion of the British Army. That is not so. The nearest I ever got to that position was winning the RAF Brigade boxing tournament during the war, and even that was a painful business. The second thing is the tale that keeps cropping up about my 'wonderful war service.' Let me say right here and now that there was nothing wonderful about it. I served just the same as everybody else. My brother is the real hero who lost his life in battle. And that truly was not wonderful."

At the urging of prominent British film figures and important personages, Reg finally allowed Universal's British distribution arm, the European Motion Picture Company or "Europeans" as they were called, to go through with certain functions which they had planned for his homecoming. Over the next couple of weeks, Reg made several personal and public appearances across England while Rene and Barbara stayed at Nora's White Lodge. Among the functions he accepted was a press reception luncheon given in his honor by Europeans. The event was held at London's Savoy Hotel and attended by three hundred of Britain's leading showmen, exhibitors, and representatives of the press including England's leading trade paper, *The Cinema*. The large ornate banquet room of the hotel had been suitably decorated with British and American flags surrounded by carnations and a welcome banner in bold type above Reg's chair with 'Welcome Home to our Denny—He's a Regular Fellow!' Large stills of Reg, in many of his popular features, hung around the walls and there was a decided Denny atmosphere about the function. All the prominent figures of Wardour Street were present. Reg found himself between Ireland's Marquess of Donegall and famous round-the-world aviation pioneer Sir Alan Cobham. Cobham testified to Lady Cobham's preference for Reg's films; he said that his wife was a severe critic of films, but she always enjoyed any Denny picture. Cobham also told Reg about the Sopwith Snipes that had just been retired from service and he'd be happy to arrange a flight for the once-upon a flyboy.

The president of Great Britain's Cinematograph Exhibitors Association (CEA), Mr. E. Hewitson, took stage and proposed a toast to the honored guest. "It was a pleasure," he said, "to congratulate a Britisher who had made good, no matter in what country." Hewitson expressed the hope that it might be possible for the European Film Company to make some Reginald Denny comedies in Great Britain. Universal's James "Jimmy" Bryson rose and stated that it might be possible for Universal to make pictures in England, if Parliament would allow it. Parliament had just passed the "quota law" which stated that a certain number of films released in the United Kingdom had to be of British origin. As he was still a British subject, Reg's work in British films would count as "quota pictures," but they had to be made in Great Britain by a British company.

After the intro speeches were given by prominent Britishers, it was time for the guest of honor to give his speech. Clad in a well-fitting light blue suit, which revealed his athletic figure and gleaming blue eyes to advantage, Reg rose to a full room of hearty applause and enthusiastic cheers. In answering the rapid-fire questions aimed at him by the reporters, Reg was perfectly at ease, his answers being pleasantly frank and direct while giving his attention to whomever asked questions. He shared that he was proud to have come from an old, old family of British actors and how his father had tried hard to dissuade him from going on the stage when he was a youth. His speech was really a heart-to-heart talk with his fellow Britishers whom he said had given him the happiest time of his life that day. It was wrong, he said, to thank him for giving his time to something which pleased his ego more than anything in his life had done. To come back to his country and to receive such a welcome, to have guests like Sir Alan Cobham present in his honor, really satiated his ego.

Reg shared his thoughts in a sentimental monologue: "America is a wonderful country and it has been kind to me, but I have had a great longing to be home. I am British, and although I have been asked to take out naturalization papers, I could not bring myself to do it. My little daughter is my gift to America. California is a fine home which gives one great opportunities for boxing, fencing, riding, and swimming; however, the chief thing that we miss is the green of England. Hollywood pays the penalty of its near-perfect climate. Nature economizes on green. We also miss those historical associations and traditions, which play so large a part in English life. These tug at the heart-strings. Hollywood's most ancient monument is the castle that Douglas Fairbanks built for *Robin Hood*, but neither the countryside nor the people are so raw and raucous as most English folk imagine them to be. America is saturated in film atmosphere, and although some of the stuff turned out is perfectly terrible, from the point of view of an ant, yet they certainly have the knack of pleasing the public palate in a general way. They have every trick in the business and all its branches at their finger-ends. England has wonderful resources to draw upon. She has the finest literature in the world, beautiful country, and fine country mansions, all useful for film production. All that is lacking is experience. Once this country gets into its stride there is no reason in the world why we should not find big stars over here. As a nation we are at least as handsome as any other, and there is always plenty of talent to be found by the earnest seeker. Besides, look at the number of British actors and actresses who have made good in Hollywood. There must be well over two thousand in Hollywood alone. And they are not out-of-work 'supers,' either. The majority of them are high up in the pay roll."

When asked when he was coming back to make pictures in his homeland, Reg responded that he would very much like to make some pictures in England. He said for the past eight years he had been dreaming of his return, but he believed in the sanctity of contracts and chose to fulfill the honorable obligations of his contract with Carl Laemmle, the great little man to whom he owed so much. "As a Britisher, it is one of my great ambitions to make pictures in Great Britain and I am actually in the process of trying to arrange it. I sincerely hope I succeed. I believe that there is real scope for them here. I want to produce for a British firm because I am an Englishman and should like to do a bit for production on this side. I am going to ask Mr. Laemmle to release me to come to England for a short time to make big films, if only to assist the quota scheme."

Reg also shared that he received an offer from a British firm who had a distribution tie-up with an American rival of Universal to star in two British-made pictures at a salary he described as "surprising." The company was Warner Bros.' newly acquired First National Pictures. "I have already received an attractive offer from a British company. It is evident there is some pretty big money floating about in the English producing business. If British companies can afford to make offers such as the one I received, then there must be a lot of money hanging around somewhere. My negotiations with a British firm are being made entirely with the sanction of Universal because although Mr. Laemmle said 'no' when I asked him for permission, it was in a hesitating way, which makes me feel he will give me permission after a while. Mr. Laemmle is a very sweet old gentleman and man I greatly admire. He has promised to consider releasing me and already we have been working on a story with an English director. At one time he suggested he would make pictures in England and that he would let me come over and make them. I have been longing for this and am waiting for that time. British films have my whole-hearted support, and if I can manage it when I get back to America, I am going to get leave to return to England to make one or two films." He closed his speech on that note and three cheers were given with good will. The guests then sang, "For He's a Jolly Good Fellow." The Marquess of Donegal rose and presented the guest of honor with a leather-bound autograph album containing signatures of all the guests, together with a playful reminder from Frank S. Ditcham that they were not to be used for checks.

After the formal luncheon, Reg took a seat on the edge of the long table and lit a cigarette for a more informal discussion. European's press manager F. W. Harland-Edgecumbe offered Reg a cigar, but he respectfully refused saying that it might make him sick. While swinging his legs casually, Reg continued that he was in England more or less as a convalescent, but at the same time he was hoping to secure film rights of a first-class boxing story originally published as a novel by a very famous British author. When asked who it was, he wouldn't answer fearing that premature disclosure might injure his chances. When the group wouldn't give up and pressured for him to divulge who it was, Reg finally confessed that it was George Bernard Shaw. "Nothing would please me more," he said, "than to appear in the screening of Mr. Shaw's work, but I am afraid of Mr. Shaw. I am going to see him and try to get him to allow me to film *Cashel Byron's Profession*, which I believe would be a good subject for me."

The press responded favorably by featuring hundreds of articles in European newspapers during his trip. *The Times* claimed, "What a charming and likeable fellow Reginald Denny is! There has never been a more unassuming film star than Reginald Denny on a visit to this country. There is nothing snobbish about this man; he is not over anxious to stress his achievements and they are such as might justify a little puff. If Reginald Denny gets *Cashel Byron's Profession*, he should make a good thing of it. He has a boxer's physique and although he spent the first five minutes of interviews denying the laudatory rumors that had made him boxing champion of the British Army, a man with a wonderful war record, and so on, it transpired that he had, during his army career, won the boxing championship for his brigade in the RAF."

Reg was then asked to attend a number of other organized British assemblies, one being in Manchester. Due to the unforeseen publicity engagements that had now been planned for him, Reg sent a telegram to Laemmle and asked for an extension of his vacation. He soon received a cable back from the Universal headquarters granting him a two-week extension providing him two months rather than the six-week vacation Uncle Carl had previously allowed.

The next day, Reg boarded the train at London's Euston Station with Jimmy Bryson and a couple of other Universal executives headed to Manchester. When the train pulled up to the station, it was literally mobbed by more than fifteen thousand Lancashire admirers. With difficulty, the police made a way for the young actor through the crowds. Cries of "Good old Denny" were shouted as he journeyed to the Midland Hotel where another luncheon was given in his honor. Thousands of people were assembled outside the building to witness his arrival, and they were so eager for a close-up of the hero that the police were powerless to hold them back. Reg was surrounded in a moment, cheered, thumped on the back, and shaken by the hand by innumerable admirers as Bryson dragged him by force into the building. "Welcome to Reginald Denny" ran a banner outside the entrance, and as Reg entered, he cheerfully waved to his fans. A group of ladies whispered, "Isn't he nice? He's even nicer off than on!"

Inside the Midland Hotel was a luncheon attended by one-hundred-sixty-five northern exhibitors. Chairman of the local CEA, H. D. Moorhouse, chaired the event and was supported by the chief constables of Manchester and Salford. The managing director of Liverpool's Granby Cinema, George Smith, owned a valuable collection of historical theater bills. He presented Reg with a very old daybill bearing his father's name in a Manchester pantomime cast of the late 1800s. Reg was exceedingly enthusiastic about the daybill, and thanked him warmly, saying how good Mr. Smith had been to think of him like that as he proudly showed it around to the guests while sharing his father's insulting plea to leave the stage.

After another endearing speech, Reg was taken through the crowds to the newly built Blackley Palaise-de-Danse Theatre on Rochdale Road. The streets around the theater were jammed with people, eager to pay tribute to "Good Old Reggie," as he was affectionately termed by his fellow countrymen. H. D. Moorhouse had just built the new theater and dance-hall where Reg officiated at its grand opening and laid a foundation stone bearing the "kinema's" name commemorating his visit. Thousands of people clustered around him, cheering him to the echo when Harry Fildes handed him a silver trowel antique cup as a memento of the occasion. After a speech by Moorhouse, they all sang "For He's a Jolly Good Fellow." Reg made a solemn promise to Moorhouse that when he next returned to Manchester, he would see the dogs. Moorhouse owned quite a number of greyhounds which ran at Belle Vue Stadium.

Afterward, Reg left for a short trip to Liverpool where he met with the film trade in that city. His welcome started at Central Station where assembled crowds of thousands waited with cheers and a throng of autograph-hunters. Reg was escorted by police to the Adelphi Hotel where a no less cordial welcome awaited him at a tea reception with over one hundred exhibitors. He was received by H.L. Williams, the American Consul, and Mr. W. Scott, prominent in Merseyside cinema circles. Mr. Scott extended cordial greetings to Reg and announced that the popular Hollywood star could be seen at the local theater, Olympia Irlams-o'-th'-Height, where *The Cheerful Fraud* was being shown.

After another fond speech, Reg returned to Manchester where he appeared at the Oxford Theatre then in another personal appearance at the Salford Palace that same evening for screenings of *The Cheerful Fraud*. Since Manchester was a major boxing hub, the press suggested that film charities might benefit if a match were arranged between Reg and Carl Brisson. Both men were amateur heavyweights, and both seemed to be in the pink of condition. Reg smiled and stated that he was there to heal from injuries, not to incur them, and possibly he would enter a fight when he next returned to Manchester in better condition.

The next day, Reg returned to London where he made a personal appearance in an English "kinema" at London's Marble Arch Pavilion for the United Kingdom premiere of *Fast and Furious*. The audience accorded a tremendous welcome to Reg when he appeared on the stage before his latest comedy was shown. Reg declared that, as a rule, he thought that personal appearances were a mistake; he would confine himself to saying how glad he was to be back in England and to have been met with so warm a reception. A large house gave both the actor and his film a hearty ovation.

Other visits included an event at the Rialto Theatre where the applause lasted many minutes and was characterized as the greatest ovation any film star ever received in the British capital. A special "Denny Repertory Week" at the Park Hall was planned with six of Reg's films screened there for the entire week in celebration of his visit.

When George Bellamy found out Reg had returned to England, he made a visit to the European Company offices in London to meet with the wunderkind and announce to his colleagues that he was the one who discovered the star. "I knew Reginald's father, the late W.H. Denny of Savoy fame, quite well," said Bellamy, "and I am the man who first put young Denny on the rungs of the stage ladder. The papers of that time praised him—now the world's press eulogizes him."

When Reg finally met with George Bernard Shaw at his home, the famed Irish playwright told him that he'd love to work with him on the adaptation of his novel and he would be honored to have the British star as his pugilist protagonist in *Cashel Byron's Profession*. Shaw, however, expressed that he didn't want to be under an American studio umbrella or under its control, and the film would have to be under British quota law. Reg was thrilled that Shaw welcomed his ideas and the two got along famously. He closed their meeting and told Shaw he'd speak with Carl Laemmle about their discussion with the hope that he'd be returning to the motherland soon to make his novel into a film.

Following his meeting with Shaw, Reg got on the train to Richmond where he joined Rene and Barbara at Nora and Tiny's White Lodge. It had been eight years since he'd seen his sister, and since he'd flown in the war. He had to see the Snipes while he was there and before he returned home. He called European's F.W. Harland-Edgecumbe and asked to make arrangements to visit the Aerodrome where Alan Cobham had told him the war planes had been put to rest. Reg, Harland-Edgecumbe, and Shakespearean actor William Stack went north of London to the Stag Lane Aerodrome where they were welcomed by De Havilland Aircraft Company Limited's business manager F.E.N. St. Barbe and other officials of the firm.

The team at De Havilland greeted Reg and first showed him their popular English light plane, the De Havilland Moth. Famous WWI aviator and noted test pilot Captain Hubert Broad took Reg up for a test flight in the two-seater dual control biplane. A thousand feet up Reg took over the plane and handled it with masterly skill. He was delighted with its performance and his soul was revived with his return to flight as he once again flew over the English Channel. After they landed, Reg was looking over the Moth for possible purchase, but was soon distracted from a vision out the corner of his eye. There in the hangar adjacent to the Moth were a couple of 7F-1 Sopwith Snipes sitting pretty. Reg walked over to the warbirds he had first flown and was chilled to the bone when he saw the tail number of one that had been engrained in his mind. It was E-6938, the same as his wingman with the RAF. He asked if he could take the reminiscent warbird up for a spin and that was it. Reg was brought back to his first days of learning to fly the warplanes and that terrifying day when he got shot down by the German Fokkers. He decided to buy both Snipes instead of the new Moth. Reg negotiated with the De Havilland team for the purchase and they told him he'd have to clear it with the British Government in order to bring the historic WWI British planes back to America. Reg made arrangements with De Havilland and the government to transport the two biplanes back to New York via a transatlantic freight carrier, which then would be trucked across the country to Los Angeles via a freight line to join his Jenny in its hangar at Clover Field in Santa Monica.

After their wonderful two-month stay in England, the Denny family boarded the *RMS Aquitania* across the Atlantic back to New York. Reg made it back to Los Angeles just in time for the premiere of *Out All Night* which he attended with Bill Seiter, who had just returned from his honeymoon. The press once again had nothing but great things to say about Reg in his newest maritime comedy and the exhibitors thanked Universal for the Denny draw. Jack O'Connell of the Vita Temple Theatre in Toledo sent a wire to Laemmle, "Holding Denny over second week first time in history in Toledo. Marvelous picture playing sensational business breaking all records." William Martin of the Patriot Theatre in Indiana said, "This Denny boy is going great guns for us. The first good crowd of the season greeted him. Everybody happy. As good as you could want."

There was talk that Reg wasn't returning to America and everyone feared that he'd chosen to stay in his homeland. To counter any such rumors, Universal issued a jovial press release about their star in *Universal Weekly* to match those released in Great Britain: "'The most likable chap in Hollywood' is the consensus of opinion of everyone who knows Reginald Denny. The good-natured, crooked grin of this most natural young actor has established him firmly in the affections of all filmgoers; nearly all his pictures are excellent and his performances always. In addition to being a born actor, Denny early acquired his love for and proficiency in all form of sport. He is generous to a fault and has personality to the 'nth degree. He is a motor boat enthusiast, owns two WWI airplanes, was the champion boxer of the Second Corps of the Royal Air Service and has a deep desire to win a long-distance automobile driving championship. He is now one of the biggest comedy stars and appears in his own productions of super quality. 'Reg,' as his friends all call him, is six feet one, weights one hundred and eighty-five pounds, has blue eyes and dark brown hair, and photographs like a million dollars."

Reg corrected the statement and responded to the *Universal Weekly* release. "People don't believe I actually fly. So, on my next vacation I am going to fly around the country from city to city making personal appearances to prove it." After all the Hollywood hoopla, he couldn't wait to try out his new British war planes and share them with his flying club.

At that same time, young Texas millionaire Howard Hughes was commencing production on his aviation war film, *Hell's Angels*. To make the film as authentic as possible for the WWI drama, Hughes had his team search all over the world for vintage aircraft. When he found out that the film star had just bought two RAF Sopwith Snipes back from England, Hughes called Reg to inquire about his warplanes for use in his film. Reg responded to Hughes that he would be happy to lease his Snipes for the production, but only for use in background shots and not to be flown. Hughes and his production chief Frank Tomick, who had just finished his work flying for Paramount's *Wings* (1927), met with Reg at Clover Field. Hughes was in awe of the British warbirds which had been used in service, bullet holes and all. He asked Reg if he could take a fly, so the two aviators took both planes up in the air together. Reg was thrilled to fly his new Snipe for its first time in America. He and Hughes had a roaring time as they soared over the Pacific, just as Reg had done with his wingman over the English Channel during WWI.

10 DENNY SWANSONG

THE STUDIO AND THEIR NEWEST DIRECTOR, Fred Newmeyer, had been anxiously awaiting Reg's return to begin filming his next pugilist comedy, *On Your Toes* (1927), written by Gladys Lehman and Earle Snell. Newmeyer was a noted comedy director who had recently been added to the Universal directorial staff following his brilliant career at Paramount Pictures. As Bill Seiter had been delegated to another film with his new bride, Carl Laemmle thought it would be good to pair Reg with Harold Lloyd's top rate director for his next action-packed film. Reg got back on his toes to work again with accident-prone leading lady Barbara Worth, along with Hayden Stevenson who had worked on his *Leather Pushers* series. Unfortunately, Reg found Newmeyer to be another Pollard who liked to use the broad comedy with which he didn't feel comfortable, nor did he appreciate working with an actress who wrecked his racecar and broke all his bones.

In *On Your Toes*, cinemagoers' first sight of the pugilist star was as an effeminate dancing instructor, Elliott Beresford, who is oblivious that his father was a one-time undefeated heavyweight champion of the world. He was brought up by his grandmother to be a little gentleman and she decided he'd be a dancer instead of a boxer. One of the first laughs in the picture is the sight of Reg's athletic waistline dolled up in a dancing costume. He finally abandons his profession as a dancer and becomes a taxi driver. While he argues with a passenger who won't pay fare, Beresford delivers the knockout blow, which lands him into the fighting game. Meanwhile, the grandmother decides to pay him a visit and when the little old lady surprises her grandson by arriving unannounced, our hero converts the gym into an impromptu dancing school and the prizefighters become his pupils. As the story unfurls, Beresford deserts the dance floor for the ring and not only wins the championship but also the love of his leading lady.

The critics and the audiences welcomed Reg's return to his earlier triumphs as a pugilist. The *Daily News* praised the film saying, "Reginald Denny returned to his old love, the prize ring, in *On Your Toes,* Universal's fight film which opened at the Colony Theatre New York last week to an enthusiastic audience. Denny puts a real kick into a fight that is as exciting as any ringside fan might wish. *On Your Toes* deals with the prize ring and is one of the most amusing and entertaining fight films we have seen in a long time. Dance scenes were a riot and the shots from ringside are excellent. The trick of having him wiggle his ears when the family dander gets up was a happy thought. Delightfully played by its two stars, it is a fast-moving action drama, which has a remarkable prize ring sequence and a distinct departure from the usual type of Denny farce pictures."

While he was recovering at White Lodge, Reg had written a story about an orphan girl who claims him as her daddy, which he called *Now I'll Tell One*. Upon his return from England, Reg presented the treatment to Carl Laemmle with the intent of Bill Seiter directing. Laemmle liked his story and decided it would be Reg's next feature, but regretted to inform him that Seiter was already delegated to another picture and the studio had instead assigned Fred Newmeyer for his upcoming pictures. Reg had no choice but to acquiesce.

Reg changed the title of this newest project to *That's My Daddy* (1927). He got to work and starred as Jimmy Norton in the romantic drama with Lillian Rich as his gold-digger fiancée, Barbara Kent as the heroine, and newcomer six-year-old Jane La Verne as the little orphan Pudge. Reg's pictures usually started out with accidents. True to form, on the first day of production, stuntman Edgar Kennedy lost control of his motorcycle and fractured his knee. Tom O'Brien, who had stunted in a number of Reg's pictures, was hastily substituted for the role and they got off to a rolling start.

Yet again there was trouble in paradise, as Reg would later recount to Kevin Brownlow in his book *The Parade's Gone By...*: "They gave me Freddie Newmeyer, who had been Harold Lloyd's director. He was supposed to direct *That's My Daddy*. But we didn't have the same ideas of comedy. So, I directed it. I came out and told him that I didn't approve of the way he wanted to do the sequences, and he said, 'Well, Reggie, go ahead.' I had already written the story myself; I refused to make the awful story they gave me. From my story, Earle Snell wrote his own scenario, which I promptly threw out the window. We shot from my original. I rehearsed the actors, and everything else, and wrote the titles. Universal took it and had a sneak preview which they tried to keep from me. I managed to go out and see it; they had gagged it up with silly titles and ruined it. It was vile. 'I refuse to do another picture for you,' I told them, 'unless I get that picture back for recutting.' 'Impossible,' they said. 'The negative's all been sent away.' I made them send the negative back. I had an awful time, but I managed to restore the cuts and the original titles. *That's My Daddy* was the story of a guy who's engaged to be married to a wealthy gal, and also the story of a little orphan. The orphan has always dreamed that she had a real daddy somewhere, a daddy with a silk hat and everything else. She runs away from home, and gets hit by a car, and is taken to the hospital. Meanwhile, this guy is on his way to his wedding. He's in a silk hat and cutaway, and because he's in a hurry, he's driving his own limousine. He's in too much of a hurry, and a speed cop stops him. I alibi to the cop: I tell him my little child has been in an accident and I have to get to the hospital. It's an Irish cop. 'Sure,' he says. 'I know. Follow me, I'll take you there.' At the hospital, they take me to the little kid, and tell her 'Your daddy's here!' It's just what she dreamed of. And I'm landed with the kid on my wedding day. The girl I had was a sweet little thing, Jane La Verne. Harry Pollard later used her in *Uncle Tom's Cabin*, and Universal put her under contract. She was only six years old; I treated her very carefully and made her really believe in what she was doing. She was terrific. Then Universal took the picture and made her a wisecracking kid with gag titles. It was terrible. After I had recut the film and it was released, the general manager called me into his office and showed me a letter from the New York office. They thought it was the worst picture they had ever seen. Old Man Laemmle wasn't there; he was at some hot springs. I got in my airplane and flew over and crash-landed at the sanatorium and went to see the old man 'Look,' I said. 'I know a report has been sent from the Universal office about this picture, but I tell you what I'll do, Mr. Laemmle. If that picture doesn't make more money than the last four pictures we've made—and it cost only half as much—then I'll work for you for nothing until the difference is made up. And I'll sign that. But if it makes more money than the last four, then you give me my own unit.' The old man said, 'Do you mean that?' I told him I did, and he almost made a final agreement. But then they got to him and said, 'He's trying to dictate to you,' and he wouldn't go for it. Of course, the picture just cleaned up. Even with bad write-ups. They got to the press, too. 'Denny Swansong' it was called. Afterward, the old man came to me and said, 'I'm sorry. I realize I listened to the wrong people.'"

Reg was upset by the company's reference to his latest film as a "swansong." It was insulting and he took offense to the comments made by studio colleagues who were supposed to have his back. The studio was surprised when the film was released, and the turnout was spectacular. Letters from Denny fans filled the Universal mail room. One patron wrote, "Today I viewed *That's My Daddy* and had to write you. I must say that this picture is Mr. Denny's best picture since *Skinner's Dress Suit* and perhaps I might add even better, due to the presence of little Jane La Verne. Little Miss La Verne is the most charming and best child actor I've seen. She belongs in a class that Baby Peggy and Jackie Coogan were once in. She can move you to tears and laughter almost at the same time. Most of my praises seem to be for the little miss just mentioned, but that is not because the rest of the cast were not good. Goodness no! Miss Barbara Kent is very talented and beautiful. Lillian Rich did her part well as did all the rest, including Tom O'Brien and the three butlers. If Mr. Denny wrote the story, let us hope he writes more, with himself taking the lead on the screen." Willie Aliene Coates, Dallas, Texas.

The critics again applauded Reg's work and the *Los Angeles Times* added to their praise in saying, "Denny knows all the tricks of the stage farceur and he uses them continually. In fact, his popularity has been so marked of late that various rival screen magnates have been bidding for his services when his contract with Universal expires shortly."

Along with Reg's ongoing conflicts at the studio, there were also conflicts at home. His marriage to Rene had been in a spiral descent during his climb to success. Although she was appreciative of Reg's ability to support his family, she was upset by her husband's indifference and irresponsibility. Rene wanted an attentive husband and father to their child, but Reg wanted and needed more; racecars, boats, airplanes, and drama were vital to his being. Rene couldn't give that to him. She claimed that he acted like a spoiled child when he argued with the studio hands that fed him and jeopardized his livelihood while being surrounded by young eager-eyed starlets. The trip to England was their final attempt to rekindle the sparks in the marriage, but it was a hopeless endeavor.

While carrying the load of a family as he played and worked overtime, Reg couldn't get his mind off a certain refreshing young actress. During production of *Skinner's Dress Suit*, he had taken notice of Universal's new "stock" actress, Isabelle Stiefel. The youngest of a large German-Irish family from Salt Lake City, the eighteen-year-old ingénue was new to the studio and frequently seen on the Universal lot. Isabelle had quit growing when she reached five feet but insisted that she'd never quit growing cinematically. Her flashing brown eyes, black hair, and tininess appealed to Carl Laemmle with whom she shared her plans to become a movie star. When Uncle Carl cast Isabelle in one of Universal's Arthur Lake comedies, she came up with the screen name "Betsy Lee" for use in her new role as a screen star. Betsy Lee subsequently played a small part in *Skinner's Dress Suit* in which Lake also co-starred. On set, Reg befriended the coy and flirtatious aspiring actress and offered to help with her career. He complimented Betsy Lee on her tiny frame and bubbling personality. He nicknamed her "Bubbles" after his favorite song, "I'm Forever Blowing Bubbles," and serenaded to her when she'd stroll by en route to the commissary. Amidst all the conflicts at the studio and at home, Reg was revived, refreshed, and rejuvenated by the youngster. Little Bubbles empathized with him about his wife, daughter, and studio problems. She was sixteen years younger than Reg, thus didn't carry the baggage of women of his age, or Rene's.

The Universal heartthrob made an even bigger impression on tiny Bubbles when he treated her to a flight aboard his Jenny on a trip to a star-studded Hollywood party as guests of William Randolph Hearst and Marion Davies. When Rene heard the news her husband and the young actress had flown to Hearst's new estate in San Simeon, she'd had it. After hearing flying rumors about Reg having an affair, which he adamantly denied, Rene went to the courthouse and filed divorce proceedings. On November 24, 1927, she took Barbara and moved out of her once happy family home to an apartment of their own. Instead of trying to win back the love and trust of his wife, Reg took Bubbles out for their first official date on the same day he was served with divorce papers. When she was first approached and questioned by the press regarding her reported relationship with the Universal film star, Bubbles acted as though she didn't know what they were talking about.

"Why, I don't even know him. I haven't anything to say," she stated.

A week after the *Los Angeles Times* released news of Reg's divorce, Bubbles responded to all inquiries as to her possible plans to marry him. "You will have to ask Mr. Denny. Friday night was the first time I have ever been out with him in my whole life."

Once their romance became public, Reg courted Bubbles and they flaunted the union by attending soirees of the rich and famous. Reg drove his convertible Cadillac down Hollywood Boulevard at night where there was always a party with movie stars waving at each other and clinking champagne glasses. Bubbles and Reg were in the heart of it all during the Roaring Twenties and having a ball.

Reg wanted to give his new girlfriend a taste of his other true love—the cabin. He invited Bubbles, and her sister Helene, Helene's husband, and their cousin Izzy as chaperones to stay at his mountain retreat in Running Springs. After a day of walking the beautiful property, the guests had a lovely dinner and settled in for the night. After showing Bubbles to her guest room, Reg returned to his suite where he was startled by a fiery surprise.

"I had gone to bed, and when I saw the red glow, thought the girls had left the light burning on the porch. I leaped up to see a roaring wall of flame rushing toward the house. I shouted to Bubbles and her friends to get out and drive up to Big Bear, called out to my care-taker, the cowboy Art Manning, to get the horses out, and some rangers luckily camping near-by came to help me. But even in the midst of the turmoil I got a laugh.

There on top of the big rock in the path of the fire, was a little squirrel who sat up chattering and scolding for dear life! It finally decided to leave, however, and the last I saw of it, it was scooting along to the spring and safety. Fire-Fighters came to help out, and we learned that the Indians are the very best firefighters of all. They adore the excitement of it, seem never to tire, and are at their best in the thickest of the conflagration battle. They'd whoop and yell and dance about as they built their backfires. These Indians came up from the Sherman school. Next morning early, with the battle still going on, the rangers sent an Indian youth out in the mountains to bring back a report of the different fires. He was gone nearly all day, running without food or water, and brought back a report and a map showing accurately where the worst fire conditions were. The Indians never let out a whimper. Some of the white fire-fighters, though, were knocked completely out. And the things they'd do! We found a lot of them sitting around burning a log which they had refused to extinguish, though it was dangerously close to some dry underbrush, because they said they wanted it for warmth!"

After the worst of the battle was over, Reg housed a hundred and fifty of the fighters in his house and over the garage. "And that's when he washed the dishes!" Art Manning told the *Los Angeles Times*. "My wife and I were worn out, serving coffee and food to the fighters. We finally went to bed late at night. Next morning, we arose to find that Denny himself had stayed up and washed up those hundreds of dishes!"

Being forever grateful for those who helped him, Reg paid it forward and gifted his Cadillac to Manning who lost his truck in the fire while trying to protect the ranch. The "Plunge Creek Fire" burned 8,000 acres on the southern slope of the San Bernardino Mountains that week which proved so deadly near that Reg thought his beautiful home was surely gone as the sea of flames licked at its very walls. He suspected Rene had followed them up and lit the fire, which reportedly started on his property.

Reg's injuries from the fire delayed yet another picture for a week while the studio waited for him to heal from his burns and bruised ego. After completion of *That's My Daddy*, Universal was ready to begin production on Reg's next Super Denny film, *Be Yourself*, adapted for the screen by two of the screen's best-known writers, Peter Milne and Philip Hurn. When Reg read the script, it had all the hokum he so despised. When he learned the studio had again assigned Fred Newmeyer to his picture, he refused to return to work.

The press got word Reg was in a standoff with the studio. Myrtle Gebhart was a fan and staff writer for *Picture Play*, feature writer for the *Los Angeles Times*, and contributor to the popular movie magazines such as *Motion Picture Magazine*, *Photoplay*, *Movie Weekly*, and *Screenland*. The writer and Universal star met often for lunch and Reg vented to her which she reported in the *Los Angeles Times*. "During his five or six years at Universal, while other stellar tantrums were spasmodic and easily solaced, Denny had a continual, somewhat muffled mad. A bomb exploded at intervals. I wrote an annual story on his grievances. Usually it was the same one—poor stories, mediocre productions. His grievance is against the stories chosen and the amount of money spent in production. It got so that we could calculate just when the next eruption was due. Over a luncheon table, or in the calming atmosphere of the Athletic Club, I listened seasonally to his vocal lava. About six years ago I called him 'an abysmal brute with dimples.' That caption seemed on the point of becoming an actuality during the Universal warfare, when the old British spunk was aroused to a dogged fight. Denny refused to make a picture because he did not like the story, or that Universal was unwilling to produce Denny's ideas. It has come to be one of those chronic battles that keep you guessing. Universal, thinking to soothe their star's ruffled feelings, stated that there was nothing to report that Mr. Denny had walked out. Denny was not so reticent himself. He talked freely and determinedly, stating that if his ideas were not met, he would leave Universal and sail for England."

At the urging of Carl Laemmle, Reg came down the mountain to meet with the studio executives. He made a few demands before he would return to work. First issue was he wanted to picturize three of his plays in Great Britain beginning with George Bernard Shaw's *Cashel Byron's Profession*. Next, it was his paycheck. The studio refused to pay Reg for his directing efforts on *That's My Daddy* and they had not increased his budget as Laemmle had promised. Instead, they changed his heartfelt story to a silly comedy and allocated the directorial funds to Newmeyer whom Reg claimed didn't do a thing for his film. The last sore thumb was the types of stories being chosen. The studio kept pushing him to the limit with the silly broad comedy which he felt made him a fool.

The farce king insisted the suits see his point. "The reason farce has been abandoned is because no one is sticking to the formula. You're trying to combine farce with pie-throwing and slapstick comedy. And the trouble is with the class of stories chosen. The fact that human beings frequently behave in real life ways twice as absurd need not be dwelt upon, because each of us thinks it is the other fellow that is crazy. My pictures made a year ago with Bill Seiter cost more and were much better."

Reg saw the disproved looks on their faces. He was fighting again, but now for his existence on the screen. "In the long run it is I who will incur the exhibitor's wrath and find my popularity gone—not the film company who will suffer. But unless some change is made, I shall not make any more pictures for Universal," he said with finality.

Uncle Carl was a fan and had been patient with the star, understanding his concerns; however, his son Carl Jr. had now taken the production reins and didn't have the same emotional attachment with Reg as his father. At the height of his bargaining power, the Universal executives told Reg, per his contract, they had ownership of all his intellectual property, and they would be the ones to option *Cashel Byron's Profession* if Mr. Shaw wanted to make an American film with their star. They also advised Reg the studio was transitioning into making sound pictures and cautioned the British actor on leaving during this epic conversion in media, especially with such a move to England where they were behind the boat, so to say. They warned him, if he left now, he would never work again. It was like a game of chess; Reg was a big money-maker for the studio, and the studio was a sure paycheck for him.

Carl Laemmle didn't want to let go of Reg, so he asked for two more years by giving him a substantial bonus and, as a Christmas present, the studio optioned the famous Taylor Holmes British play *The Third Party* for him. *The Third Party* was based on a vogue practice at the Café Royal in London and enjoyed a successful run in New York. In addition to better stories and more money allocated to his projects, Laemmle also told Reg he had taken Fred Newmeyer off his next film and instead assigned Bill Seiter to direct. The parties agreed to the terms and Reg got back to work.

With their reunion, the actor and his director changed the name of their next Universal film from *Be Yourself* to *Good Morning, Judge*. In *Good Morning, Judge* (1928), Reg played a rich young idler, Freddie, who meets Julia, a wealthy social service worker, played by Mary Nolan, who runs a haven for reformed criminals. By telling her he is a hardened criminal, Freddie is allowed to stay at her mission. At a charity ball given by his sister in honor of his homeless colleagues, Freddie discovers some of the men are stealing jewelry from Julia's friends. He reveals his true identity, rounds up the thieves, recovers the jewels, and wins the girl. The cast also included Dorothy Gulliver, Otis Harlan, Bull Montana, and Sailor Sharkey.

The press loved the reunion of Reg and Seiter. *Universal Weekly* featured the exhibitor reviews with, "Universal thought the Denny picture, *On Your Toes*, was about the high mark of Denny production for this year until they saw *Good Morning, Judge* last week. The unanimous opinion now is that *Good Morning, Judge* is the best Denny yet."

At the same time Universal was fine-tuning their silent films, Warner Bros. had been working on the new medium of sound pictures with their release of the first feature with synchronized dialogue, *The Jazz Singer* (1927). Warners had tapped in on the market and was way ahead of the game with the newest in recording technology. They were the first to make the transition from silent films to sound pictures and already had a division with their own patented equipment, "Vitaphone," allocated to the new medium. Universal was behind the bandwagon and Laemmle needed to regroup or else he'd quickly be out of business. Just as Seiter and Reg finished work on *Good Morning, Judge*, Universal shut down the studio and put a halt on all their productions while they figured out a strategy to transition their existing slate of films to talkies.

Reg was at once free. He finally got the break he needed, without the pressure of a studio, the press, his fans, or a wife. He got in his Jenny and flew up to the cabin where he spent time alone chopping wood from his Ponderosa pines, reading by the fire, and riding his horses until the studio advised him to report for his next picture. He loved taking morning swims across Lake Arrowhead and formed his own swimming record, thinking nothing of a ten-mile swim after having to paddle the English Channel. Reg became a real mountain man and used his marksmanship skills acquired during the war to hunt venison for his meals. He took up archery and held contests with the local Serrano tribe who had helped him during the fire. When a mountain lion entered his paddock and threatened to kill the horses, Reg used his bow and arrow to kill the predator instead of using a gun so as not to scare his equine friends. Reg also used the time to reunite with his daughter. He picked up Barbara in the Jenny and they flew to his new landing field at the ranch to reunite with Georgie flying overhead. Barbara was having a hard time adjusting to the family change. She had been through enough abandonment issues with her father and was now heartbroken with the separation. Reg did his best to continue a loving relationship with her while he courted a woman only ten years her senior. He also had Bubbles up to the cabin so his daughter and girlfriend would get to know, and hopefully like, each other.

A month later, Universal resumed business and Reg returned for the filming of his next picture, the boxing comedy *The Night Bird* (1928). The studio wasn't quite prepared to make it a sound picture, so they kept the silent format. Bill Seiter was already assigned to another picture and the studio executives again assigned Fred Newmeyer to megaphone. Newmeyer had cast accomplished silent film actress Jocelyn Lee to play the female lead; however, Reg insisted his new girlfriend get the part as he had promised Bubbles the lead role in his next picture. Another disagreement ensued between Denny and Newmeyer when the director refused the star's demand. Reg stomped into Carl Laemmle's office and insisted that "Betsy Lee" play the female lead opposite him in his newest film or he'd walk. The studio subsequently placed Bubbles in the lead role of Madelena and relegated Newmeyer's pick to a smaller role in the film as The Redhead.

Bubbles was overjoyed Reg had kept his word by giving her the film role. She was excited about the prospect of becoming Reginald Denny's next leading woman. She promoted her film career, certain her boyfriend would make her a star. Bubbles wanted her stardom to be official without any confusion in her screen name, so she went to the courthouse to file a legal name change before production of *The Night Bird* began. She showed up before Judge Marshall McComb along with another young lady, Dolores Asúnsolo Martinez del Rio, and the two feminine screen players asked for legal aid in changing their names. Bubbles stated her case to Judge McComb. "That's the way I am known on the screen and the name Betsy Lee is worth much money to me." The other young lady asked that her name be legally shortened to Dolores Del Rio. The judge granted Dolores Del Rio hers, but the hearing was interrupted when Bubbles' boyfriend showed up and persuaded the actress not to legally change her name as he had other plans. At the onset of production of *The Night Bird* and on Bubbles' twenty-first birthday of May 8, 1928, Reg publicly proposed to her with a two-carat square-shaped diamond engagement ring. Bubbles was ecstatic and showed the ring to everyone at the studio. Reg announced to the press their plans to marry that fall, once Reg's divorce was final. Reg also announced that Miss Stiefel had been chosen as the leading woman in his next picture which would also be released that fall.

The Night Bird was written by Frederick and Fanny Hatton and adapted for the screen by Earle Snell. Reg portrayed a champion New York City pugilist, Kid Davis, who is a bear in the ring but a lamb among women. He ditches a party and while walking through Central Park he runs into an abused Italian girl, played by Betsy Lee. Reg once again rescued the damsel in distress by leaving in the middle of a boxing match to beat up her abusive fiancé. The two fall in love to live happily ever after. The film premiered on September 16, 1928, with the critics having fabulous things to say about Reg and his new leading lady. *Universal Weekly* featured news about the theatrical exhibitor results. "Reginald Denny is a knockout in *The Night Bird* at the Uptown this week. This picture, while it has a pugilist for its central character, is a comedy of manners rather than a drama of the ring. Knee deep in the plot the hero meets a little Italian girl whom he thinks he is adopting, but who he soon discovers, has adopted him. This part is cleverly taken by Betsy Lee, a newcomer to the screen who is given more than her share of the picture by the gallant Mr. Denny. The picture is droll from start to finish. The few fight scenes are acted with a lambasting earnestness that makes them exciting and those of the audience who have poor control will be disposed to whistle when the hero leaves the ring clad in a pair of sateen trunks and boxing gloves to bust up the wedding of his rival."

The *Toledo Times* made a typo by using the original cast choice in their review with, "Denny makes a handsome champion and gives to the part everything that it requires. Jocelyn Lee, a new 'discovery,' appears opposite him as a little Italian girl he befriends in Central Park." They got Bubbles' name wrong, which upset her, but it was revenge for the actress who originally had the part. The *Tribune*, however, got it right" "Betsy Lee's work as the little Italian immigrant girl is a performance second only to that of Denny. There promises to be no stopping Miss Lee's ninety-eight pounds of feminine vividness on the climb to stardom; for she makes no secret of her greatest ambition—to be a motion picture star."

11

I'M FOREVER BLOWING BUBBLES

CARL LAEMMLE CELEBRATED UNIVERSAL PICTURES' 23rd Anniversary by making a formal announcement in *Universal Weekly*: "Talking pictures, instead of being detrimental to the silent drama, will give the present style of soundless films an attendant impetus such as it has never experienced before. It will also add an interesting angle to the silver screen without overturning the silent drama. When the movies first gained their foothold, calamity howlers claimed that they would sound the death knell to the stage. Time proved that they were wrong. The movies, instead of devitalizing the stage, became merely another form of entertainment, in addition to, not instead of, the drama. Now the sound film has made its appearance. Calamity howlers are once more in evidence. 'The silent picture is doomed,' shrieks one. 'Talkies cannot last,' cries another. 'The industry is in a panic,' moans a third. This is all poppycock. The talking picture is here to stay. It is another cog in the wheel of progress. Progress will not be halted. And you will see that the talking picture will develop into an additional form of entertainment, taking its place in the amusement world along with the stage and the silent film. One hears talk of television. If it is perfected you will hear the calamity howlers once more. But it, too, will take its place as an added contribution to the world's entertainment appetite. Of course, we have had our troubles. Many difficult problems were unexpectedly encountered and had to be solved in the field, so to speak. The delicate microphone picked up all sorts of noises inaudible to the human ear. The twittering of birds a block away disturbed an intense love scene. A dramatic moment was utterly spoiled by the droning of the propeller of an airplane sailing by several thousand feet overhead. But those were details, some mechanical and some human, that, mosquito-like, plagued us for a while and eventually will be overcome. In the meantime, we sawed wood. Universal's first one hundred percent talking picture and the world's first all-sound feature movie-tone production, *Melody of Love,* has been completed and will be released shortly. I modestly think it will make screen history, but, excellent as it is, even *Melody of Love* will not supplant its silent prototype. *Lonesome,* the Paul Fejos masterpiece, with Glenn Tyron and Barbara Kent, is almost one hundred percent talkie. It will open next week at the Colony Theatre in New York, and I am so confident of its tremendous success and unusual audience appeal that I am going across the continent to see the opening."

That fall, Universal released its first round of sound pictures with Hungarian director Paul Fejos' *Lonesome* (1928), then Arch Heath's *Melody of Love* (1928) with Walter Pidgeon and Mildred Harris. *Red Hot Speed* (1928) would be the studio's next talking picture with Reg as its protagonist. The studio had assigned Fred Newmeyer for the film, but the actor refused to work with anyone who made a fool of him, especially now that his voice would be heard. Carl Laemmle assigned accomplished actor and director Joseph Henabery to the action-packed comedy. Henabery had a similar personality as Reg; he was an actor who had eloquently portrayed Abraham Lincoln in *The Birth of a Nation* (1915), and who also had the same "professional disagreements" with the likes of Louis B. Mayer at Metro-Goldwyn-Mayer and Adolph Zukor at Paramount Pictures.

Red Hot Speed was the pair's first full-talkie and their first project together. Reg starred with Alice Day in this fast and thrilling racing comedy about a mix-up at the court, in which the daughter of a newspaper mogul who is about to start a campaign against speeding is herself given a speeding ticket. Under an assumed name, she is given a suspended sentence and put under parole of prosecuting attorney Darrow, played by Reg. The film was released in both silent and sound, two negatives—one silent, one with dialog.

The press reacted in a great way to the British native's voice. *Universal Weekly* said, "Reginald Denny's following among fans of the silent screen has been immense and enthusiastic for seven years; just how Denny would register in the talkies was a problem only recently solved upon the release of *Red Hot Speed*. Of course, Denny's stage career pointed the way to successful voice reproduction, but that is not always an infallible guide. There is no longer any question about Reginald Denny as a sound star. He has clicked. The critics are unanimous about the fact that his voice is exceedingly pleasant and his English accent an added attraction."

According to A. Fulton Gillaspey of the *San Francisco Bulletin*, "In the matter of these talkies one of two things occur, a fan becomes more enthusiastic about a movie star or in case the voice and diction is disappointing the unfortunate falls from the pedestal. There are no doubts about the favorable impression made by Reginald Denny in his first talkie, which made its debut on the screen at the Pantages Saturday. He lives up to all expected of him. For one thing Denny has a fine voice. He can sing and has several times appeared on the local stage and won the admiration of his hearers with his baritone solos. This voice goes a long way in making his dialogue picture a success. *Red Hot Speed* is a comedy. It is ingenious and the sound of the voices enhance the enjoyment of the picture. Denny makes the chatter fit entirely with the theme and Alice Day, his leading woman, who also has had stage experience, follows the pace set by the star."

The Chronicle claimed, "The fascinating game of 'Voices' goes on among movie enthusiasts. The latest to submit samples of his manly tones to the public is Reginald Denny. Unlike a few who have emerged gruff where they should be dulcet, or reedy where they might better be commanding, Reg's voice in *Red Hot Speed* on the Pantages screen this week is everything to be desired. *Red Hot Speed* is one of those brisk well-tailored, thoroughly entertaining and somewhat foolish comedies of which half a dozen have been turned out by Universal for this particular star."

Reg sighed in relief to hear of the positive responses to his voice for the first time on the big screen.

He then got to work on his next sound picture, *Clear the Decks* (1929), also directed by Henabery. The film was based on E.J. Rath's novel, *When the Devil Was Sick* and adapted for the screen by Earle Snell and Gladys Lehman. Reg reunited with Otis Harlan and Lucien Littlefield who had worked with him in *What Happened to Jones* and *Skinner's Dress Suit*. The company proceeded by boat to Seattle for the purpose of talking scenes on a cruise ship. Onboard the ship, Reg played a young society man who replaces a friend on an ocean voyage, using his friend's name and stateroom. He falls in love with a pretty fellow passenger, then learns he's supposed to be mentally ill and confined to his stateroom on a diet of goat's milk. His efforts to escape custody, establish his sanity, and convince the girl of his true identity gives rise to a rapid succession of funny incidents and dialogue.

Reg was going crazy missing his tiny Bubbles and couldn't wait to finish the picture. Upon his return from Seattle, the same week his divorce from Rene was to be final, Reg took his fiancée to meet his friend Judge Samuel R. Blake in the Los Angeles Courthouse corridor. He approached the judge with a request.

"Sam, will you do me a favor? Reg asked. "You're my friend, you know."

"Reg," said Judge Blake, "I'll do anything unless it interferes with my position as judge. What is it?"

"Marry me? Meet the future wife."

Whereupon Reg, Bubbles and Judge Blake went into the marriage license bureau and the couple took out a notice of intention to wed. Upon finalization of Reg's divorce on November 24, 1928, Reg and Bubbles were married at the bride's parents' home with a star-studded reception at the Hollywood Athletic Club. *Los Angeles Times* columnist Grace Kingsley attended the reception with "Stella the Star-Gazer." Kingsley was the first motion-picture editor and columnist of the *Los Angeles Times* and top Hollywood writer with the *Los Angeles Sunday Times*. She featured a story in her *Los Angeles Times* column about the star's marriage. "We are going over to Reginald Denny's wedding reception! We found Denny and Bubbles, his adorably sweet little bride, who was looking radiantly lovely in her wide white skirt and tight-fitting bodice, her veil of exquisite white lace, and her huge bouquet of gardenias, in the big reception room upstairs at the Hollywood Athletic Club, where they were surrounded by scores of friends."

When the photographer popped shots of the new bride, Bubbles looked at Kingsley and smiled. "I didn't say 'obey' in the wedding ceremony. I would have, though, only the preacher didn't put the word in."

Obey him she did. After working together in *The Night Bird*, Reg had decided he didn't want his new wife to be "Betsy Lee" any longer. Based on experience, he insisted two actors couldn't maintain a successful marriage and the only condition of theirs would be Bubbles must give up her dream of becoming a motion picture star. Bubbles' dream had always been to be an actress; now, she agreed to give that up and become a supportive housewife to her enigmatic husband. When asked by Kingsley about her future plans as a film star, Bubbles had a different tone than before.

"No, I'm not going to work any more in pictures," the bride said. "I'm going to make a career of home-making."

Reg had to get back to work the next day but promised his new wife he'd take her on a honeymoon once he finished completing his next film. The newlyweds celebrated their wedding night at Reg's home in the Hollywood Hills, where they would reside together.

Clear the Decks was advertised as "a gale of fun on a sea of hilarity" and the film was released on March 3, 1929. The exhibitors were happy and the press again raved about Reg's speaking voice. In *Universal Weekly*, an announcement was made regarding his second sound picture. "Denny's first talkie, *Red Hot Speed,* established without question that the comedian is a success via Movietone, and now *Clear the Decks* backs up his earlier achievement. Reginald Denny revealed a solid speaking voice in *Clear the Decks*." The *Wisconsin News* said, "Patrons at the Alhambra are enjoying a hilarious talking picture starring Reginald Denny and a cast of capable actors. It is called *Clear the Decks*, a rollicking farce comedy of life and adventures aboard an ocean liner. Denny has the sort of voice you'd expect him to have and his current comedy is just the light sort of medium he excels in."

Both Reg and Laemmle were happy to hear the positive reviews about his British voice in the American-made films.

In his next film, Reg returned to the prize-ring in another part-talkie, *His Lucky Day* aka *You've Got to Fight* (1929), written by John Hymer and Gladys Lehman and directed by Edward "Eddie" F. Cline. Co-starring Lorayne Duval, Otis Harlan, and Eddie Phillips, Reg played real estate agent Charles Blaydon who mistakes a gang of bank robbers for respectable, prospective tenants and is forced to pull out his boxing gloves. The critics favorably reported they were happy to see Reg in his element acting again as a boxer and now with a speaking voice.

Reg then wrote his own first full-talkie, *One Hysterical Night* (1929) aka *No! No! Napoleon* directed by William James Craft. He created the role of William "Napoleon" Judd for himself and starred alongside a talented cast of characters which included actress Nora Lane as Nurse Josephine, E.J. Ratcliffe as the Duke of Wellington, Slim Summerville as Robin Hood, and future star Walter Brennan as Paul Revere. The crew had a hoot acting as though they were insane, and the press caught on to the contagious hilarity with more positive reviews about Reg's first self-written talkie.

The *Los Angeles Times* wrote, "Reginald Denny has himself written the story for *No, No, Napoleon*, which assures a vehicle providing the happiest material for the comedian's breezy type of humor. The scheming aunt and uncle of William Judd, heir to the family fortune, persuades him to pose as Napoleon at a fancy masquerade ball, but they are actually having him committed to an insane asylum. Since all the other inmates/attendees think they are historical figures such as Robin Hood, the Duke of Wellington, Paul Revere, William Tell, Salome, Robinson Crusoe, Sherlock Holmes, and others, it takes a while for Judd to separate the wheat from the chaff and prove he is not deranged. His quest becomes more urgent when he falls in love with a nurse named Josephine, who does not think she is Napoleon's 'Josephine' but is convinced Judd thinks he is Napoleon."

On May 16, 1929, the first Academy Awards ceremony was hosted by Reg's friend Douglas Fairbanks at the Roosevelt Hotel in Hollywood. Even though none of the Universal films were nominated, Reg attended the event where he and Bubbles ran into Howard Hughes whose film *The Racket* (1928) was up for Outstanding Picture. Hughes had just wrapped the airplane scenes for *Hell's Angels* (1930) and thanked Reg for the use of his planes in his film that took two years to shoot. As films were still silent in 1927, Hughes' film was originally shot as a silent. When he learned the studios had begun to make sound pictures, Hughes ordered his team to reshoot all the flying sequences to make it a sound picture costing him $5 million more and a year longer to complete. To add to the delays, there were also numerous plane crashes in the making of *Hell's Angels* due to the elaborate direction of the daring aviator, and Hughes had just survived a plane crash himself while flying in his film. When Paramount Pictures' *Wings* (1927) won for Best Picture, Production that night, Hughes was more determined to get his aviation movie done as quickly as possible.

When Reg introduced his new wife to the newly divorced aviator, Bubbles made a sarcastic comment that it was time for Hughes to get a divorce from Reg's airplanes. The socially awkward millionaire assured Reg his biplanes were in excellent shape and had been stored in his hangar while not in use for background shots. He invited Reg to come to his hangar so he could hand over the Snipes, only if he could take one of the historic warplanes up for one last flight.

That week, the two met at Hughes' hangar at his Caddo Field just north of Van Nuys Metropolitan Airport. Reg and Hughes took off in the Sopwith Snipes and flew in formation over the skies of Hollywood as if they were in a dogfight. Neither of them crashed and both landed safely at Clover Field where Reg's Snipes joined his Jenny in the hangar. Afterward, Hughes had his driver pick him up and Reg took the Jenny out for a fly as it had been grounded for quite a while. Soaring over Downtown Los Angeles, his engine sputtered. He tried to get it restarted up in the air, but it was no use; he was forced to make a crash landing at Mt. Vernon and Highland Avenue in the heart of Los Angeles. Reg wasn't hurt, but his stunt plane was wrecked, and the near-death crash was announced in the papers.

Reg was lucky to have survived another accident; but Bubbles demanded her new husband stop flying. The Black Cats were disbanding anyway and with his secure contract coming to an end, along with a large divorce settlement, Reg could no longer handle the cost of maintaining the two historic warbirds. He decided to loan out one of his Snipes to the Los Angeles County Museum and donated the other to Los Angeles High School as a gift to inspire youth to learn the art of flying. Reg wanted to encourage the study of aeronautics for the school's physics classes and its aviation club, so he personally presented the Snipe to Lt. William Williams, the high school's aviation night class instructor. As he was letting go of his airplanes, Reg also gifted the *Barbarene* to his ex-wife and daughter for which the boat was named.

Reg was grounded and his new wife wanted her long-awaited honeymoon. He had planned on taking his bride to Europe or on a cruise to Honolulu, but Reg didn't want to be exposed to the public or press with stories of his divorce still circulating and rumors of his leaving the studio. He instead opted to go to his cabin and hibernate with his new bride. The press was dying to find out what was going on with Reg. He wanted to dispel all the rumors flying around town, so he finally allowed one columnist, Grace Kingsley, to stay at the cabin to see the other side of Reggie and his idyllic life with his new wife.

That June, Kingsley and "Stella, the Star-Gazer" made the trip to Reg's cabin and featured a narrative of their Denny visit in the *Sunday Los Angeles Times*. "'And Reginald Denny and Bubbles call this a cabin!' exclaimed Stella, gazing about her, enraptured at the lovely surroundings in which we found ourselves. What Reggie didn't tell us is that he owns a bit of Paradise! We had just arrived, after travel through the most breath-takingly beautiful mountain scenery, on a winding road, at Reggie's mountain home. It is situated in a sheltered valley that nestles, oddly enough, high up between two of the tallest peaks of the San Bernardino Mountains, in a natural park gorgeous with wild flowers, tall pines, ferns and springs. The house sits pertly on the very edge of a magnificent precipice overlooking the green wooded hills and valleys below. That cabin is really a beautiful mansion. It is made of pine logs, cemented between, treated in some fashion to make them a rich brown, while the ceilings are made of plain pine boards, but somehow smoked and oiled so that they suggest seasoned age. The beauty and coziness of the great living-room envelope you the moment you enter. There was a huge fire in the fireplace—a half a tree had just been thrown upon it—and its cheery warmth was most grateful after the icy mountain air blowing in from the mists that were beginning to sweep in from the valleys. There were great bear rugs on the beautifully polished floors, a table entirely covered with a throw made of fox skins, a lamp the feet of which were dainty, polished antelope hoofs, a long sofa with cushions, and the most charming curved divan, not to mention easy chairs that you sank into with such comfort that you felt you could never get out. Our bedrooms were just dreams of comfort, with their varnished log dressers and huge mirrors, their great, soft rustic beds, their bright Indian rugs and their cheerful yellow chintz curtains. Stella may be rather dance-mad, but she turns girl of the big out-doors at a moment's notice, so we all went out for a little archery practice with the big bows and arrows, and Bubbles easily beat us all, even Reginald. She is a great shot with a rifle, too, and loves going hunting, does this dainty, pale, Madonna-like little lady. Then there were charming little walks about, under the trees and down to some springs, and Stella went horseback-riding on Peanuts, Reggie's tamest horse, with Bubbles. Out in front of the house, on the ledge, the trees are all cruelly blackened and warped. That's where the great fire of last year was. We danced to the music of the radio, and then went out on the veranda to view the most beautiful night scene it has ever been my joy to see. We were away above the clouds, and the moon was lighting the mountain tops gorgeously, while below us in the valley, the clouds lay, all softly silver pillows, in the moonlight. As I said before, Denny has an upright front yard, so to speak, and you have fairly to slide down it to get to some springs below, but that we all accomplished next morning. All, that is, except our host. Reggie arose at dawn to pack into Greyback Mountain, whither some forest rangers were moving for a better outlook over their territory with the coming of summer. Denny was going to help them get their belongings up there. Art Manning told us that Reginald is such a willing worker, getting in and working like a section hand himself, that the rangers are always most delighted when he offers to aid them. Just one person wasn't pleased that Reggie was getting up so early. That was his tiny wife, Bubbles. Because her husband regularly awakens her when he is getting up early for any of these excursions, bringing her a cup of coffee and telling her it is time to get up. She never, never does, but he goes on with the custom just the same. After he is gone, Bubbles curls up and goes to sleep again. This morning he was up and gone before the rest of us were awake; but when we arose, we decided to drive over to Big Bear, and in the wine-like air we sped around those curves over to the beautiful spot where the turquoise of the lake is a gem in the bosom of that lovely valley, returning starving at lunch time. Earle Snell, the writer, was there, and Vernon Woods, Denny's manager; also Mrs. Arthur Todd, wife of Denny's cameraman, and

Helen Ludlam, fan magazine writer; and late in the afternoon William J. Craft, the director, arrived. Another merriest of evenings, while the rain and sleet fell outside, and then we retired to await the morning and a much-regretted departure. We were so comfortably tired that even the roar of the wind through the pines, sounding like the noise of a tumultuous sea, could not keep us awake. The morning came crisp and cold and like a draught of wine, and we took a hike about, looking for wild flowers, gathering in glorious bunches of yellow wild primrose, branches of white dogwood, a honey-sweet yellow flower, wild iris, almost as large as the cultivated variety, little yellow violets, lupine and the gorgeous red snow flowers, which grow, we hear, while the snow is still on the ground. And such a fast, invigorating race around that curved road, after we had bade our well-beloved hosts good-bye! 'We shall never,' we declared in a breath, 'forget that!'"

Neither would Reg. He loved that cabin more than anything in the world, as well as his Bubbles. On their romantic honeymoon, Reg shared his favorite getaway with his new wife in splendor. They were both truly high on each other in heaven.

When the honeymoon was over, Reg returned to the Universal lot to star in his next contractual obligation with the studio, *Embarrassing Moments* aka *Compassionate Troubles* (1930). A crafty crass comedy directed again by William James Craft, the sound picture had artist Marion Fuller, played by Merna Kennedy, inventing a husband, Thaddeus Cruikshank, to avoid an arranged marriage. The invention turns to reality in the shape of Reg. The couple meet, fall in love and marry within a twenty-four-hour period. While working out scenes on *Embarrassing Moments*, Reg met another newcomer in the Universal commissary.

Bette Davis had just moved from New England to Hollywood with her mother Ruthie to pursue a film career. The twenty-two-year-old East Coast stage actress had made arrangements for a screen test with Universal Studios. Davis and her mother traveled by train to Los Angeles and when they arrived at Le Grande Station, nobody from the studio was there to meet them. Bette took a cab to the studio only to fail her arranged screen test. She and Ruthie headed to the commissary and that's where they met Reg. Being Universal's ambassador of sorts, Reg became a mentor to the new arrival. After lunch, he drove Bette and Ruthie to their hotel and the two became good friends. Both were honest, to the point, and loathing the business of Hollywood.

Reg later shared his thoughts about the actress with author Charles Higham in the biography *Bette: The Life of Bette Davis*. "… I knew Bette was hating it in Hollywood. She longed to go back to the theater. But I encouraged her to stay. I knew that although she wasn't conventionally pretty, she would outlive all the platinum blondes who were walking around trying to be noticed. Her face was made for the camera. It was amazingly open. The emotions weren't hidden by deceit. You could read all her feelings in those hauntingly expressive eyes. I suggested to her that, instead of fretting over lost theater, she should immerse herself in good movies. She should see the stars who counted—Garbo especially. Garbo had done very little in theater, yet her face told millions about her most secret feelings. Bette, I felt, could do the same."

Carl Laemmle Jr. was casting for his production *The Bad Sister* (1931) based on Booth Tarkington's 1913 novel *The Flirt*. Hobart Henley was set to direct and he had cast actress Sidney Fox as the lead Marianne Madison with Conrad Nagel, Humphrey Bogart, and character actor Slim Summerville in supporting roles. Reg urged Junior and Henley to give Bette a chance for the role of Fox's sister, Laura Madison, in the film. After the screen test, Carl Laemmle Jr. told Reg that Bette had about as much sex appeal as Slim Summerville and felt she'd never last in Hollywood. Reg, however, believed in her. He coached Bette and stood behind the scenes as the petite actress acted with an edgy sharpness while studio executives insulted her.

Reg felt Bette needed support, so he introduced her to one of his loyal assistants, Bridget Price, to help her with her work at the studio. Bridget became Bette's closest confidant who helped the actress get through the crap of hardcore Hollywood. Bubbles observed Reg's interest in the newcomer, reminding her of the same care he had taken in her when she was new at the studio, and when he was married. She didn't like the devoted attention her husband was giving to the aspiring film actress and prohibited him from spending any more time with her.

Just as Bette was beginning her screen career at the advent of talkies, Reg was ending his stardom at the studio. Members of the press had met him in person during the silents, so they knew he had a refined British accent. Most of the paying public, however, Reg's fans, had never heard his speaking voice. *Embarrassing Moments* garnered good reviews from the critics but the public had a different reaction. To them, he had been the all-American hero who made them laugh. In fact, his characterization had been that of a typical young American entangled in the problems of suburban life. Hearing Reg's English accent, they were confused; his voice contradicted the roles he was playing. His refined British accent was not befitting to the all-American characters previously stereotyped on his road to stardom. Exhibitors reported for the first time they were now losing money with their Super Denny films.

This hit Reg and proved what he had been fighting for—the typical American dummy hero was against his true nature and his character. He felt sabotaged by the studio. He didn't want them to continue making of fool of him with the same roles and thus ruin his career in the world of sound pictures. "I felt something like the man who tried to live for a year on nothing but Limburger sandwiches. Limburger undoubtedly is tasty, occasionally, but can you imagine it as a steady diet? Having to eat Limburger without a break is one of the definite penalties of achieving stardom."

Reg went to Laemmle and asked if they'd let him out of the contract for his final contractual obligation of *The Third Party*. Uncle Carl was disappointed but understood the challenges Reg had faced for quite some time. He reluctantly acquiesced and signed to end their contract together.

Reg spent one last bittersweet moment reminiscing in his bungalow which had been his home at Universal City for eight years. Laemmle gave him a fatherly hug, thanking him for being his top comedy star and as a son throughout the past decade. Uncle Carl said, "I'm sorry to see you go, Reggie. Most people feel good when they make people laugh, but you. You're wired differently. You're on some sort of different frequency, another brain wave above us all. Spread your wings, son, and fly."

Reg flashed his crooked smile at the man whom he owed his life, thanked him, and gave him a warm hug. He had been with Universal as their top comedy star for a record term and now the cord was cut.

12 OF HUMAN BONDAGE

ON OCTOBER 29, 1929, the economy took a severe downturn when the U.S. stock market crashed. The Roaring Twenties had fizzled out leaving an insecure feeling for the country, the entertainment industry, and Reg. After it had all set in, reality slapped the film star in the face. He had left such familiar shelters of the studio and his family to expand his horizons for greener pastures and bluer skies at the time of The Great Depression. With the advent of sound, Reg was no longer the king of laughter at a major studio, and no one was knocking down his doors. The studios were themselves going through huge changes with their contractual stars during the talkie transition and none of them were willing to take the gamble on Universal's ex-silent film star. Consequently, the drop had been a lot further and the inevitable bump had been a lot harder.

"A star never realizes when he begins to slide off the top. Each feel that the public, and all the other producers, are crying for his services. He is the last man in the world to understand that he is through. So, when a contract ended, and a star was released, he used to wait for offers from other studios. Of course, they didn't come. His pride wouldn't let him play minor roles. There was no fighting to regain a lost prestige. They just sat and waited. Eventually, the truth dawned—they were passé, done for, finished. Nobody wanted them. Then came a frantic, panicky examination of the bank account. Usually, there was nothing left."

Now a free agent, Reg contemplated his return to England. He had been contacted by Sono Art-World Wide Pictures, who was doing British deals, and Reg finally met with the ambitious independent foreign production company. Sono Art-World Wide Pictures was the original U.S. distributor of Alfred Hitchcock's British films made in the late 1920s and they were willing to take a chance on the silent film star's voice that had been heard in musical stage prior to his screen career. The company was funded by British capital which gave Reg the chance to move back to the homeland to possibly produce Shaw's piece. After the meeting, Reg signed a three-year agreement with Sono Art to make four full-feature all-talking productions at $150,000 per picture, with two to be in made in England and two at Metropolitan Studios in the heart of Hollywood.

The first of the four Sono Art films was *What a Man* (1930) based on a novel by E.J. Rath and adapted by Harvey Gates from the play *They All Want Something* by Courtenay Savage. The company chose to make the film at the Metropolitan Studios in Hollywood with cinematography by Reg's familiar cameraman from his Seiter days, Arthur Todd.

In the romantic comedy directed by George Crone, Reg played Wade Rawlins, a former British Grenadier Guards officer, who masquerades as a chauffeur to win the love of his employer's daughter. Bubbles wanted to act once more and have the lead opposite Reg in his new sound picture. Instead of suggesting her for the role, Reg insisted his wife stick to their deal and support him in this new chapter of his career. The company instead hired Miriam Seegar for the role of Eileen Kilbourne.

The press responded favorably to Reg's performance in his first film away from Universal. Myrtle Gebhart wrote for *Motion Picture* magazine, "*What a Man* revealed Reg could still carry a tune engagingly. Not only do Denny's fans get to hear his British accent and operatic singing voice, but they now have the chance to find out the real color of their favorite's eyes and hair and complexion, inasmuch as the picture was made in full color as well as sound."

Unfortunately, the deal at Sono Art was too good to be true. The film did okay, but neither Reg nor Sono Art were pleased with the box-office results. The independent company couldn't pay him the amount agreed upon and subsequently defaulted on his contract.

Metro-Goldwyn-Mayer (MGM) was the last studio to buy into the new medium of sound pictures. They released their first talkie effort in the form of two musicals, *The Broadway Melody* (1929) and *The Rogue Song* (1930). Carl Laemmle's former secretary and manager of Universal Studios, Irving Thalberg, now headed production at MGM. When Thalberg found out that Laemmle's favorite comedic star was no longer obligated to their top competitor, he got a hold of Reg and called him in for a meeting. Thalberg said he couldn't provide the handsome salary Universal had paid him, but asked Reg if he'd be interested in using his singing talent to star in four of their new musicals. As his first love was song, Reg was appreciative the musical studio wanted him and signed with MGM. Thalberg had married Reg's original *Leather Pushers* co-star, Norma Shearer, and Reg felt right at home with the studio that treated him like family, at a time when he was feeling insecure about his future in the business. Although he was disappointed the profitable contract with Sono Art had abruptly ended, he was humbled and relieved to be back at a major studio, and to be working.

To get started on his first film at MGM, Thalberg arranged for Reg to meet with one of the studio's top directors who was making the transition from silent films with his second talkie and first musical talking picture. Cecil B. DeMille called Reg in for a meeting about his upcoming talkie, *Madam Satan* (1930). "We had only a bowing acquaintance. On a friend's recommendation he sent for me. 'I understand you sing?' he inquired. I replied that I, also, understood that to be a fact, though it had been disputed in some quarters. He arranged tests. *Madam Satan* was a medley of farce and melodrama, but I'm more grateful for his faith in me than I could ever express. He fought for me. I'm terribly happy not to have disappointed him."

Reg began his second career, at MGM, as a featured player. In his portrayal of cheating husband Bob Brooks, he acted and sang baritone as the lead, with Kay Johnson playing his wife, aka "Madam Satan," in Cecil B. DeMille's classic cult-noir musical thriller comedy. The supporting cast included Roland Young as Reg's comedic buddy and Lillian Roth as his mistress, Trixie. The pre-Code film was way ahead of its time and off the charts crazy with a mix of music, comedy, and a thrilling climax with a Zeppelin crash in New York City. Reg returned to his role of hero who saves the day, in a twisted DeMille sort of way.

Once Reg completed his stellar job in *Madam Satan*, MGM put him to work in three more pictures that year. He starred as Larry in *Those Three French Girls* (1930) with French-Canadian star Fifi D'Orsay, then as lead Paul Brandt in the mildly entertaining film directed by Sidney Franklin, *A Lady's Morals* (1930), starring with Grace Moore and Wallace Beery. Thalberg loaned Reg out to Fox to go Irish as thief Barney McGann in *Oh, for a Man!* (1930) with Jeanette MacDonald and Bela Lugosi (who would star the following year as *Dracula*). Back at MGM, Reg appeared as Jeffrey Haywood in *Parlor, Bedroom and Bath* (1931) with Buster Keaton and Charlotte Greenwood, then starred again with Greenwood in *Stepping Out* (1931) directed by Charles Reisner.

Douglas Fairbanks' wife, Mary Pickford, had been cast by United Artists in the remake of the successful silent film *Kiki* (1931). The silents' leading lady specifically requested her husband's good friend be cast as the male lead opposite her. Even though the film's producer, Joseph Schenck, had previously told Reg he'd never work in film due to his crooked smile, blah personality, and waddle of a walk, he hired him for the role of Victor Randall at the insistence of Ms. Pickford. Mr. Schenck (or "Mr. Skunk" as Louis B. Mayer reportedly called him) congratulated Reg on his successes; happy the actor didn't listen to his insulting advice ten years prior. During production of *Kiki*, Bubbles happily announced she was pregnant with their first child together. Reg was overjoyed to start a new career and a new family.

That same year, Reg portrayed Victor in Noël Coward's MGM production of *Private Lives* (1931) with Norma Shearer and upcoming film star Robert Montgomery. On set, Reg and Bob Montgomery developed a close friendship and partook in various sportsman activities together off-set. Bob was into polo and as Reg was now a skilled rider, Montgomery talked him into joining the Riviera Country Club where polo was quite the sport among Hollywood's elite. With fellow member player pals Leslie Howard, Walt Disney, and Will Rogers, they had a rollicking time during practice and rode in weekly tournaments.

On September 28, 1931, Reg's son, Reginald Denny Jr. was born healthy. Reg was the proud father of a son who could carry on his legacy. Motherhood didn't come so easily to Bubbles; she was still childish and faced challenges caring for the infant. Reg hired a nurse to help care for the baby while Bubbles recovered from childbirth.

Reg was filled with gratitude when he received an invitation from Morris Gest to be his honored guest at a special reprise production of *The Miracle* (1931) given for President and Mrs. Herbert Hoover at the Lyric Theatre in Baltimore, Maryland. Although their new son was only two months old and Bubbles didn't feel she could travel, Reg accepted the invitation, which would take place, by chance, on his fortieth birthday. He flew solo to Baltimore and attended the celebratory event. Afterward, Gest handed him the memorable program with a handwritten note, "To Reginald Denny, the only actor who ever payed [sic] me back." It was a nice birthday present to remind him of his past and how far he had come in ten years.

When Reg returned home for the Thanksgiving holiday, Bubbles greeted him with disdain. She was angry her husband had left home after she had given birth to their son, and he hadn't even celebrated his own milestone birthday with them. She handed him a notice that Rene was suing him. Reg had only paid his ex-wife one third of their agreed divorce settlement having stopped payments when his salary decreased. When the notice was publicly announced in the newspapers that Rene had filed legal attachments to the house and his two automobiles, Bubbles was furious. In addition to Rene coming after him for the remainder of their settlement, the IRS was after Reg for the large bonus Universal had provided him, which he hadn't claimed on his tax return. The City of Los Angeles was also after him for unpaid speeding tickets resulting from his reckless driving. The walls were closing in and Reg was paying for careless mistakes he'd made when he was a gay blade about town.

He needed an escape from his newfound stresses, so the young family went up to the cabin for the holidays. After a snowy and quiet New Year celebration in the mountains with Bubbles' family and the baby boy, Reg returned home to the Hollywood Hills and hit the polo fields with his buddy Bob Montgomery. While the celebrity team practiced on the grounds of the Riviera polo field for an upcoming tournament, another player's mount collided with Reg's. Both ponies fell with their riders in the saddle and rolled over several times crushing the players. Montgomery rescued Reg from under his horse and got him to the hospital where he was taken to the emergency ward. X-rays revealed Reg hadn't broken his back, but he had sustained injuries in the region of his spine and could barely move. After a few days in the hospital, the doctor sent him home and told Bubbles to keep him stationary in bed for at least a couple of weeks.

The polo accident forced Reg to take a break and to finally spend time with Bubbles and Reggie Jr. While he recuperated, it was difficult to lay still in bed. Reg needed something to do. He was too weak to do the normal activities to which he was accustomed, such as auto racing, yachting in the Pacific, flying British warplanes, and recently polo playing, as his outlets. He needed a new one, but with less risky action. He thought about taking up hobbies such as painting and carving models, like he'd done as a kid. When he was able to get up and move around, Reg went to the hardware store to buy art supplies and carving tools. There, he met a skilled model maker who recognized the film star and asked him what he was doing there. Reg shared that carving models had been a childhood passion of his and he needed a simple hobby to decompress while he recuperated from an injury. The man said he wanted to share something Reg might appreciate and asked him to take a ride in his car.

"He took me to his workshop and pointed out, among other models, one of a river boat that was the most marvelous piece of work of its kind I'd ever seen. Then he told me why he'd built it. He was an oil man and during the depression, he said, he lost $20,000,000, a statement I later verified. When he discovered he was actually broke, he went home, he confessed to me, with the full intentions of committing suicide. He was on his way to his den to get a gun when his little son interrupted him. The boy had a picture of a boat, which he asked his daddy to make into a real boat. This man then realized what a fool he'd been. He wondered whether, if he concentrated on the boat model, he would be able to forget his worries. He started working on plans, and months later, working night and day, he had it built. He told me that that boat became the all-important thing in his life. By the time he had completed it, some of his stocks had come back and, when I talked with him, he had made another fortune."

The oil man's experience left a lasting impression on Reg and as a result of the man's insightful message, he decided to whittle away his stresses. Once he was mobile, Reg drove to his cabin getaway where he collected leftover firewood. He sat under a tall Ponderosa tree out in the open and began carving a boat. His hawk Georgie flew overhead while Reg whittled away and quickly forgot his cares, just as the once suicidal multimillionaire had done. Walter Huston and his wife had just bought the land next door and they were remodeling the existing cabin there. Reg helped Huston draft his plans and gave advice for his rustic remodel, and gifted him the new yacht he had carved as a housewarming present.

When Reg returned home, he got a call with an offer to return to the stage, this time for many weeks and on tour while Reggie Jr. was just seven months old. That May, he left for San Francisco where he opened at the Alcazar Theatre starring as Alvin Roberts in *Blessed Event* (1932). After a three-week run there, he returned home where the play ran another three weeks at the El Capitan Theatre in Hollywood. After the stage run, Reg worked on only two films that year while he spent time with the family and whittled. He turned villain for the first time in his screen career with the lead role of Judson in Radio Pictures' *Strange Justice* (1932) directed by Victor Schertzinger, and then as Steve Mason in an independent film directed by Chester Franklin, *The Iron Master* (1933).

John Barrymore had stayed in close touch with Reg throughout their work schedules and their marriages. Barrymore knew Reg was out of work and shared an idea to get his friend back in the saddle. He said he enjoyed their Shakespearean stage debut together and he wanted to perform as they had in *Richard III,* only this time in a sound motion picture version of *Hamlet.* Reg loved the idea and told his friend he'd do anything to help get it made. Barrymore asked cutting-edge set designer Robert Edmond Jones to stage a screen test so they could pitch it to RKO as a full-length feature film. Jones had been the set designer on *Richard III* and had also designed Barrymore's stage production of *Hamlet* back in the twenties. He had been experimenting with a new three-color Technicolor process and thought this would be a great opportunity to test it out.

Reg and Barrymore reunited to perform "The Ghost Scene" in the first film version of *Hamlet* (1933) with Barrymore as Hamlet, Reg as Horatio, Donald Crisp as Marcellus, and Irving Pichel as Claudius. The six-minute Technicolor scene was amazing and when Barrymore pitched it to Merian Cooper at RKO, they immediately signed a contract to make the picture with consideration of Gloria Swanson or Helen Hayes to play Ophelia. Reg loved his troubled friend, and not only did he play the loyal Shakespearean role on set, he was the real-life Horatio to the tormented Barrymore. Unfortunately, Barrymore developed health issues associated with his alcoholism and another project shut down.

It was a thin year of work for Reg. He was disappointed that the *Hamlet* project was cancelled, and he wasn't getting calls for parts. He decided he'd better create his own roles if he wanted to make pictures again. In between his whittling at the cabin and spending time with his new family, Reg returned to writing. One of the stories which he called *The Worthy Deceiver* was about an actor who is hired by a wealthy woman to impersonate a British lord who gained his status through an advantageous marriage. The woman throws a party and the entire crowd falls hard for the bluff as they find all their valuables are missing.

Reg began the rounds of pitching his story to producers and met with Paramount Pictures' former head of sales, George Weeks. Weeks had formed his own production company and was looking for projects to fill his slate. Reg told Weeks he had some ideas for dramas that allowed him to display his full scope of acting and presented his latest written effort. Weeks liked Reg's proposal and signed him to direct and act in his own story and to co-produce the film with his recently formed Angelus Productions. Writer Faith Thomas had adapted Reg's story for *That's My Daddy*, and also his first talkie, *Red Hot Speed*. Reg asked the writer if she would adapt his new story for the screen as a starring vehicle for himself. Thomas wrote the screenplay and, with the "big bluff" in the story, they changed the title to *The Big Bluff*. Reg wanted to direct his film, but he needed help with the technical aspects of directing such as camera angles, lighting, and cutting. Weeks hired assistant director Leigh Smith to help with the mechanics and aid Reg in bringing his vision to life. Reg hired a young divorcee and former Ziegfeld Follies girl, Claudia Dell, to play opposite him in the leading lady role. Tower Productions financed the film with George Weeks' Angelus Productions and with the help of Smith, Reg directed *The Big Bluff* (1933), in which he also starred with Dell, Jed Prouty, Cyril Chadwick, Donald Keith, and Phil Tead.

Bubbles was again upset Reg didn't hire her as his leading lady. She suspected her husband was having an affair with his new co-star. When Reg missed dinner and came home late one evening after having dined with Dell after work on set, Bubbles went mad, threw a carved model at Reg, and then informed him she was pregnant with their second child.

While working on the production of *The Big Bluff*, Reg was awarded the role of Gerald Hume in Sam Wood's controversial MGM film, *The Barbarian* (1933) with Ramon Novarro, Myrna Loy, Edward Arnold, and soon-to-be-famed journalist Hedda Hopper. While on set, Reg confided to Hopper that he and his "jealous wife" had fought and she had thrown a terrible temper tantrum. When Reg was seen out again with Claudia Dell, rumors circulated around town that there was trouble at home and Reg was going through another divorce. When *The Barbarian* premiered on May 12, 1933, a *Los Angeles Times* columnist announced the film's release and asserted that "the Reginald Denny screen couple had 'phfft,' which in English means separated, and were Reno-bound." Bubbles was enraged when she read the newspaper headlines. She was upset her husband had shared their private arguments with others and that someone had the nerve to report of her temper tantrum. In order to counter the negative rumors and appease Bubbles, Reg bought a full-page ad in the Hollywood film trades to deny claims that the couple was on bad terms. In the ad, Reg claimed that he and Bubbles had not separated and that everything was swell in the Denny household. He stated, in fact, they were happily expecting another baby.

Following a couple slim years of work, Reg was surprised to get a call from Carl Laemmle Jr., who had reached a commanding position at Universal with his success in making the first sound versions of *Dracula* and *Frankenstein*. At the suggestion of his father, Laemmle offered Reg a nice role in Universal's *Only Yesterday* (1933), megaphoned by accomplished director John Stahl. Reg gladly accepted the offer and returned to his home studio to play Bob Warren in the film opposite Billie Burke. Based on the book by

Frederick Lewis Allen, the pre-Code drama is about a young woman who becomes pregnant by her boyfriend before he rushes off to fight in World War I. It starred Margaret Sullavan in her film debut and John Boles as the war vet who forgets who she is. Reg played a charming young swain who sang tenor for Billie Burke and was praised for his versatility in his acting, now as a supporting character.

After he finished work on *Only Yesterday*, Columbia Pictures offered Reg a supporting role in Valentine Williams' murder mystery *Fog* (1933). The film was directed by Albert Rogell and starred "the sweetest girl in pictures," Mary Brian, along with Donald Cook. In *Fog*, Reg played the colorful part of Dr. Winstay, personal physician to a multimillionaire who is murdered shortly after a transatlantic liner leaves New York en route for Europe. Other murders are committed in swift succession onboard the liner crossing the Atlantic in a dense fog, and many of the passengers come under suspicion before the actual killer is brought to justice with the aid of a ghost. Reg was happy to have continual work in dramas, now with another baby on the way.

Radio Pictures' head of production Merian Cooper was greatly disappointed that the *Hamlet* project was put on hold. He liked Reg's work in the short, so he called him in for a meeting. Merian said he was a fan of the British actor and asked if he would like to work at RKO. Reg was thrilled to receive another studio offer. Without hesitation he signed a generous six-picture contract with Radio Pictures. Reg got to work on his first project at the studio with *The Lost Patrol* (1934) directed by John Ford. Adapted by Garrett Fort from the novel *Patrol* by Philip MacDonald, the WWI drama is about twelve British soldiers who are stranded in the Sahara Desert and are menaced by Arab enemy snipers.

In *The Lost Patrol*, Reg played a British soldier named Brown and starred with fellow actors Boris Karloff, Wallace Ford, Alan Hale, and Victor McLaglen whose older brother was the jiu-jitsu scoundrel, Leopold McLaglen. It was an all-male cast and, for authenticity, Ford had the crew film the scenes of the deserted men on location near Yuma in 120-degree temperatures of the Arizona desert. One of the producers was hospitalized due to sunstroke, and afterward the crew was limited to working only two hours a day. One of the actors was so deathly afraid of sunstroke he hired a detective to shadow him while they were in the middle of the desert. The conditions were unbearable and Reg was uncomfortable working with the brother of a man who had robbed him. While they were out in the desert, Reg shared with his co-star of the experience he had with Leopold while they were in India twenty years earlier. McLaglen revealed his brother was a scandalous con-man and he'd been forced to bail the cheat out of many situations while constantly helping him get work in Hollywood. Although several horses and mules died from heat exhaustion, the cast made it out alive and John Ford told Reg he was extremely happy with his performance.

Once Reg completed work on *The Lost Patrol*, two of the films in which he had appeared during that year were released. On November 1, 1933, *Only Yesterday* premiered at the Pantages Theatre in Hollywood where members of the cast were presented in person at the food show preview, exclusively for local grocers and their families. Critics nationwide praised the film and its performers. *New York Movie Magazine* said, "Lavishly staged, attractively costumed, skillfully directed. *Only Yesterday,* Universal's greatest film effort since *All Quiet on the Western Front*, comes to the screen with the greatest galaxy of stars, near-stars, one-time stars and stars-yet-to-be, ever assembled. It makes Margaret Sullavan a new star, heightens the popularity of John Boles, Reginald Denny and Billie Burke, and brings before you probably the longest roster of film talent ever to grace one screen. In his come-back, Reginald Denny has now proved he is not a has-been histrionically by turning in a splendid bit in *Only Yesterday*. He has much to say of the extravagances of yesterday, but his wisdom will be unheeded by those who need it most. He said that he will be satisfied with minor roles and he has found a contentment that his old stardom could not bring."

The following week, *Fog* premiered with more great reviews coming in from the critics. Reg was again complimented for his superb acting in a drama. Waldon Yerger of the *Times Union* said, "Reginald Denny as Doctor Winstay, personal physician to the millionaire, shows his versatility by being able to enact various roles with equal dexterity." The *San Francisco Chronicle* said of him, "Reginald Denny, who usually conducts himself in such debonair, gentlemanly fashion, lays himself open to some harsh charges by his behavior as the ship's physician."

Reg was relieved to once again receive positive reviews from the press, as well as his top-rate directors.

During the release of his most recent films, Reg got a call from producer Harold Hopper asking for a favor. Hopper said that Melvyn Douglas had been cast for the lead role in Al Ray's *Dancing Man* (1934), but he suddenly had another obligation. He pleaded with Reg to fill the role. Reg had some time between RKO films, so he accepted Hopper's offer and played Paul Drexel in the comedy-mystery opposite beautiful actress Judith Allen.

On November 25, 1933, just days after his forty-second birthday and a day after their fifth wedding anniversary, Reg and Bubbles celebrated the birth of their daughter Joan. The little angel was a small 5 lbs. 13 oz. at birth and the spitting image of her petite brown-eyed mother. A number of Hollywood press agents came to the Queen of Angels Hospital to see the new Denny princess and interview her mother for the public birth announcement. Bubbles got all prettied up, but instead of providing a glowing display of the couple's new baby, she made sarcastic remarks to the columnists as punishment for their previous gossip.

"We had thought of nicknaming her 'Phfft' because some gossip writer published an item saying that's what Reg and I had done," the ex-actress said in the hospital. "But we reconsidered when we thought of the child's future. We have given her a prettier name, we think, in Joan Dionne."

Reg wasn't happy with the mockery and when he read his wife's sarcastic announcement in the papers, he vowed he would never share his personal drama with anyone again and that his affairs would remain private.

The week after his daughter's birth, Reg's directorial effort, *The Big Bluff*, was finally released. He was broadsided when the critics killed the film. *Variety* posted their scathing review with, "Reginald Denny wrote, acts in, and directed this one. It's a colorless farce in which the hero is hired to impersonate an English lord by a social climber and, being the hero, he turns out to be the McCoy. This version develops no new angles. Sloppy mounting, in spite of one elaborate set, and frequent soft spots, where they stand still to tell all about it, are of no particular help, and the lighting adds from five to 15 years to the women players. Sound registration seems to be good (the horns were off at the show caught), which merely helps to emphasize the flat quality of the dialog. Denny, generally able to dash through a part, seems to be weighed down by his responsibility as megger and little more than walks through, leaving Phil Tead and Jed Prouty to do what they can with the comedy. Usually a breezy bird who can waltz through a comedy part; Denny plods in this one—probably due to added cares as author and head man."

This was the first bad review Reg had ever received. He was devastated to hear the critics tear up his latest film release and he questioned his place in the business. Just as Reg was Barrymore's Horatio, Robert Montgomery was Reg's. Montgomery had just finished his picture *Transcontinental Bus* aka *Fugitive Lovers*, and had a new baby, Elizabeth, at home. The two busy actors needed some manly time away and took off together to spend a week at Reg's cabin in the snow while their wives spent time with their babies. There the two men lit up their pipes, drew up chairs to the log fireside, and confided in each other. Reg shared with Montgomery that things weren't going so well at home or with his new film career. Bob shared the troubles he was having with his ex-Broadway actress wife, Elizabeth. Both wives were temperamental women and jealous of their husbands' time away with their all their sports activities while they were at home with the babies. News got out that the two men had taken off together as "manly mountain men chopping wood," which confused Bubbles even more. She couldn't understand why her husband was gone all the time. She felt abandoned and alone to raise the children.

Reg returned from the cabin and got to work on another film with director John Ford in *The World Moves On* (1934). In the post-WWI film, Reg played a stiff-backed German officer, Erik von Gerhardt, with an impressive cast including English actress Madeleine Carroll, Franchot Tone, and Nigel Bruce. At the same time, Reg doubled up and appeared in his next RKO film, *Of Human Bondage* (1934) directed by John Cromwell. Reg had convinced Bette Davis to stay in Hollywood when she was just starting her film career at Universal a few years earlier; now they finally had the opportunity to work together.

In *Of Human Bondage*, Reg played playboy Harry Griffiths with his friend Leslie Howard in the lead role of Philip Carey who is hopelessly in love with a cold and indifferent waitress played by Davis. Reg not only enjoyed working with his gal pal Bette, but he had a great time reminiscing with his polo pal Leslie Howard. Reg and Leslie had quite a time on set swapping horror tales of their days in the war. Reg also enjoyed working again with his *Madam Satan* co-star, Kay Johnson, as well as friends Alan Hale and Reginald Owen. A great time for all was celebrated on set. This was Bette's come-out role which would lead the way to her stardom.

Reg worked all the time while he doubled up on two films, leaving Bubbles alone with her nurse, three-year-old Reggie, and newborn Joan. The feisty childish brunette now had two young children to care for and she was mad that Reg was gone all the time surrounded by actors and actresses whom she suspected were after her handsome husband. Bubbles became enraged when she learned Reg had reunited with Bette; she was insanely jealous of the actress knowing of the interest Reg had taken in her at Universal. Then, one evening on the set, Reg and Leslie Howard worked out a scene at Radio Pictures' ranch in the San Fernando Valley, twenty-five miles outside of Hollywood. The scene takes place while the two walk down the foggy streets of London. Coincidentally, there was intense fog that night, so the crew didn't have to use equipment to simulate the thick London fog. When they finished at ten o'clock, it was so foggy it took them each a couple extra hours to drive home. After driving in the intense fog, Reg finally got home at midnight. Bubbles greeted him furiously at the door. She accused her husband of having an affair with Davis and they got into a heated fight. Reg got in his car to escape an attack in front of his small children, who were woken up by the yelling. He headed up to his cabin where snowdrifts piled high and it was bitter cold.

Reg got a comforting log fire underway. He had gone outside and down to his basement to get some supplies when the big cellar door slammed shut. Unbeknownst to Reg, Bubbles had followed him up and snapped the lock down. Reg yelled through the door for Bubbles to let him out. When she thought he had learned his lesson, she tried to lift the handle on the heavy log door, but it was frozen stuck by ice. Reg was trapped. He yelled and pounded at the doors, hoping one of the neighbors would hear him. Fortunately, he had on his overcoat, as he spent a night of horror locked in the cellar of his mountain cabin while Bubbles stayed warm by the fire upstairs, worried she may have overreacted. When daylight came, Reg's caretaker Art Manning arrived. Bubbles came out crying that the wind had blown the cellar door shut. When Art heard Reg pounding from inside, he pried the heavy door open and let his boss out. It was a good two-hour drive back into town. When Reg showed up late to work on set with a heavy cold, everyone asked what happened. Leslie and Reg had shared their WWI horror stories, and now Reg had a new one to share with he and Bette.

When the press found out about Reg's night in the big freeze, they questioned him. Reg did his best to deflect any further rumors of the couple splitting up. He made up a story about how Bubbles just happened to drive up on her own and rescue him. In the newspapers the next day, writers made a satirical joke about the experience and tied it in with the film Reg was working on with, "Fate cruel and kind to actor in 'cold storage' and 'of human bondage.'"

Just as Reg had tantrums on set when previously asked to go against his nature, Bubbles had tantrums at home because becoming an abandoned wife and mother were against hers. The reactive way his wife now behaved worried Reg; it was a complete contradiction from the cute, innocent, adorable actress he had courted. Not wanting to trigger anything to upset his reputation or their livelihood, Reg put on a happy face in public regarding his wife and family. His life had now become the farce he had so desperately fought to evade.

13

DENNYMITE

REG MADE IT OUT OF HIS COLD STORAGE and back to work on *Of Human Bondage* while the rest of the films in which he appeared from the previous year were released in succession. On February 16, 1934, *The Lost Patrol* opened in theaters nationwide. For the opening of the film, Reg and Boris Karloff flew to San Francisco where they made a personal appearance for its world premiere at the Golden Gate Theatre. After the film's release, the press presented outstanding reviews about the realistic acting of its cast and superb direction of John Ford, as well as the eloquent musical score and panoramic photography. Blackford of *Billboard* said, "… Once again RKO hits the bell with this fascinating and interesting story of the desert. The photography is the finest ever shown in desert scenes."

Louella Parsons said in the *Examiner*, "*The Lost Patrol*, which RKO officials considered important enough to give a television premiere at RKO Theater, is no ordinary papier-mache model. Unique in its treatment, impressive in its dramatic strength, this picture is not the usual lace-trimmed, valentine idea with love sonnets written in dripping dialogue. There isn't a love scene, there isn't a woman, and there isn't a fireside chair, yet seldom has there been a picture with such powerful, dramatic situations. John Ford, who directed this amazing picture, should be congratulated for never once permitting his story to be spoiled by conventional action. Reginald Denny should have hundreds of offers and this picture should bring him back."

Doris Arden praised the film in the *Chicago Illustrated Times*, "The film is superbly acted by a masculine cast—each characterization is a magnificently sincere and vivid performance."

The *Washington Post* said of Reg, "Denny turned up again in *The Lost Patrol* to do a great job of straight dramatic acting. It's a swashbuckling soldier—a member of a doomed patrol trapped in the Mesopotamian desert—he is in the new cinema. Quite unlike the polite parts he has been doing of late is his portrayal of the likeable soldier Brown. Now, doing a comeback, he attempts parts that call on his abilities as an actor." *The Lost Patrol* did so well it was listed as one of the top ten films of 1934 and nominated for Best Music Score at the 7th Academy Awards. The following week, Reg's *Dancing Man* premiered at the Pantages Theatre bringing in more accolades from the critics and the public.

Reg was at once relieved to hear such complimentary reviews after the horrible feedback he'd gotten from his work in *The Big Bluff*. Just as he had suddenly found out he was no longer the huge box-office draw and that his magnificent salary was a thing of the past,

Reg was humbly happy to be working again as an actor. It was a successful year with many good supporting character roles; however, the parts Reg now played didn't pay enough to keep up with the extravagant lifestyle in which he and his wife had become accustomed. In addition, Reg had made generous investments in Bubbles' family with her brother's attempt to run a cattle business and gold mines; both turned out to be false promises resulting in a major dent in the bank account. They now lived on what was left of the savings of his past salary and Reg worked paycheck to paycheck to pay the bills.

He needed an outlet within his reach, so in between filming Reg continued the hobby of model making. By concentrating on the problem of crafting from pieces of balsa wood, he persisted to whittle away his worries. Working on the models was cheap, tangible, and satisfying; he could start a project and complete it without disruption or distraction. By intently focusing on something without risking his life or spending his life savings, Reg was able to calm his mind in a Zen way, as the Maharajah had taught him. For guidance in carving and gluing and such he went to his friend, fellow actor Rod La Rocque, whose workshop had been his hobby for many years. La Rocque had tools and equipment worth $40,000 and could make anything from any material. Reg took lessons from his fellow hobbyist to perfect his model making skills. He designed blueprints of various scale-model ships and airplanes based on the large-scale craft with which he was familiar. From his blueprints, Reg carved and built an exquisite model schooner in perfect miniature for young Reggie. The library in the Denny hilltop home eventually resembled a toy shop with the shelves and floor adorned with all kinds of ship and airplane models in various stages of construction. Reg dedicated the room to designing his models with a full HO scale model train set on tracks circling the perimeter and blowing off steam to entertain his son.

The artistic carvings looked nice on his shelves and as gifts for family and friends, but Reg wanted to put them in motion. At first, he used the propeller rubber band method from available kits. World War I veteran Paul Guillow had designed a line of balsa flying model construction kits built from a wood frame, then covered with light tissue stiffened with a substance called dope. These stick-and-tissue kits included pre-cut strips and blocks, detailed instructions, and pre-formed parts and decals. The scope of these models was limited and there was no controlling the plane; all Reg could do was throw it in the air and watch it crash to the ground. When completed, the models were able to be hand-launched or flown using a small gas engine or rubber-band-powered propeller, but since one rough landing was likely to ruin as much as forty hours of work, most ended up on the shelf. It was entertaining for three-year-old Reggie, but not enough for Dad.

With his passion for model making and aerodynamics, Reg wanted to find a way to operate a model plane and fly it like the real thing; not just throw it in the sky for it to fall to the ground. He was intrigued with Nikola Tesla's concept of wireless radio control and hadn't forgotten about the telemetry technique he'd witnessed in use with the falcons. He also remembered the electronic devices used with the observation hot air balloons during his service in the war. Reg wanted to be able to use his models as if he were at the controls inside the cockpit, only remotely and from the ground. He built a workshop in the basement of his home where he got to work on the telemetry radio-control technique like a mad scientist. With the electric supplies available, he made a radio transmitter and bought some small motors which he attached to the inside of his homemade plane's nose along with wired servos on the wings with which the transmitter could communicate. He tested them out on the ground to make sure he had communication and it worked. He then attached a tether to the plane so when he started it up and threw it in the air, he'd have control. It worked, but the plane only went around in circles while he held the line. He did the same with the boats. Fun for a moment, but the craft only went around in circles.

Reg decided to test his models without the tether. He designed a radio-controlled sailboat with a moving rudder and brought it to the cabin. When he took it out to the dock at Lake Arrowhead and set it on the water, it sailed like a charm. He was able to send it out several feet and bring it back in remotely. He had done it with a boat and now wanted to take the telemetry technique a step further with the airplanes. He designed a plane just like the real thing with ailerons, flaps, rudders, elevators, and stabilizers. He took his models to the cabin and used his airport runway for take-off and landing. He launched the planes from his homemade runway and tested them out in the open skies on the ranch property. After numerous crashes, Reg was ecstatic that not only could the non-tethered planes fly, but he could control them from the ground while they were flying in the air and then eventually bring them in for a smooth landing on their own.

Back in the Hollywood Hills, Reg rounded up the neighborhood kids to test out his new airplanes. He started a ground school where he gave "flying lessons" to the youth from his home basement using his scale models to simulate the real thing. Reggie Jr. was a little young to join in, but he was an eager audience. Being a flyer himself, Reg was sympathetic to all youngsters who were keen over airplanes so in the basement classroom, the teacher-actor used his miniature models to explain his points. When the youths finished a thorough elementary training course, he took them to the nearby park to fly his model planes. He loved his new teaching job and took it quite seriously, declaring it was more interesting than any of his other hobbies. The kids loved it, too.

Bubbles, however, wasn't too happy about all the attention her husband gave to his new hobby. While Reg became obsessed with his models, Bubbles became obsessed with his not wanting to spend time with the family, nor give her the attention she demanded. She sarcastically said he behaved like a child who played with toys and he should work instead of hanging out with the neighborhood kids. While his wife made fun of Reg, newspaper columnists got wind of his flying school and released news of the film star's new hobby. With his newfound popularity as the movie star who made models and gave flying lessons to youth, Reg was contacted with an offer to exclusively sell his models to the large department store chain Montgomery Ward. Reg thought it could be a lucrative business and accepted the offer to sell his planes at their stores and mail order catalog. In order to make the sale of his planes official, he formed his own company.

In 1934, Reg incorporated his Reginald Denny Industries as a California corporation. Wealthy socialites and one of the founding families of Los Angeles, Paul and Olive Whittier, were close friends of Reg and Bubbles'. When Reg shared with Whittier that Montgomery Ward had offered him a contract for worldwide distribution of his model planes, Whittier's company invested in Reginald Denny Industries to help the modeler get his business off the ground. As a result, the M.H. Whittier Company held the controlling stock in Reginald Denny Industries.

Now that Reg had an investor with start-up funding for his radio control hobby business, he needed a place other than his home where he could make the planes and sell them to the kids. He located a commercial storefront building at 5751 Hollywood Boulevard where he opened the Reginald Denny Hobby Shop. There, he hired a team to build and sell rubber band-, electric-, and gasoline-powered flying models as well as model plane kits, supplies, and miniature gas engines. Reg recognized the "build rubber power until you can afford gas" phenomenon, so his ads featured several attractive rubber-powered models as well as the gas-powered. He designed and sold the first model airplane kits based on the popular adventure serial radio show *The Air Adventures of Jimmie Allen*. In addition to the Jimmie Allen model kits, Reg also designed rubber band and motor models named after birds: "The Condor," "The Skylark," and "The Starling." He also designed a crack-proof plane he called the "Bullet." The models caught on quickly and became immensely popular, William Randolph Hearst being one of his first customers.

The fervent modeler ultimately designed and developed his first signature gas-powered plane which he called "Dennyplane." The radio-controlled gas model was a miniature 1933 Fairchild 24 Model G based upon planes owned by his friend Cecil Smallwood, who had a flying service operating from Clover Field. The Dennyplane used an experimental engine developed and produced by Major Mosely's Aircraft Industries in Burbank. The model featured wing halves that plugged into the fuselage top, a rather complex undercarriage, a solid-sheet empennage, and wire wingtips. To accompany his Dennyplane, Reg also designed inflatable wheels just like the real thing which he called "Denny Streamline Airwheels" and "Dennywheels."

The Dennyplanes were manufactured at the Reginald Denny Hobby Shop and also sold to the public there. A modeling-press advertising campaign, most notably in *Model Airplane News*, generated worldwide sales. Bob Montgomery bought several which were personalized for him and used in the ads. Even though the country was still trying to recover from The Great Depression, people found a way to buy Reg's planes; when they couldn't, he created a "Denny Jr." model which was less expensive than its more costly, larger parent model. The Denny Jr. was a design featuring a one-piece wing, simplified landing gear, and overall simplified construction. It was sold as a lower-priced kit, eliminating much of the deluxe hardware and liquids of the more expensive Dennyplane. For promotion, Reg sold or gifted his Denny Jr. model to such child actors as Mickey Rooney, Jane Withers, Freddie Bartholomew, and Jackie Cooper. Many of them flew at miniature air races with competitions at Mines Field, now Los Angeles International Airport (LAX). Reg was also asked by the studios to design model planes to simulate real aircraft for use in their films. To support the new hobby and its enthusiasts, the Academy of Model Aeronautics (AMA) was formed in New York City.

Reg became *the* builder of scale models and kids of all ages flocked to his hobby shop to buy his planes. In addition to the model planes, Reg developed and sold radio-controlled model boats and cars making him the founding father of the radio control or "RC" hobby industry we know today.

While Reg ran the business of his hobby shop, he continued with film work under his contract at RKO. He reunited with his old friend Bill Seiter and starred once again with Marian Nixon and Billie Burke in RKO's farcical comedy *We're Rich Again* (1934).

Reg returned to the type of farce that made him famous at Universal. He played young stockbroker Bookington Wells who is lucky on the market but unlucky in love. Engaged to a selfish city girl, Wells is captivated by a dumb little country girl from Texas, played by Nixon. It was Reg's first romantic lead in some time and he loved working with his Universal family again. Seiter and Laura La Plante had just divorced, and the director had become very close with Marian Nixon following her own divorce. The two were happy to announce their engagement on set and the cast celebrated while they were on location at a Beverly Hills home.

During filming of *We're Rich Again*, Carl Laemmle Jr. called Reg and asked if he'd return to Universal for an important supporting role in the John Galsworthy drama *One More River* (1934) directed by James Whale. Reg said yes under one condition—that he'd put his daughter to work with him. Barbara had just graduated high school from the Flintridge School for Girls and was contemplating a screen career. When Whale met the beautiful seventeen-year-old, he cast her in a small role with her father. In *One More River*, Reg played the role of David Dornford, a young candidate for Parliament in the all-British story about spousal abuse and divorce starring English actors Diana Wynyard and Frank Lawton in the leading roles. Reg had the opportunity to revel in having an English accent and used it to the hilt. Barbara was thrilled to make her first professional appearance on the familiar Universal lot which she had come to know as home when her father was their top star. She rehearsed her courtroom scene at her old family home with her father, but Bubbles wasn't happy about it. She was upset that Reg had cast Barbara in the film, but he wouldn't even think about casting her in another movie. Bubbles and Barbara were close enough in age that Bubbles constantly competed for her husband's attention, like another daughter.

Reg was at work on set when he received another call, this time from Irving Thalberg. MGM was producing the musical *The Merry Widow* (1934), with Ernst Lubitsch directing. Thalberg and Lubitsch wanted Reg to play the lead role of Prince Danilo, as he had done on the English stage. Reg regrettably told Thalberg he was committed to RKO for three more films and the dates conflicted with his shooting schedule. Thalberg was disappointed, but for their second choice he cast Maurice Chevalier to star with Jeanette MacDonald in the film. Reg's silent films had become quite popular in France where Chevalier had billed himself as "The French Reginald Denny." As a result of Reg's successful silent film *That's My Daddy*, Paramount Pictures modeled their own sound film *A Bedtime Story* (1933) after Reg's hit which starred Chevalier as the adopted father of the little orphan girl.

Around that time, Jack Warner contacted Reg for a meeting with him and his Warner Bros. production chief, Irving Asher. Warner and Asher told Reg they were planning a twenty-six-picture schedule at their new Teddington studio in Surrey, England, close by Nora's White Lodge. Warner had been busy lining up talent and wanted to reunite Reg with his silent film colleagues Laura La Plante, Hoot Gibson, and Edward Everett Horton to take back with him to England for work at Teddington. Reg said he was open to it and shared with Warner and Asher his idea for a couple of films he'd like to make in England. One was Shaw's *Cashel Byron's Profession*. The other was a story he'd written about a man who helps a kid from the slums of London, similar to his own experience with Sir Harry Preston, which he called *The Cockney Kid*. Warner loved Reg's ideas and offered him a three-picture deal to begin filming at the onset of 1935. He asked if Reg would travel with Asher and La Plante to London the following month to take a tour of the studio in preparation for their upcoming productions.

Reg was overwhelmed with this serendipitous string of offers. He was at another crossroads with decisions to make. As Barbara expressed her interest in being an actress, Reg told his daughter about his offer to work in England and that the world's best dramatic school was located there, Sir Beerbohm Tree's Royal Academy of Dramatic Art. Reg said she could travel with him for the Teddington meetings and stay with her Aunt Nora while studying drama abroad. Both father and daughter were excited about the prospect of returning to England, so Reg took Barbara downtown to get her passport in order for their trip to London. When he brought Barbara home after the travel plans were made, they shared news of the British film deal with Bubbles. She threw a fit and protested; she wasn't about to be left alone once again with two small children while Reg went off as a traveling player, and she certainly wasn't going to leave her family in America to move to England. It was an ugly scene and the argument upset Barbara. Reg decided it was best to make his wife happy and not leave his new family or his hobby business, so he regretfully let Warner and Asher know he wouldn't be returning to England for work at their Teddington studio the following year. Warner was disappointed as he already had made an announcement in the papers, but he understood and contritely released Reg of any obligation.

Barbara, however, still wanted to go. She had already spoken with her Aunt Nora who welcomed her to stay at White Lodge while she attended the prestigious drama school. After they wrapped work on *One More River*, Reg helped his daughter prepare for the move, then he and Bubbles hosted a farewell supper honoring Barbara at the home in which she grew up. Guests were a few close friends which included the Paul Whittiers, the Robert Montgomerys, the Paul Gerard Smiths, Reg's talent manager Vernon D. Wood, and writer Franc Dillon. The next day, Barbara flew with Laura La Plante and Irving Asher to England where she stayed with her Aunt Nora at the luxuriant White Lodge. Nora was tight with British royalty. She threw her niece an elaborate welcome party, along with a royal engagement party for La Plante and Asher. La Plante commented in *Picture Play* magazine, "… Incidentally, Reg Denny's sister, Mrs. Nora Albertini, gave the most brilliant party of the season. After that affair I came to the conclusion that we have never 'seen' a party in Hollywood!"

Meanwhile back in Hollywood and upon his return home from dropping his daughter off at the airport, Reg was caught off guard when a sheriff served him a summons. Rene would take her ex-husband to court as he had yet to pay the remainder of their divorce settlement. That week, Reg went to the courthouse to face Rene regarding the unpaid debt of five years prior. At the hearing, the judge ordered Reg to pay the remaining $30,000 (approximately $500,000 today) or go to jail. When Reg returned home and told Bubbles he had written a large check to his ex-wife, she lost it. She cried that she had given up her screen career because she thought she was marrying a wealthy, established movie star, but instead suffered with the timing of his fall from grace, his irresponsible nature, and his unfinished business. Reg took off to the hobby shop and focused on his model planes instead of engaging in the rage.

Reg was relieved to jump into his next RKO film, *The Richest Girl in the World* (1934). He was put even more at ease to again work with Bill Seiter and that the director had chosen Lake Arrowhead for the film's location. Since he'd be filming near the cabin, Reg decided it was time to take his new family on their first vacation together. That June, they all headed up to their mountain lodge retreat for the summer. Reg was happy to be back at his cabin, and Bubbles was even happier to have Reg all to herself now that Barbara was gone, and they were far away from his "silly hobby shop." At the cabin, the couple entertained guests from Hollywood while they relaxed with their two small children.

After a week of relaxation, Reg and Seiter began work on *The Richest Girl in the World* with Miriam Hopkins, Fay Wray, and Joel McCrea. The story is about an heiress, played by Hopkins, who switches places with her secretary, played by Wray, in order to find a man who will love her for who she is and not for money. Reg was cast as Wray's fiancé, Phillip Lockwood, and McCrea as the man who proves his love to Hopkins. The crew had a great time working together and would joke around constantly. In one scene, Reg was eating candy and mistakenly grabbed Fay Wray's lipstick. He bit into the end of it and everyone howled when Reg flashed his crooked smile with red lipstick on his teeth. While filming scenes at the dock of Lake Arrowhead, Reg bet Seiter he could swim the three-mile lake in less than two hours. Seiter laughed thinking it was impossible and took the bet. Little did he know, Reg had been practicing swimming in the lake. Having negotiated ten miles of water on several occasions, he already held the present record of one hour and twenty-seven minutes.

The next day, with official Amateur Athletic Unit (AAU) timers on hand and fellow members of *The Richest Girl in the World* troupe looking on, Reg entered the west side of the lake and began cleaving the water with a powerful breast-stroke. There was a spanking breeze from the east, but the star scarcely noticed it. It was Sunday and hundreds of cars had driven up from the city for the weekend. When the swimmer was identified, there was a scramble for rafts, canoes, speedboats, and chugging outboards. Halfway across the lake, Reg was soon surrounded by boats with passengers pleading for autographs. They circled around the furious swimmer, again and again, and many came alongside, as they urged the star to catch hold for a minute and sign his autograph. By the time the exasperated actor could reach the east side of the lake, one hour and fifty-three minutes had passed. He won the wager by seven minutes, but was twenty-six minutes over his former record, all because of his fans. If it hadn't been for autograph seekers, Reg may have held a new record for the three-and-one-eighths-mile swim across Lake Arrowhead. He wasn't satisfied with his mark and told the reporters he was going to try for a new record in the near future. Then, he said, he would announce his time and be willing for any other swimmer to shoot at his new record.

On July 13, 1934, Reg and Seiter's previous RKO film, *We're Rich Again*, was released with great reviews. *The Hollywood Reporter* praised the comedy with, "A cockeyed little opus, fairly alive with amusing ideas, most of which come off to make a comedy that any exhibitor can be grateful for in these dull days." Wanda Hale said in *New York City News*, "To sit through *We're Rich Again*, the current film at the Roxy Theatre, and see and hear Edna May Oliver, Billie Burke, Marian Nixon, Reginald Denny, Joan Marsh, Grant Mitchell, Gloria Shea, and Larry Crabbe is a pleasant enough experience. One feels most grateful that precisely this cast and no other was chosen to execute the rather difficult formula of keeping *We're Rich Again* out of the slapstick bracket. This is another way of saying that William Seiter's direction has been quite expert."

The following week, *Of Human Bondage* was released and it was critically acclaimed by the press who had complimentary reviews about Reg's performance. New York's *Silver Screen* said, "In *Of Human Bondage,* Reginald Denny plays the blithe and philandering Englishman—a role which suits him best. Denny's work in *Of Human Bondage* has been hailed among the finest of the season." The *Washington Star* said, "Reginald Denny, as the bounder friend, is believable in those gay and insincere moments when he is calmly walking off with Miss Davis and then leaving her flat on his doorsteps." The *Youngstown Vindicator* said of Reg, "Reginald Denny gives an admirable performance as Howard's best friend, Griffiths, as does the blond Kay Johnson, as Norah. The whole cast, in fact, has been remarkably well chosen by the director, John Cromwell. He has caught the tone of Somerset Maugham's novel to perfection, making the picture version easily as fine as the story." Bette Davis did such an outstanding job with her role as Mildred Rogers she was nominated for Best Actress, but lost to Claudette Colbert who won the award for her work with Clark Gable in *It Happened One Night* (1934).

Once *The Richest Girl in the World* wrapped at Lake Arrowhead, the family returned to their Hollywood home after spending an enjoyable summer at the cabin. The following week on August 6, *One More River* premiered at the Hollywood Pantages Theater with the press raving about the British drama. The *Los Angeles Examiner* said, "As scripted by R.C. Sherriff, *One More River* emerged as a solid, well-carpentered drama, whose climactic courtroom scene kept audiences on the edge of their seats. Reginald Denny, who is appearing currently in an intriguing role in John Galsworthy's *One More River* at the Hollywood Pantages Theater, is himself British and consequently interprets the role with the dignity and realism which this English-written story requires. Denny typifies perfectly the best-known English type. His daughter, Barbara Denny, recently appeared in courtroom scenes for *One More River* and begins her screen career at the same studio where her father first began."

On August 31, *The World Moves On* was released and the press had more great things to say about Reg. Cleveland's *The Plain Dealer* said, "After looking at *The World Moves On* in the RKO-Allen Theater last week, I was more than ever reminded that the old-timer is coming back again. That the industry is making special efforts to give those shunted out when the talkies came gives a second chance to recover lost fortunes. There were more old-timers in it than any other single picture I've seen in a long time, Reginald Denny being one of the best."

The *Baltimore Sun* called his return to films a "Denny Renaissance" with, "Speaking of things English, one is reminded of the come-back now being staged by the English actor, Reginald Denny. Mr. Denny has had many ups and downs in his screen career, and came near dropping out of sight with the advent of sound. In the last two weeks, however, he has been seen in three major films, *Of Human Bondage, The World Moves On* and *One More River*. He is a capable actor and should be able to maintain his ground."

Reg welcomed his renaissance in sound pictures and delighted in reading such complimentary reviews. He immediately got back to work on set to close his last contractual obligation with RKO as Captain Halliwell in *The Little Minister* (1934) directed by Richard Wallace. The film starred Katharine Hepburn and John Beal. During that time, *The Richest Girl in the World* made its premiere and Seiter's film again received accolades from the press. It ended up being nominated for an Oscar for Best Original Story.

Back home and in-between films, Reg continued his work at the hobby shop to perfect his model planes. While at the cabin, he had demonstrated his Dennyplane to guests from the mountain runway. While showing it off, Reg discovered that the larger plane needed a more powerful motor in order to conduct the aerial maneuvers he had done during the war. In his search for a better motor, Reg put on a contest at Mines Field. Several backyard shop machinists, who were likely unemployed at the time, submitted their engines for the competition. Cal Tech graduate and engine designer Walter Righter entered his powerful miniature engine. When Reg mounted Righter's motor in the Dennyplane, he was amazed at the power that little gasoline-powered engine provided. He selected Righter's winning engine as it was easiest to start, the most reliable, and most powerful. Reg put Righter to work and they called the new motors "Dennymite" for use with his signature Dennyplane. When Christmas orders started flying in from Montgomery Ward and ads in *Model Airplane News*, Righter moved production of the Dennymite motors from his home garage to a warehouse shop in Burbank.

Reg went hard to work at the shop while he balanced acting in films and spending time with his family. It was the busiest he had ever been in his life juggling his resurrected motion picture career with back-to-back filming, two homes, his family, and his new hobby.

14 RADIOPLANE

AFTER AVERAGING ONE PICTURE per month during 1934, Reg brought in the New Year with a slew of new films, working back to back while he managed the hobby shop and his mounting debts. He returned to Fox as Captain Payne in the Parisian musical comedy *Lottery Lover* (1935) directed by noted Viennese artist Wilhelm Thiele and starring with Lew Ayres, Pat Paterson, Peggy Fears, and Sterling Holloway. Reg was then awarded the role of Phil Graham in *Without Children* (1935), directed by William Nigh from a story written by Woodrow Wilson's wife, Nancy Mann Waddel Woodrow. At MGM, he worked on three films: as Johnny Spear in Hal Roach's *Vagabond Lady* (1935), directed by Sam Taylor with Robert Young as the lead; as Oliver in *No More Ladies* (1935), directed by Edward H. Griffith and an uncredited George Cukor, he appeared with good friend Bob Montgomery, along with Joan Crawford and Franchot Tone; and he played the role of Yashvin in *Anna Karenina* (1935), directed by Clarence Brown with Greta Garbo, Basil Rathbone, Fredric March, and Reginald Owen. Reg returned to Fox as Emery Gerard in Alfred E. Green's musical *Here's to Romance* (1935) with Nino Martini and Genevieve Tobin and then had the starring role of Oliver Keith in the indie crime caper *The Lady in Scarlet* (1935), directed by Charles Lamont, with Claudia Dell again as his leading lady.

Back at Universal, Reg was awarded the role of Jack Whitridge and was happy to once again work under the direction of James Whale in *Remember Last Night?* (1935). The murder mystery was adapted from Adam Hobhouse's novel *Hangover Murders* and also starred Robert Young, Constance Cummings, and Edward Arnold. Next, Reg took the lead role of Professor David Graham in another crime-mystery drama, *Midnight Phantom* (1935), directed by Bernard B. "BB" Ray, in which he again starred with Claudia Dell.

Meanwhile, Reg was unable to let go of his haunting obsession with radio-controlled airplanes. His hobby shop business thrived while a major clash for survival existed in Europe, much different than the peaceful climate in America. Nora and Barbara shared with Reg how unsettled life had become in Europe since Adolf Hitler's rise to power. The Nazi party was gaining dominance and Reg was all too aware of the atrocities taking place in his homeland. His brother had died at the hands of Germans and Reg wanted to help protect his daughter, his sisters, and his home country. At age forty-four, he thought about returning to the battlefront until another idea hit him. He thought there must be a way to use his popular radio-controlled devices in place of the real thing to help those on the front line so they didn't risk harming each other or being killed by the enemy.

Given his hands-on experience in aviation combat during WWI and rumblings of war in Europe, Reg wanted to share his new vision of using pilotless craft to help the Allies fight wars more strategically, efficiently, and with less human casualties. While at one of his model plane competitions, he heard an anti-aircraft officer complaining about the inadequacy of the target tugs they used for gunnery practice with the U.S. Army. Reg told him he saw no reason why a target plane couldn't be sent up by radio control. Then a lightbulb went off. The military could save a lot of money by using his radio-controlled planes as moving targets rather than real ones used for anti-aircraft gunnery practice.

Reg began experimenting with his radio-controlled airplanes as though they were real ones in mock war games. He took a few of his planes up to the cabin and from his flying field he created a shooting range in the air. He operated his Dennyplane from the ground and conducted aerial maneuvers as a warbird while Art Manning and friends of the Serrano tribe aimed and shot at the pilotless craft. After several rounds and days of practice, Manning's crew hit the target on the spot.

Back at his home workshop, Reg went hard to work on designing his new models throughout the night and took his planes to another height. With his unrelenting passion for radio-controlled models and his knowledge of fighter plane dynamics and reconnaissance, Reg incorporated his Reginald Denny Industries to expand his product line of hobby airplanes into radio-controlled target "drones." He hired a young radio ham and electrical engineer named Kenneth "Kenny" Wallace Case to refine the transmitters and receivers he'd been using for the Dennyplane. Along with Walter Righter, Reg and Kenny Case went to work on developing the radio controls and engines necessary for Reg's larger scale gas model planes to present to the U.S. Army as target drones. Everyone thought he had taken his hobby a little too far and that he was going, well, a little crazy. Bubbles especially. She was concerned about the time and money he spent on his hobby. Reg didn't care; he knew he could make it work and he just had to convince everyone else that it would. He shared his crazy idea with Paul Whitter who loved it and jumped onboard.

With Whittier, Kenny Case, and Walter Righter, Reg designed and developed his first prototype radio-controlled target plane and named it "Radioplane." Built of balsa and plywood, the high-wing monoplane had a nine-foot wingspan. It was powered by a 2½-horsepower engine driving a single two-bladed propeller and achieved a top speed of 50 mph. The control box was a device very similar to a telephone dial. The radio control system was modern in concept, consisting of a 73-megacycle transmitter modulated by any one of five audio tones, each tone representing a single command to the drone. The drone operator wore headphones and listened to the command tones as they were transmitted while he guided the plane with the control box. Up, down, left, and right commands could be sent to the aircraft; the fifth tone indicated "normal" flight and was audible when no other commands were present.

Meanwhile, Reg continued working as an actor while moonlighting as a drone designer. He played the lead role of Johnny Morgan in Paramount's *The Preview Murder Mystery* (1936) directed by Robert Florey and in which fellow hobbyist Rod La Rocque also appeared. Then, Reg landed the lead role of Greg Stone in an independent production of *It Couldn't Have Happened (But It Did)* (1936), followed by Universal's *Two in a Crowd* (1936) as James Stewart Anthony with Joan Bennett and Joel McCrea as the stars. While

Reg was filming on the Universal lot, he learned the studio executives had forced Carl Laemmle and Junior out of running the studio. They basically fired the father and son team from the company which Laemmle founded, and Standard Capital had fully taken over Universal City Studios that week. Reg stomped into the executive offices and chewed out the money men for such a heartless act against the warm-hearted man, especially during the Great Depression. He stormed out and vowed never to return to Universal again.

Back at Columbia Pictures, Reg went to work as Bill Houston in *More Than a Secretary* (1936) starring Jean Arthur and George Brent, followed by Talisman Studio's *We're in the Legion Now* (1936) which was directed by Crane Wilbur and filmed in Magnacolor at the Vasquez Rocks north of Los Angeles. In the adventure comedy, Reg played the lead role of Dan Linton and appeared once again with his favorite leading lady, Claudia Dell.

Reg then returned to MGM in Irving Thalberg's *Romeo and Juliet* (1936) directed by George Cukor. He was delighted to be cast in the role of Romeo's cousin and family peacemaker, Benvolio, and to be reunited with John Barrymore in another Shakespearean effort, as well as act once again with Leslie Howard, Norma Shearer, and Basil Rathbone. Reg also enjoyed working again with director Cukor and shared how he used his radio-controlled airplanes in films. Intrigued, Cukor asked Reg to bring his plane to the set. Reg brought one of his radio planes to the MGM studio where he demonstrated it to Cukor and Thalberg while donning his 17th-Century costume. John Barrymore got a kick out of the air show and wanted to fly the plane. Reg told his friend he'd better stay at the controls for fear the plane and its operator could go out of control and possibly kill someone on the set.

After *Romeo and Juliet* was wrapped up and ready for release, Irving Thalberg came down with pneumonia. On September 14, 1936, the night of the film's Los Angeles premiere, Thalberg died at his home at the young age of thirty-seven. The stars were just arriving on the red carpet of the Carthay Circle Theatre when they learned of their producer's death. It became a somber affair, so the press didn't interview any of the film's stars as they entered the theater. Reg and Barrymore attended together distraught by the loss of their dear colleague and amazing producer. *Romeo and Juliet* was hailed as a critical success in motion picture history, being nominated for Best Picture at the 9th Academy Awards ceremony.

Reg continued to work hard during the day at the studios to make money and harder at night in the garage to build his dream. Finally, the new "Radioplane-1" (RP-1) target plane was ready for Reg to demonstrate to the military. He contacted the United States Army and after numerous phone calls and letters, they told him they'd like to meet with him for a demonstration at their base in San Pedro. The following week, Reg met Lieutenant Colonel C.M. Thiele and his military team at the U.S. Army Air Corps installation of Fort MacArthur at the Los Angeles port. The Army had been experimenting with anti-aircraft weaponry there due to the location being a logical threat for attack and they had been conducting target practice with real planes and tugs. During the initial test for Colonel Thiele, Reg found that his first model didn't fully adhere to the military specifications as it achieved a speed of only 50 mph and the control reaction was not completely satisfactory. Unfortunately, the craft spiraled after being pushed and crashed to the ground. Reg returned home with the destroyed drone and got to work with Walt and Kenny on improvements.

During that time, Reg was approached by Paramount Pictures to appear in a series of films they were producing based on the detective-adventurer *Bulldog Drummond* stories created by H.C. "Sapper" McNeile, which Oscar Apfel had made into a 1922 silent film. Reg signed for an eight-picture deal with the new series and was featured as Algernon "Algy" Longworth in Paramount's *Bulldog Drummond* films. Throughout production, there were several changes in the cast, but Reg remained throughout the entire series. The first was *Bulldog Drummond Escapes* (1937) directed by James Hogan with Ray Milland as the light-hearted Captain Hugh C. "Bulldog" Drummond. Also starring with Reg and Milland were Sir Guy Standing as Scotland Yard chief Colonel Nielson and Heather Angel as Phyllis Clavering. Next in the series was *Bulldog Drummond Comes Back* (1937) directed by Louis King. Sir Guy Standing had died, so John Barrymore replaced him as Colonel Nielson and had a ball working with Reg in his extraordinary disguises while carrying on with the party. Milland was in too much demand to continue with the series, so John Howard replaced him as Bulldog, and Louise Campbell replaced Heather Angel as Phyllis. That same cast continued on with the next two in the series, *Bulldog Drummond's Revenge* (1937) directed by Louis King, then *Bulldog Drummond's Peril* (1938) directed by James P. Hogan. While filming on the Paramount lot, Reg brought six-year-old Reggie Jr. for set visits along with his Radioplane prototypes. He once again demonstrated to the crew how his planes flew just like the real thing, and this time let Barrymore take the controls.

In 1937, in addition to working on the *Bulldog Drummond* films at Paramount, Reg did seven more movies that same year while perfecting his Radioplane and managing the hobby shop. Reg played Steve Lodge in Republic Pictures' *Join the Marines* (1937) directed by Ralph Staub. Then it was back to Columbia for three three films: as Fritz "Frederick" Eagan in *Women of Glamour* (1937) directed by Gordon Wiles; as George Willoughby in *Let's Get Married* (1937) directed by Alfred E. Green with Ida Lupino and Ralph Bellamy; and as Ralph Marshall in three chapters of the Frank Buck serial *Jungle Menace* (1937) directed by Harry L. Fraser and George Melford. Back at Paramount, Reg acted in B.P Schulberg's *The Great Gambini* (1937) directed by Charles Vidor in a melodrama of a clairvoyant who predicts other peoples' deaths and causes his own. Then it was back to MGM as Clifton Summitt in *Beg, Borrow or Steal* (1937) directed by Wilhelm Thiele, and finally as the Master of Ceremonies in *Sunday Night at the Trocadero* (1937) directed by George Sidney in an entertaining musical variety show with various singing stars. While Reg doubled up on set and at work in the garage, Bubbles gave birth to their second daughter, blue-eyed Deborah.

At home in the evenings, Reg, Walt, and Kenny diligently worked on the military drone design which evolved into the "Radioplane-2" (RP-2). With improvements, the high-wing monoplane was slightly larger than the RP-1 model with a square fuselage. Reg called Colonel Thiele and asked if they could give it a second try. This time, the basswood plane was flown in the desert at the military's Twentynine Palms Base outside Palm Springs where it still only demonstrated an airspeed of 50 mph. It was going fine in the air; but when pushed to the limit, it sputtered out and soared to the ground with another destructive crash. The RP-2 model still hadn't met the specs necessary for their use, but Colonel Thiele was intrigued with the concept and wanted to see more, so it was back to the drawing board.

Reg was determined to fulfill the military specs and told his team it was time to get serious about increasing speed and resolving the landing issue. He, Walt, and Kenny continued to improve and test the Radioplane, but it kept crashing when they'd push the speed. Then another lightbulb went off influenced by Reggie Jr. Reg had taken his six-year-old son to many military air shows and at one of the aerial performances there was an Army parachute jump demonstration. Little Reggie was in awe of the way the parachute stopped the plummeting man from crashing to the ground and floated him safely to a smooth landing. At home while his dad and the team busily worked on the drones in the garage, young Reggie pestered them with all sorts of questions. When he was bored, he'd throw dirt bombs at the windows to get their attention. After listening to the men in the garage constantly complain about their crashing dilemma, Reggie Jr. came inside.

"Why don't you just land your drone by parachute like those guys in the air show?" the boy asked.

Reg smiled, turned to his fellow inventors and said, "But then, out of the mouths of babes come words of wisdom."

Reggie Jr. watched as his dad, Kenny, and Walter hit the drawing board while they figured out how to design and attach a parachute to the Radioplane with a remote release. After many months of work, Reg and his team finally got the parachute mechanism figured out so once the plane got shot it would gently glide back to earth instead of crashing and being totally destroyed.

The team improved upon the RP-2 with the new and more advanced "Radioplane-3" (RP-3). The high-winged monoplane was similar in size to the RP-2 and featured a new welded steel-tube fuselage with a single propeller and an increased airspeed of 60 mph, and it now had the new parachute feature. Reg thought they had it right this time, so he contacted the Army to set another test flight. Reg and the team met with Brigade General Archibald Henry Sunderland of the United States Army Antiaircraft Forces at March Field located in Riverside, California. During the tests, the RP-3 still couldn't handle the stress of the military specifications; however, the new parachute proved to be a handy recovery device. Instead of crashing, the Radioplane-3 glided slowly to the ground, undestroyed.

Even though Reg's drones still hadn't successfully met the military specifications, both Colonel Thiele and General Sunderland were impressed with the Radioplane and wanted to learn more about his proposal. At the urging of Thiele and Sunderland, Captain George V. Holloman contacted Reg and invited him to attend a top-secret meeting at the United States Army Air Corps Base at Wright Field in Dayton, Ohio. The U.S. Army Air Corps was the flight division of the U.S. Army which would later become the U.S. Air Force. Captain Holloman had been experimenting with a similar concept of automatic landing systems and wanted to learn what Reg envisioned with his remotely controlled devices.

Reg traveled to Dayton where he appeared before a board of ten military leaders with the U.S. Army Air Corps Special Weapons to prove his invention could be of use to the military. At the meeting, he explained while the government was spending millions of dollars building their manned war machines such as tanks, airplanes, and ships, he was building less costly unmanned drones. He said they could eventually save a lot of valuable time, money, and lives by using radio-controlled devices in place of the larger manned devices for use in the military. He added that his "flying robots" could be used for reconnaissance missions and also for what he termed as "aerial torpedoes." One of the captains scoffed at that idea as being only good for indiscriminate area bombing. Reg countered that they could refine the "torpedo" with radar devices for better accuracy.

He continued to share his vision by expressing that the future troops wouldn't have to fight battles from their airplanes, their tanks, or their ships; let the Radioplane, the Radiotank, or the Radioship do it remotely while the soldiers operated them safely on the ground from home base. In addition to being used as target planes, aerial torpedoes, and reconnaissance craft, Reg said his drone could also be used for exploration of unchartered and hostile environments. With further development and improvements in the technology available, he stated that these unmanned devices could eventually reach the depths of the ocean and even travel to the Moon and into outer space.

Reg gave the men examples of what his model planes had accomplished. He said that his Denny Jr. model, with a 6-foot 1-inch wingspread, had flown nearly five hours. In the record flight, the model flew approximately eighty miles and attained an altitude of 3,000 feet. When Reg wagered one of the military experts that he could hit a bull's eye thirty miles away with a model plane that had a twelve-foot wing span and a pay load of ten pounds of simulated cargo, they thought he was joking. They all laughed at the man whom they had known as a comedian on the screen. Their laughter and their questions frustrated Reg. He felt like he did when he met with studio executives trying to explain his vision of how farce should be done; yet they wouldn't listen.

After four days of pleading his case and negotiating with a very doubtful board, Reg urged the military team to at least give him the opportunity to show them how his Radioplane could work for anti-aircraft gunnery training. He continued that the type of target plane he could produce "would be of inestimable value" and stressed that his drones could be used like real planes for anti-aircraft gunnery training. One of the members, Major Greene, was particularly against it with his chief objection being that the proposed size and speed of the target plane was too small. Reg argued they were both relative, the smaller was cheaper and actually better for practice, and they could increase the speed as necessary. He became frustrated with the ignorant challenges being presented by those who were supposed to be experts in defense and felt that they didn't get it or him. He sighed and knew he'd be going home with bad news to share with Whittier, Walt, and Kenny. Until Captain Holloman and Major F.M. Borum stood up. Holloman and Borum were fascinated with what Reg shared and, as crazy as it seemed, they agreed the project should be given a trial. They argued that size and speed of the drone could be increased later if necessary, and that its cheapness was a great factor. Captain Holloman stated his case, further explaining how Reg's drone could work for the military and suggested everyone take a vote. After a nine to one vote in favor of his Radioplane, Reg left Dayton with Captain Holloman's letter of intent for a military contract to be negotiated and executed in the near future whereby they'd test "Reggie's Robots" as drones for target practice.

Reg was ecstatic that someone believed in his vision, was willing to take the chance on him, and it was someone who could make it happen. When he returned home with the Air Corps' letter of intent, Reg sent Captain Holloman one of his homemade Bleriot scale model planes to express his gratitude for this opportunity to prove his invention.

The Bleriot was the first military aircraft to fly across English Channel in 1909. Captain Holloman sent Reg a note expressing his thanks and to tell him how expertly the model was assembled. He was in awe of the craftsmanship that "elicited considerable commendation from the officers and civilian engineers at Wright Field." According to one of his engineers, he said "the completeness and fidelity of detail were perfect and showed careful study on the part of the model builder." He even observed that the U-bolts and turn-buckles in the fuselage structure were true reproductions of the type used by Bleriot. Holloman closed the letter in saying he placed the model in a locked glass case for display at the Army Aeronautical Museum and had a suitable legend prepared acknowledging Reg as the donor.

Upon his return home from Dayton, Reg celebrated Bubbles' thirty-first birthday with a family gathering at the house. Later, Bubbles told him she was glad he was given the opportunity to prove his invention; however, she wasn't happy her husband was spending all of their money on a pipe dream. They had bigger worries. When Bubbles showed Reg their bank statements and piling bills, he realized they were going broke. In addition, she said she couldn't handle a hyperactive son whose father was away all the time while she and their nurse cared for Joanie and the baby.

While Reg focused on his work and his drone, the Denny homelife became more chaotic. After Beverly Hills shopping sprees and evening cocktails, Bubbles would unleash her frustrations on the family. During her nervous breakdowns, she'd scream and throw objects at Reg in fits of anger. Reggie Jr., now seven, imitated the madness of his mother's tantrums. He'd throw rocks through the living room windows and set fire to the drapes to get attention. Meanwhile, five-year-old Joanie had developed a nervous eating disorder. At the dinner table during parental arguments, she'd pretend to swallow her food only to hide it in her mouth and then, before she went to sleep, she'd place it in the drawer of her nightstand for their nurse to find the next morning. Vine Manor was across the street where several little people resided and where Joanie would escape. She'd watch the "munchkins" rehearse their song-and-dance acts for work on *The Wizard of Oz* (1939) as a joyful distraction from her mother's mania.

If the home environment wasn't bad enough, Reg's overhead continued to increase while he purchased the necessary materials for his drone and paid Walt and Kenny for their work. His funds were quickly being depleted while his obsession with building the expensive drones caught up with him. In order to continue on with his hobby and have a home, Reg was forced to file bankruptcy and sell his cherished haven—the beautiful cabin retreat in the mountains. He was brokenhearted to let go of his idyllic escape. On the day he sold the cabin, Reg went up alone for one last visit to his beloved sanctuary. Georgie circled overhead. He called the hawk down to where she landed on his arm. For the first time in his life, Reg broke down and cried from such an emotional crash. Before the movers came, he grabbed a carved model of the hawk from his cabin suite and brought it home to place in his Hollywood library.

Meanwhile, Reg had to get back to work. He played the role of Captain Douglas Loveland in Fox's *Four Men and a Prayer* (1938) directed by John Ford with Loretta Young, George Sanders, David Niven, and Alan Hale, then as Edward Grant in Walter Wanger's *Blockade* (1938) directed by William Dieterle with Madeleine Carroll and Henry Fonda.

Reg also continued his role as Algy Longworth in the *Bulldog Drummond* series. His good friend John Barrymore had left the production for another Paramount film and actor H.B. Warner replaced him as Colonel Nielson in the next of the series, *Bulldog Drummond in Africa* (1938) directed by Louis King, followed by *Arrest Bulldog Drummond* (1938), *Bulldog Drummond's Secret Police* (1939), and finally *Bulldog Drummond's Bride* (1939) all directed by James P. Hogan. Reg then returned to Fox as Dr. Pilcoff in *Everybody's Baby* (1939) directed by Malcom St. Clair.

With all the drama and disturbances at home, Reg decided to move his drone project and his team to Righter's shop in Burbank; they now also needed more room to develop the larger planes and parachutes. At Righter's shop, they went hard to work on designing the prototypical planes with the military specifications to win the government contract.

With prominent British film trade figures at European Motion Picture Company's
London office (1927). Courtesy of Reginald Denny Collection.

At European's London office with novelist Andrew Soutar, Universal's James Bryson, and Rene (1927). Courtesy of Reginald Denny Collection with photo credit to Johnson's Court, Fleet Street Photography.

With actor William Stack, F.W. Harland Edgecumbe, and F.E.N. St. Barbe of de Havilland Aircraft Company beside de Havilland's new Moth at England's Stag Lane Aerodrome (1927). Courtesy of Reginald Denny Collection with photo credit to *The Central News London*.

Getting ready for test flight in de Havilland's Moth at the Aero Drome (1927). Courtesy of
Reginald Denny Collection with photo credit to The Central News London.

Ready for take-off with Captain Hubert Broad (1927). Courtesy of Reginald Denny Collection with photo credit to The Central News London.

As Jimmy Norton with Barbara Kent and Jane La Verne in *That's My Daddy* (1927).
Courtesy of Reginald Denny Collection.

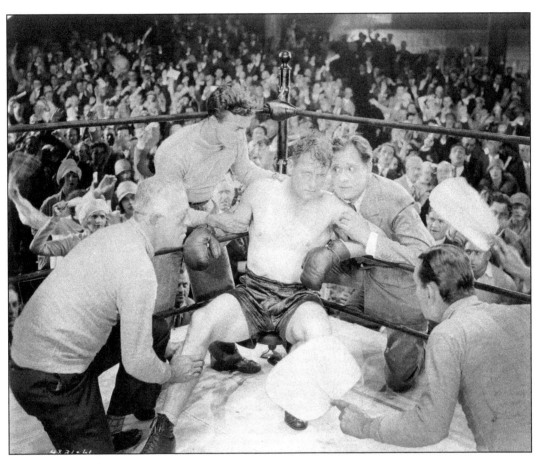

As pugilist Kid Davis in *The Night Bird* (1928). Courtesy of Reginald Denny Collection.

Universal executives and public relations team with Reg and cast of *The Night Bird* (1928).
Courtesy of Reginald Denny Collection.

With Betsy Lee in *The Night Bird* (1928). Courtesy of Reginald Denny Collection.

As Darrow with Alice Day in *Red Hot Speed* (1929). Courtesy of Reginald Denny Collection.

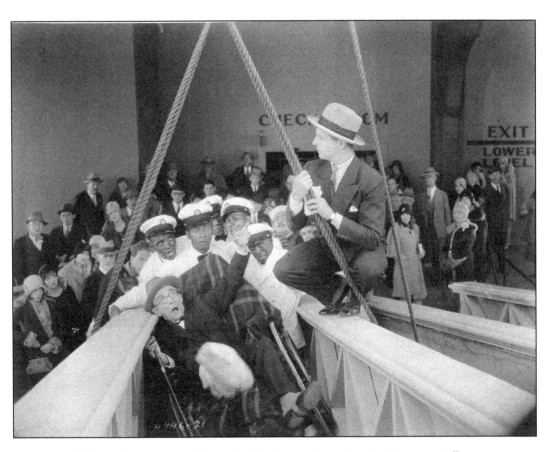

As Jack Armitage in *Clear The Decks* (1928). Courtesy of Reginald Denny Collection.

At Los Angeles County Courthouse with his fiancé Bubbles (1928).
Courtesy of Reginald Denny Collection.

Mr. and Mrs. Reginald Denny November 24, 1928. Courtesy of Reginald Denny Collection.

As Charles Blaydon with Tom O'Brien, Lorayne Du Val, Eddie Phillips, and Otis Harlan
in *His Lucky Day* (1929). Courtesy of Reginald Denny Collection.

As William "Napoleon" Judd in *One Hysterical Night* (1928). Courtesy of Reginald Denny Collection.

At 1st Academy Awards ceremony Hollywood Roosevelt Hotel (1929).
Courtesy of Marc Wanamaker/Bison Archives.

Portrait of the newlyweds (1929). Courtesy of Reginald Denny collection with photo credit to Ball.

At mountain lodge haven in Running Springs (1929). Courtesy of Reginald Denny Collection with photo credit to George Hurrell.

Bubbles at the cabin retreat (1929). Courtesy of Reginald Denny Collection with photo credit to George Hurrell.

British cowboy and his favorite steed (1929). Courtesy of Reginald Denny Collection with photo credit to George Hurrell.

Skeet shooting off the cabin deck (1929). Courtesy Reginald Denny Collection
with photo credit to George Hurrell.

Cozy by the fire inside their cabin (1929). Courtesy of Reginald Denny Collection.

As bartender (1930). Courtesy of Reginald Denny Collection.

As Thaddeus Cruikshank in *Embarrassing Moments* (1930).
Courtesy of Reginald Denny Collection.

As Wade Rawlins with Miriam Seegar in *What A Man* (1930).
Courtesy of Reginald Denny Collection.

Bubbles set visit on *What A Man* (1930). Courtesy of Reginald Denny Collection.

Rehearsing the "Madam Satan Waltz" with Kay Johnson and Hal Findlay on piano (1930).
Courtesy of Marc Wanamaker/Bison Archives.

As Bob Brooks with Kay Johnson, Roland Young, and partygoers on the Zeppelin stage of *Madam Satan* (1930). Courtesy of Marc Wanamaker/Bison Archives.

With a visiting Prince and Princess on MGM set of *Madam Satan* (1930).
Courtesy of Reginald Denny Collection.

Taking cigarette break at MGM stage doors on set of *Those Three French Girls* (1930).
Courtesy of Marc Wanamaker/Bison Archives.

As Victor Randall with Mary Pickford in *Kiki* (1931). Courtesy of Reginald Denny Collection.

With Mary Pickford in *Kiki* (1931). Courtesy of Reginald Denny Collection.

Publicity portrait by Freulich (1931). Courtesy of Reginald Denny Collection
with photo credit to Roman Freulich.

With Douglas Fairbanks, Norma Shearer, Robert Montgomery, and director Sidney Franklin on set of *Private Lives* (1931). Courtesy of Marc Wanamaker/Bison Archives and Academy of Motion Picture Arts and Sciences.

Playing polo at the Riviera Country Club (1931). Courtesy of Reginald Denny Collection.

Marlin catch with Paul Whittier on Catalina Island (1931).
Courtesy of Reginald Denny Collection with photo credit to H.G. Boscell Catalina.

SAG meeting along with Edward Connelly, Robert Montgomery, Stuart Erwin, Frederic March, Jimmy Gleason and other actors (1932). Courtesy of Marc Wanamaker/Bison Archives.

Taking a break with Ramon Novarro and Myrna Loy on set of *The Barbarian* (1933).
Courtesy of Marc Wanamaker/Bison Archives.

As Brown with J.M. Kerrigan, Victor McLaglen, and Wallace Ford in *The Lost Patrol* (1933).
Courtesy of Marc Wanamaker/Bison Archives.

As Harry Griffiths with Leslie Howard and Bette Davis in *Of Human Bondage* (1934).
Courtesy of Everett Collection.

With Claudia Dell, Bubbles, Olive Whittier and Paul Whittier in front of Patio Entrada at Agua Caliente Resort (1934). Courtesy of Marc Wanamaker/Bison Archives.

Carving one of his model boats (1934). Courtesy of Reginald Denny Collection.

Reginald Denny Hobby Shop at 5751 Hollywood Blvd.
Courtesy of Marc Wanamaker/Bison Archives.

Viewing model plane at his hobby shop (1935). Courtesy of Reginald Denny Collection.

Proudly showing off one of his model planes to kids at the hobby shop (1935).
Courtesy of Reginald Denny Collection.

At Motion Picture Hall of Fame during San Diego World Fair (1935).
Courtesy of Marc Wanamaker/Bison Archives.

Robert Montgomery with his Dennyplane (1935). Courtesy of Reginald Denny Collection.

As Oliver with Robert Montgomery, Edna May, and Joan Crawford in *No More Ladies* (1935).
Courtesy of Reginald Denny Collection.

As Yashvin with Greta Garbo in *Anna Karenina* (1935).
Courtesy of Moviestore Collection Ltd./Alamy Stock Photo.

As Oliver Keith with Claudia Dell and James Bush in *The Lady In Scarlet* (1935).
Courtesy of Marc Wanamaker/Bison Archives.

Nora Reynolds Albertini with son Bill Albertini, Barbara Denny, Madge Dugmore, Mona Dugmore, and others at White Lodge (1936). Courtesy of Gerry Albertini with caption provided by Nora Reynolds Albertini.

Family portrait photo with Bubbles, Reggie Jr., and Joanie (1936).
Courtesy of Reginald Denny Collection.

As Benvolio fencing with Basil Rathbone in *Romeo and Juliet* (1936).
Courtesy of PictureLux/The Hollywood Archive/Alamy Stock Photo.

Taking a break with John Barrymore on MGM set of *Romeo and Juliet* (1936).
Courtesy of Marc Wanamaker/Bison Archives.

With George Cukor, Walter Brisbane, Leslie Howard, John Barrymore, James Hilton, Irving Thalberg, Basil Rathbone, and visiting writers on set of *Romeo and Juliet* (1936). Courtesy of Reginald Denny Collection and Marc Wanamaker/Bison Archives.

15 TARGET DRONE DENNY

ON SEPTEMBER 1, 1939, THE ALLIES declared war on the Axis powers, marking the official beginning of the Second World War. That same week, the United States Army Special Weapons contacted Reg and awarded Reginald Denny Industries an official contract to use his prototype Radioplane as target drones for anti-aircraft gunnery practice. The contract stipulated for the demonstration of three experimental "Radio-Controlled Target Planes," which would take place at the United States Army's aircraft testing facility at Muroc Dry Lake in the Mojave Desert of California during the Spring of 1940. Reg had six months to get it right in order to fulfill the contract.

Now that he was doing business with the United States government, Reg formally applied for his U.S. citizenship. As part of his process for obtaining citizenship and while developing drones for the military, he wanted to prove he was now a true-blue American. Due to his expression of patriotic conscience and the work he had conducted in the country for over twenty years, Reg was elected chairman of the Americanism Educational League and, with director Hobart Bosworth, he opened a court fight to bar the Communist party from all voting polls in the state of California.

Reg was happy to receive the military contract and start the process to become an American, but was saddened that week when he got a call from Carl Laemmle Jr. Junior told him that his father had a heart attack and died at the age of seventy-two on September 24, 1939, at his home in Beverly Hills. Along with over two-thousand mourners, Reg attended the touching service for Carl Laemmle Sr. which was held at the Wilshire B'nai B'rith Temple in Los Angeles. He remembered how the kind-hearted German-Jewish immigrant studio head had taken him in when he was a down-and-out British war vet and paid his heartfelt respects to the man he once fondly called "Old Man Laemmle."

Now more than ever, Reg was driven to continue with the enhancement of his Radioplane for use in the war and also prove to the U.S. Government he wasn't crazy. The government wouldn't provide funding for development of his prototypes, so he had to figure out how he was going to build the three experimental planes. He needed $12,000 to continue with the production of his dream child or let it all go to hell. Paul Whittier was away in Hawaii and the M.H. Whittier Company refused to allow any of Reginald Denny Industries' money to be used in financing the contract, so he had to raise outside funds. Reg went to Union Bank and met with his banker William Neary to apply for a business loan. When he told Neary he needed the money to fund his top-secret radio-controlled airplanes for the military, the banker declined on the loan. He explained to Reg, as he didn't have any collateral and had filed bankruptcy, his credit was shot.

Instead of lending money to the bankrupt actor, Neary introduced Reg to wealthy business magnates Whitley Collins and Harold Powell of the Elastic Stop Nut Corporation for possible investment in his Radioplane. Collins had been an executive at Lockheed Aircraft Corporation and recognized the groundbreaking opportunity, especially given there was a military contract in place. Both men took great interest in Reg's invention and offered to invest $10,000 as working capital with one-third interest in his dream. Reg failed to hire an attorney and being in his dire situation, he immediately agreed to the businessmen's terms. Although Paul Whittier wasn't involved in the military contract, Reg nevertheless gave him half of his interest for his support in helping him develop his Radioplane.

At the same time, Reg took a job on the stage while his engine developer and radio specialist perfected the target drone. He starred as a depressed drunk in *Outward Bound* (1939) with Scottish actress and singer Cissie Loftus. The Brits played several weeks in San Francisco and then at the Biltmore Theatre in Los Angeles for a month. In the story about alcoholism Reg played the afflicted man in a remarkable performance, but in real life Loftus was a known alcoholic and morphine addict who would sadly die a few years later from her addictions.

One night after another sold-out show, David O. Selznick showed up at the Biltmore and met with the play's star backstage. Selznick told Reg he was producing a movie based on a popular gothic novel written by English author Daphne du Maurier and asked if he'd be interested in the opportunity to work with British director Alfred Hitchcock. Reg replied that he would and gladly accepted Selznick's offer for the role as Frank Crawley in Hitchcock's first American-made movie, *Rebecca* (1940). He acted in the thriller with Laurence Olivier, Joan Fontaine, and George Sanders at Selznick's studio where Reg and Hitchcock became close friends. Reg shared with Hitchcock his deal with the military and the director was respectful of Reg's insight. Hitchcock's twelve-year-old daughter Patricia was five years older than Joan and babysat the Denny kids while Reg and Bubbles attended the premiere of *Rebecca* with its director and his wife, screenwriter Alma Reville.

Back at Righter's shop in Burbank, Walt and Kenny continued their work on the Radioplane. With funding from Collins and Powell, they were able to upgrade Reg's target plane to the new and improved "Radioplane-4" (RP-4). The high-wing radio-controlled monoplane had a wingspan of just over twelve feet with an 8½-foot square welded steel-tube fuselage and an open hatch for the recovery parachute landing device. Walt designed a new 6.5-horsepower two-cylinder engine that drove two outrigger-type counterrotating propellers that increased its airspeed to 70 mph. They replaced the phone dial transmitter with a joystick for easier radio control to the plane. The team also designed a metal twin rail apparatus which they used to launch the drones from a limited space for quicker takeoff.

On April 10, 1940, Reg was proudly awarded his United States citizenship. That same week he put his flying robots to the test. Reg, Whittier, Walt, and Kenny met with Captain Holloman and his Army Air Corps team to demonstrate the three Radioplanes at the dry alkaline lake beds of Muroc Lake, now Edwards Air Force Base. The military specifications called for a one-hour flight with a rate of climb at 500 feet per minute to an altitude of 5,000 feet, then a parachute recovery landing within a quarter of a mile from take-off point with minimal damage. When Reg launched the first RP-4, Captain Holloman was extremely impressed with its sweeping aerobatics. When it temporarily went out of control, the guys thought it was part of the test. Reg was relieved when he was able to recover his plane before it dove into the nearby reviewing stands and parachuted to the ground. One of the military guys tried out the next RP-4. The looks on the operators' faces when they launched the drone from the rail apparatus and were then able to maneuver the airplanes high in the air a half-mile from take-off, which until that point had only been flown with manned aircraft, were that of excitement. They made aviation history as they flew the target planes remotely.

He was accustomed to applause for his work on stage, but when Reg heard the spirited cheers as the three planes slowly parachuted to the ground, after performing the required maneuvers, and none of them crashed, his heart filled with a new kind of joy. Captain Holloman signed his acceptance on the spot and secured the contract with Reginald Denny Industries for development of his Radioplane target drones to be used by the U.S. Army Air Corps.

Reg had fought in one war with Germany and won; now he was ready to fight another, only this time he'd stay on the ground from his new home turf. He knew the military orders would start rolling in quickly, and by the thousands. Reg wanted to implement the drones in action to help the troops as soon as physically possible, but he needed a larger facility with equipment and employees in order to manufacture the target drones as outlined in the $33,000 government contract. Now that he was officially a U.S. citizen and had financial backing, Reg and his financiers agreed to form a business together to get the drones built for action.

On June 20, 1940, Reg, Paul Whittier, Whitley Collins, and Harold Powell formed the Radioplane Company as a California Corporation. Reg again failed to hire an attorney to negotiate terms of the business deal and proceeded with blind faith that his radio plane was in the right hands. He still hadn't filed a patent for his invention and even though Walt and Kenny had filed a patent for the parachute recovery system, Collins made it part of the deal that the Radioplane Company took ownership of that. As Collins had the most professional expertise in running a business and had put up most of the finances, he became majority owner and president of the new company. Officers were voted and a Board of Directors assigned with Whitley C. Collins as President, Harold H. Powell as Executive Vice President, William Larrabee as General Manager and Treasurer, Ferris M. Smith as Vice President Engineering, and Reginald Denny as Vice President and Secretary.

Once the business terms were worked out, the team located a vacant commercial warehouse in Van Nuys and got plans in motion to set up the drone manufacturing plant. Collins and Powell purchased the equipment necessary and hired the best of the best in the engineering and aviation fields to put Reg's blueprints to work on the assembly line. Reg was awarded the working title and role of vice president with paid salary to oversee development of the drones and run the daily operation of the new facility. Production of the military drones began that summer at the new Radioplane plant located at Metropolitan Airport, now Van Nuys Airport.

Reg hadn't negotiated a profitable deal for himself: his was a minimal salary and proceeds from sales were at a very low percentage as compared to his wealthy business partners. When the initial investment of $10,000 was made, Reginald Denny Industries was to be reimbursed $6500 which was due Reg for expenses to make the three planes. This left a working capital of $3500. Reg and Whittier were assessed according to their interests for the amount necessary to complete the contract. This first contract was for $12,000 and when the money was paid after fulfillment of the contract, Collins and Powell took out the $6500 paid to the Industries claiming it was not working capital as called for in the original agreement. They twisted the deal to their advantage, both financially and with controlling percentage of the business.

Being broke and not yet making a penny from the deal, Reg doubled up with his work in film as the plant was being set up. Nearing fifty years old, he appeared in several more major motion pictures as war echoed overseas. Producer Joe Pasternak called Reg and offered him a role in his upcoming production at Universal. Reg was hesitant to work for the studio that betrayed his former boss, but he needed the money. He returned to Universal as The Major in the musical comedy *Spring Parade* (1940) directed by Henry Koster with Robert Cummings, Deanna Durbin, and Henry Stephenson. Pasternak liked Reg's work so much that he offered him another role in his next production at Universal. Reg accepted the role of Captain Church in *Seven Sinners* (1940) starring John Wayne and Marlene Dietrich. The new American citizen had a lot to discuss with Wayne as their beliefs on Americanism were similar being screen actors involved in the cause.

While her father had been developing his drones, Barbara had returned home from England. She had spent five years staying with Aunt Nora and Reg was happy to have his daughter back home safe in America as the dangers of the new world war were a big part of daily existence in England. Barbara had grown into to a beautiful young lady and, on her own accord, she auditioned for and landed the role of Alice in *All Women Have Secrets* (1939) with Virginia Dale, Jeanne Cagney, and, in a small part, Veronica Lake (billed as Constance Keane). On set, she was introduced to Howard Hughes' TWA publicity executive, James Simmons, and the two started dating. On August 25, 1940, and just after her twenty-fourth birthday, Barbara and Simmons were married. Reg was happy his daughter had pursued a film career in America and she was in a healthy relationship with a man who had a dependable career with Hughes' new airline.

Once the Radioplane facility was up and running, Reg invited Major Dan Goodrich of the U.S. Army Air Corps to the new Radioplane plant to show them his target drones and to obtain their first order. Reg and the team had continued to refine the design of the RP-4 by adding better aileron control, larger engines, and increasingly more-reliable radio equipment making the target drone even more like a real plane. Per Reg's meeting with Major Goodrich, the new and improved RP-4 design led to a contract with the U.S. Army to become the first military target drone, the Army's "OQ-1." This first major contract was for 10,000 drones at $600 each ($10,000 per unit today). The Army replaced their old-fashioned target tugs with their new OQ-1 at the same time the United States military was developing nuclear energy with the code named "Manhattan Project" at Hanford, Washington, and Germany was developing their "V1" flying bomb, or "aerial torpedo" as Reg had called it in his proposal to the Army.

After touring the new Radioplane facility, Reg invited Major Goodrich and his Air Corps team over to his home for dinner along with his daughter and first son-in-law to celebrate the Army's first order and also the newlywed's union. The officers were impressed with Reg's family and grateful for Bubbles' hospitality in hosting the formal dinner. After the visit, Major Goodrich wrote to Reg. "Dear Reginald: All hands agree that our stay in Hollywood was the highlight of the entire trip and as far as I'm concerned it was the most interesting experience in my whole checkered career. Without doubt your efforts in our behalf were instrumental in making the visit so enjoyable, and I want to thank you again for all you did for us. It was grand meeting you and your family and I sincerely hope that I will have the pleasure of seeing you again in the not too distant future. With best wishes, I remain, Sincerely yours, Don Goodrich, Major, Air Corps, War Department Office of the Chief of the Air Corps, Washington, DC."

In the Spring of 1941, Reg attended another Academy Awards ceremony, this time at the Los Angeles Biltmore Hotel. Selznick's *Rebecca* was up for eleven Oscars that night, including Best Picture and Best Director. The stars with their producer and director attended the ceremony and all were ecstatic when Hitchcock's first American directed film won the Oscar for Best Picture at the 13th Academy Awards. The cast, their producer, and director had a big celebration following the ceremony that night.

During a year of the Army's successful use of the RP-4 target drone, Reg's team made improvements which evolved into the "Radioplane-5" (RP-5) prototype for more sales to the military. This high-winged monoplane target had a triangular, welded steel-tube fuselage, stamped aluminum wing ribs, two contra-rotating propellers and attained an increased airspeed of 85 mph. In June 1941, the Army placed more target drone orders with the new RP-5 and referred to their upgraded model as their "OQ-2."

Reg invited Captain D.S. Fahrney of the United States Navy to the Radioplane plant for a personal tour of the facility and to show him the new RP-5. After hearing of the success that the Army was having with its target drones, Fahrney immediately placed the Navy's first order for the RP-5 under the designation of "Target Drone Denny" (TDD). The "TDD-1" was the Navy's version of the OQ-2, but without the landing gear. The military branch subsequently put out a classified monthly booklet called *T.D.D. News* and in their first published issue featured a story about Reg in honor of the drone's namesake.

As the news got out about Reggie's Robots for use in the war, Reg started hearing various rumors that his business partners were telling employees they had developed the drone and Reg was just a "crazy actor." Reg also learned that Whitley Collins was upset the Navy had named their military drones after him, and that letters addressed to Reg from the Navy were being intercepted, as well as invitations to important government events. All this made Reg distrustful of his business partners, the military, and their agendas, so he wrote to Captain Fahrney requesting clarification that the Navy's drone was indeed named after him. Reg was relieved to receive a response from Fahrney confirming he wasn't crazy. "Dear Mr. Denny, You are entirely right—the initials 'T.D.D.' stand for 'Target Drone Denny' and is named in your honor in keeping with your long association and pioneering on this radio control project. I feel that you should be given great credit for this work because it is the early pitfalls and headaches of the development program which deserves the commendation and not the smooth flow that is involved in production. I believe that the Denny target will be of great service in training gunnery crews and we are eager to get some into the service to prove the point. Very best wishes. Sincerely yours, D. S. Fahrney, Capt. USN."

War films were now popular and Reg did several WWII aviation adventure dramas that year. It was back to work at Paramount where he played Erich Strasser in *One Night in Lisbon* (1941) directed by Edward H. Griffith. Reg reunited with Billie Burke in a drama involving a Nazi spy which starred Fred MacMurray and Madeleine Carroll. Reg then returned to Universal as Michael Dailey in a fun comedy, *Appointment for Love* (1941), which reunited him with his pal Bill Seiter who directed the film which starred Charles Boyer and Margaret Sullavan. Reg then portrayed Wing Commander Severn in Warner Bros.' *International Squadron* (1941) starring Ronald Reagan. The film is based on the Eagle Squadrons, American pilots who volunteered to fly for the Royal Air Force during World War II. Reg had the opportunity to reprise his role with the Royal Air Force, this time in a movie and in another war while working with a future president.

On July 24, 1941, Reg's film *It Couldn't Have Happened (But It Did)* was featured on New York City's newly launched, first full-time television station WNBT (Channel 1). Upon the first televised broadcast of one of his films, Reg was contacted by stage producer and director Lee Ephraim. Ephraim made Reg an offer to return to New York and star in his stage production of *All Men Are Alike*. Reg accepted Ephraim's offer and was thrilled at the opportunity to be back on his home turf in front of a live audience while he took the welcome break from Hollywood. On October 6, 1941, he returned to Broadway at the Hudson Theatre where he co-starred as Alfred J. Bandle with Bobby Clark in *All Men Are Alike* directed by Harry Wagstaff Gribble.

After spending two months in New York, Reg returned home just in time for Thanksgiving while war continued. That week, he received a telegram from Nora that the Germans had been invading London with what they referred to as "the Blitz" and White Lodge was nearly destroyed several times from the extreme bombing. She said she and Tiny would be coming to the States for a stay at their East Coast residence for safety. Reg was gravely worried for his home country and for America. The following week on December 7, the Japanese military launched their surprise attack on the United States Naval Base at Pearl Harbor and one of the naval officers whom Reg had met was killed. The radio plane inventor stressed to the military the need for his robotic advancement to win wars and reiterated his drones could also be used for surveillance to watch for enemy attacks. At Reg's suggestion, one of the naval officers who originally tested the Radioplane drones was sent to the Pacific onboard an aircraft carrier with an urgent request to utilize the new devices in warfare against Japan's offensive attacks following the Pearl Harbor incident. As he was the most skilled, the nineteen-year-old soldier went on the dangerous mission aboard an aircraft carrier near Guam to test out the drones for reconnaissance and observation. Reg tried to stay in touch, but lost contact with the brave young man shortly after he left.

In more WWII films, Reg played the Commanding Officer in *Captains of the Clouds* (1942) directed by Michael Curtiz with Ronald Reagan's good friend James Cagney. It was back to Fox as Barrett in *Thunder Birds: Soldiers of the Air* (1942) directed by William A. Wellman, with a screenplay by Lamar Trotti adapted from a story written by Darryl Zanuck, starring Preston Foster and Gene Tierney. Reg then got an offer from Universal to work on another *Sherlock Holmes* movie, *Sherlock Holmes and the Voice of Terror* (1942), directed by John Rawlins. He returned to the home studio as a Nazi spy, Sir Evan Barham aka "Heinrich von Bock," with Basil Rathbone as Holmes and Nigel Bruce as the faithful Dr. Watson. In this version, Holmes is hired by the British Inner Council to track down a Nazi agent who is responsible for Nazi propaganda broadcasts, "The Voice of Terror." It was an interesting conflict of real life versus acting for Reg to play his home country's enemy spy.

While in the midst of filming *Sherlock Holmes*, Reg and Basil received disturbing news about their friend, John Barrymore. Barrymore had returned to the NBC Radio network for Rudy Vallée's the *Sealtest Show*. He recorded seventy-four episodes of the program, continuing in the vein of self-parody with jokes about his drinking, declining career, and marital problems. On May 19, 1942, while on air recording a line from *Romeo and Juliet* (in which he had earlier appeared with Reg and Rathbone on film), Barrymore collapsed. He was taken to the Hollywood Presbyterian Hospital and died there on May 29 from cirrhosis of the liver and kidney failure, complicated by pneumonia. On June 2, Reg attended the service at Calvary Cemetery with Rathbone to pay respects to their friend who was now at peace. Another irony as Reg reminisced about working with Barrymore on their first *Sherlock Holmes* film together, and his friend died just as he was working on another with their *Romeo and Juliet* castmate Basil Rathbone, who this time played the role of Holmes. The stars were all connected like constellations in the night sky.

Following his success with murder mysteries during the thirties, Reg was cast in couple of urban moody mysteries while he moonlit at the Radioplane plant. In MGM's *Eyes in the Night* (1942) directed by Fred Zinnemann, Reg appeared as Stephen Lawry with Edward Arnold and Donna Reed, then as Dick Brenner in Fox's *Over My Dead Body* (1942) directed by Malcom St. Clair and starring Milton Berle. As Reg got busier with the drone operation, he only worked on one more film the following year, playing Paul Ashley in Columbia's *The Crime Doctor's Strangest Case* (1943) directed by Eugene J. Forde and starring Warner Baxter.

Back at the drone plant, the improved prototype RP-5A was completed and evolved into the Army's "OQ-3" and the Navy's "TDD-2." It differed from the RP-5 in that it had a heavier steel-tube construction, no landing gear, a single two-bladed propeller driven by an 8-horsepower engine and attained an increased airspeed of 103 mph at sea level. Radioplane produced a total of 5822 RP-5 targets for the military.

Reg worked on only one film at the onset of 1944 while his drones were being improved upon with large orders from the Army and Navy. He returned to United Artists as Director Curtis in the comedy-musical *Song of the Open Road* (1944) starring Edgar Bergen & Charlie McCarthy and W.C. Fields with Jane Powell making her film debut. Reg now devoted all his spare time to management of the Radioplane plant and eventually sold his mortgaged home in the Hollywood Hills of twenty years with a family move to the San Fernando Valley where he'd be closer to his office in Van Nuys.

On June 13, 1944, Germany bombed London with their first use of the V1 flying bomb "Cherry Stone." It was the first cruise missile and the same type of "aerial torpedo" that members of the Army had joked about when Reg made his proposal six years prior. In July 1944, a totally new drone design was introduced to the military as the "RP-8."

Although similar in appearance and general construction to the RP-5, the RP-8 was a faster, sturdier target. It was powered by a new Righter 22-horsepower engine, allowing it to reach 141 miles per hour. The RP-8 was taken into service by the U.S. Army as the "OQ-14," and by the U.S. Navy as "TDD-3." A total of 5204 RP-8A drone targets were manufactured by Radioplane. At that same time, Paul Whitter told Reg that Collins and Powell had bought him out. Collins had paid Whittier a substantial sum to edge him out and thus gained more interest in the company. Reg wasn't advised prior to the buyout, but he couldn't do anything about it anyway as he had no funds. He was worried the guys with the money were taking over his baby and when his partners called a meeting to announce Whitter was no longer on the board, Reg was advised not to share his invention with anyone in Hollywood and to remain a "silent partner."

That same week, Reg was invited by the Navy to attend a dress rehearsal of the first atomic bomb tests which were going to be conducted on a future date at Bikini Atoll in the South Pacific under the code name "Operation Crossroads." He had been invited to the rehearsal in recognition of inventing the "Robot Plane" and was flown down to San Diego with a bunch of Los Angeles newspaper reporters who covered the show. The dress rehearsal took place on the aircraft carrier *Shangri La* commanded by Rear Admiral C.A.P. Sprague. When Reg arrived onboard the naval vessel, everyone was curious to know why a film star was along. Knowing the feelings of Collins' confidentiality regarding his involvement in the military drone, Reg just told them he was representing the Radioplane Company.

U. S. Navy's Admiral William H. P. Blandy approached Reg and took him aside. He said he wanted to discuss the possible use of his drones in testing the new atomic bombs. The military had been planning on using manned aircraft to test its reaction once the bomb was dropped over the ocean and, after the nuclear explosion, how the plane would manage once it exploded in the air. He also asked if the drones could carry a load. Reg shared with Admiral Blandy not only could his drones be used for target practice, but they could be developed for testing bombs so as not to expose soldiers to radiation, as well as for surveillance missions and even as "fighter planes" which could carry a load and take off from aircraft carriers. Any replacement of the unmanned for manned—gunnery practice, aerial torpedoes, defensive protection, reconnaissance—could work with his drones.

After the dress rehearsal, a cocktail party was given by Admiral Sprague for the newspapermen and other guests. Reg was talking to Admiral Sprague and Captain J.W. Davidson, who was in charge of all robot operations, when Don Ryan of the *Herald Express* joined them.

Ryan pointed at Reg and asked the men, "Will somebody tell me what this guy is doing here?"

Captain Davidson replied, "This guy? Why, he's the father of the robot plane."

Don Ryan seemed dumfounded and turned to Reg, "Is this true, Denny?"

"I'm sorry." Reg said. "But I do not want to get into any trouble so do not want to be quoted. If Captain Davidson is willing to give you the story, that would be wonderful as it would be official, and I could not be accused by my company of violating security regulations."

Captain Davidson gave Ryan the story which resulted in his article being featured in the *Herald Express* with the headlines, "Bare Navy Robot War on Japs. Reginald Denny Revealed as Father of War's Robot Plane." Ryan issued releases about Reg's achievements, but when questioned about a top-secret project which he was known to have developed, Reg kept his mouth shut. "Mr. Denny was one of the men who developed a radio device now used by the war department in gunnery training. He said he couldn't elaborate on it because it is a military secret. Mr. Denny is well known for his achievements not only in the theatrical world, but for his accomplishments in the aviation field. His radio-controlled plane plant has been turned over to the government for the duration."

Upon returning home from the Naval event, Reg was confronted by Whitley Collins. Collins expressed his displeasure in reading the newspapers about Reg attending the event and being hailed as the founder of the Radioplane with no mention of him. Reg argued he didn't say a word and asked Collins why he was upset the press had exposed the truth. Collins subsequently called the Navy and ordered them to stop designating the Radioplane drones as "Target Drone Denny" for future models.

Meanwhile and back at home, Bubbles was having a terrible time managing the household while Reg was away. Reggie Jr. continued to cause trouble around the house without a father to mentor him. Bubbles told Reg she couldn't handle their hyperactive adolescent son any longer. Even though they couldn't afford it, that September, Reg sent Reggie Jr. off to the Mahon School for Boys in Claremont.

A couple weeks after Reggie's thirteenth birthday, Reg sent a letter to his son: "My Dear Reg, Was so glad to get your letter. Of course, you would rather be home, I'm glad that you feel that way, it would be terrible if you didn't. We too would rather have you home, and we miss you very much, but it is better for you to be at school, and as a matter of fact, actually you are happier there and always have something to look forward to. Well I have quite some news for you. I have the fuselage of your gas model all finished—and it really looks beautiful. I have the wing construction well under way and hope to have it finished by the time you come back. Walt Righter has promised me one of the new Dennymite engines in about three weeks so you really will have a 'snazzy' plane. Lieutenant Simmons returns from Camp Train (sp), on the desert near Barstow on November 3, and then there will be more night filming at Redondo, so you see you have something else to look forward to. Well good-bye old boy. I love you very much and am really looking forward to seeing you again. Your loving Dad."

Reg enclosed a photo of the custom model plane which he made for Army General Douglas MacArthur's son and wrote on the back, "My Dear Reg, Here is a picture of the plane I sent to General MacArthur's son. Thought you would like to have it. Mr. Mahon says you are behaving splendidly, which makes me very happy and very proud of you. Am taking good care of your fish, and so far, none of the young guppies have died. I miss you very much but feel so happy that you are at this school and I'm sure you feel the same way about it now. We'll be seeing you soon. Your loving Dad."

In November 1944 and after further upgrades on the Radioplane drones, the new and improved "RP-14," "RP-15" and "RP-16" prototypes were completed all under the Army designation of "OQ-6." The more streamlined RP-14 had a wingspan of fourteen feet, an overall length of ten feet, and a gross weight of 295 pounds. This model also had an uncowled engine, a sharp-nosed propeller spinner, and wing struts with an increased airspeed of 168 mph. The RP-14 was the first to be powered by McCulloch Motors four-cylinder engine instead of Righter's engine. The similar RP-15 was completed in January 1945, had a speed of 195 mph and was powered by a four-cylinder 60-hp McCullough engine.

Just prior to the Christmas holiday, Reg was offered another stage role to star as Charles Condomine in Noël Coward's British fantasy comedy, *Blithe Spirit* (1944-1945). With Reg Jr. away at boarding school, Reg accepted the offer and, against Bubbles' wishes, left the family and the Radioplane plant to go on a seven-month stage tour. *Blithe Spirit* opened at the Alcazar Theatre in San Francisco and ran for two months there. The company's next stop was in Salt Lake City where Bubbles, with daughters Joan and Debbie, met up with Reg and also made a visit with Bubbles' family there. Reg made his performance with *Blithe Spirit* at the Uptown Theatre in Salt Lake City with several great reviews and a warm welcome for Bubbles on her first hometown return since girlhood. Following the one-night performance in Salt Lake City, Reg continued on to Denver and spent five more months as a lone traveling player across the country without his family or his drones.

16 GOODBYE NORMA JEANE, HELLO JACK NORTHROP

AT THE ONSET OF SUMMER, Reg finished his *Blithe Spirit* tour and returned to Los Angeles just in time to approve the new top-secret Radioplane brochure for the government (Appendix A). By this time, the company's factory floor had expanded from 979 square feet in 1940 to 69,500 square feet spread over five buildings delivering fifty drones per day.

During his work on the film *International Squadron,* Reg had confidentially shared his Radioplane with Ronald Reagan, who was intrigued with his drone concept. When Reg invited Reagan to his office at Radioplane, Reagan was so impressed he sent the First Motion Picture Unit (FMPU) to the Van Nuys plant to get a glimpse of the drones everyone in the military was talking about. The FMPU provided newsreel footage of the homefront to be shown as informational movies for the overseas troops' morale program. One sunny June day, the film crew arrived at the Radioplane manufacturing plant accompanied by one of their photographers, David Conover. While the film crew ran coverage of workers in the plant, Conover took still pictures of women in war work for an August 1945 issue of *Yank, the Army Weekly* magazine. One of Reg's stellar employees on the assembly line especially caught the photographer's eye.

Norma Jeane Mortenson had lived in foster homes since she was a young girl due to her mother's mental illness. One of her mother's friends, Grace McKee, took in the abandoned and abused fifteen-year-old girl to live with her at her home in Los Angeles. Their neighbors had a twenty-year-old son, James "Jimmy" Dougherty, whom Norma Jeane got to know well. When Norma Jeane turned sixteen, the two started dating. Grace and her husband had to relocate to the East Coast, so they urged Norma Jeane to marry Jimmy instead of being left behind as a homeless orphan again. The two became engaged and in 1942 they were married. Just as Norma Jeane turned eighteen, Jimmy enlisted with the Marines and went off to war. As many women had to work during WWII while their husbands were overseas, Mrs. Dougherty was hired by Reg to work at Radioplane as a painter and assembler of the red drones. When she initially interviewed with Reg, he felt bad for her and treated her as if she were his own daughter. The next year, after celebrating her nineteenth birthday with Grace in New York, Norma Jeane wrote a letter to her foster mom to tell her the exciting news of the day she returned back to work in Van Nuys.

On that day, Conover noticed the photogenic young lady doping target drone panels. In the *Sun Sentinel* he recalled, "I moved down the assembly line, taking shots of the most attractive employees. None was especially out of the ordinary. I came to a pretty girl putting on propellers and raised the camera to my eye. She had curly ash blond hair and her face was smudged with dirt. I snapped her picture and walked on. Then I stopped, stunned. She was beautiful. Half child, half woman, her eyes held something that touched and intrigued me. I retraced my steps and introduced myself. 'And you?' I asked."

"'I'm Norma Jeane Dougherty.' She smiled and offered her hand."

Conover took several more photos of Norma Jeane while she proudly posed with the newer "RP-18" drones in hand. Her appearance and ease in front of the camera captivated Conover. Upon hearing she wanted to become an actress, he told her she would need to model first. Conover suggested she pose for more natural and glamorous shots. Norma Jeane gladly agreed, so they met at various locations for additional photos. These photo sessions soon ended the auburn beauty's role with Radioplane, as well as that of Dougherty's wife, and launched her into films to begin her career as the blonde bombshell known as "Marilyn Monroe." Army and Naval officers overseas might have cherished the drones they were launching even more had they known the actress who would become Hollywood's most iconic sex symbol of all time had assembled them.

When Norma Jeane gave her notice, she wanted to personally tell Reg. She thanked the film star for giving her the job, for being such an inspiration, and ultimately for being the catalyst in her modeling career. Reg gave the aspiring actress a few last words of advice about life and the biz, as if talking to himself. "You're striving for something you don't quite yet understand. Don't let people in this business turn you into something they want and someone you know you are not."

At the same time, Reg returned to Paramount Pictures as Defense Counsel Phillips in Ayn Rand's *Love Letters* (1945) directed by William Dieterle and starring Joseph Cotten and Jennifer Jones. Reg received a nice review, in addition to the other stars, and the film was nominated for four Oscars at the 18th Academy Awards ceremony.

On July 16, 1945, the first nuclear tests using the plutonium from Hanford were successfully conducted by the U.S. Army Corps under the code name of "Trinity" at Jornada del Muerto near Los Alamos, New Mexico. In response to Japan's attack on Pearl Harbor, the U.S. Army used their new bomb and dropped its "Little Boy" above Hiroshima on August 6, then "Fat Man" over Nagasaki on August 9. Japan was devastated and subsequently surrendered to the United States. On September 2, 1945, World War II ended. In all, 15,375 models of the RP-4 through RP-18 series of TDDs were built and used to train American antiaircraft gunners during the war. General MacArthur called Reg to personally thank him for the model plane he had gifted to his son and for his valuable contribution to the military during the battle.

Even though the war had officially ended and Radioplane's bombshell had left her drones behind, the company kept up their assembly and became highly successful with their post-war drone launch. Radioplane followed up the success of their military target drones and made improvements on the design which evolved into the "RP-19." The fabric fuselage was replaced with a metal skin and the drone was streamlined, like a missile. The military suggested a more powerful engine for the targets to travel faster, so the company switched from using Righter's engine to the larger McCulloch Motors engine that was used for the RP-15. The previous drone engines were built at Walter Righter's shop in Burbank; however, now that the power source contract was with McCulloch Motors, Collins made Walt an offer to purchase his Righter Manufacturing Company in Burbank and make it part of Radioplane. Walt took the money and that was the end of his involvement with Radioplane.

The new and improved RP-19 traveled as fast as 250 mph and to altitudes as high as 27,000 feet. Flying at a 300-yard range from firing batteries, the RP-19 presented the appearance of fighter aircraft of normal size flying at 700 yards distance at 700 mph. The military quickly placed their orders for production of the RP-19, which the U.S. Army designated as their "OQ-19." The new drone could be controlled from stationery and truck-mounted ground-command control stations making the Army's OQ-19 operations to be as mobile as training required.

With their order, the U.S. Navy obeyed Whitley Collins' directive and changed their updated drone designation from TDD to the "Basic Training Target" (BTT) or "KD-2R5." Captain Fahrney called Reg and apologized that the Navy would no longer be using his name for their drone designation. Reg told Fahrney he understood it wasn't by their choice and he was still happy the Navy had utilized his invention with such success. All the drones came equipped with parachutes for recovery on land or at sea; as Reg had come up with the parachute landing system, he suggested adding a flotation device for recovery of the Navy's drone when it parachuted to the ocean for its retrieval in the water. Fahrney liked the idea and Radioplane then developed such a device and called it the "Radioplane Flotation-1" (RPF-1).

At the same time, Edward Churchill of *Flying Magazine* released a story called "Aerial Robots" about Radioplane and its history. Instead of conducting the interview with Reg, the writer met with Whitley Collins. In the article, Collins made false and incorrect statements about the history of Reg's invention and made no mention of Colonel Holloman, who had just been killed in a B-17 plane crash while traveling from Shanghai to Manila. Reg couldn't understand why his business partner had such a problem giving him, as well as the military man who facilitated the deal, credit for their work and its proper history.

Following massive worldwide press headlines announcing the end of World War II, the *Los Angeles Times* contacted Reg for an interview. Now that the war was over, he could discuss his invention publicly and didn't care what anyone thought. The *Los Angeles Times* praised Reg for his invention with their newfound news of the actor. "Film actor Reginald Denny, a British Royal Air Force machine gunner and observer in World War I, yesterday revealed that he had invented a pilotless, radio-controlled airplane used in World War II by the Allies to train aerial and anti-aircraft gunners. Denny stated that he and 'associates' made the first test for Army observers in 1935. In 1939 the Army ordered its first three radio-controlled craft, and after that his plant at Van Nuys continued to turn out the craft, reaching a peak of fifty planes a day at the end of the war. Reg won recognition for his development of the 'Radio-controlled Target Plane,' a pilotless fighter aircraft used effectively by both the Army and Navy against the enemy. This was considered a very important contribution to the winning of the war."

Upon reading the article, Collins met with Reg and stressed that he wasn't happy about his "employee" speaking to the press without his consent or involvement. Reg smiled his crooked smile at Collins, said "Cheerio!" then waddled out of his office.

Reg had taken a couple of years off from acting in films while he worked at Radioplane. After the war ended, he jumped back into action at the studios. He returned to RKO as Mr. Wendell in John Brahm's *noir* classic *The Locket* (1946) starring Robert Mitchum and Laraine Day, then as Fernandez in Universal's *Tangier* (1946) directed by George Waggner. Reg played James Collins in Paramount's *My Favorite Brunette* (1947) with Bob Hope, Dorothy Lamour, Peter Lorre, and Lon Chaney, Jr. Next, he was the Police Inspector in Ernest Hemmingway's *The Macomber Affair* (1947) with Gregory Peck, Joan Bennett, and Robert Preston, then the Colonel in Goldwyn's *The Secret Life of Walter Mitty* (1947) starring Danny Kaye, Virginia Mayo, and Boris Karloff. Reg closed out the year as Mr. MacLean in Warner Bros.' *Escape Me Never* (1947) with Errol Flynn, Ida Lupino, Eleanor Parker, and Gig Young. Reg and Flynn hit it off and became good friends who shared stories about their divorces, marriage, and the loss of their mutual friend, John Barrymore.

That fall, Reg was again contacted by David O. Selznick who offered him a great supporting role, this time opposite Cary Grant and Myrna Loy in Eric Hodgins' comedy *Mr. Blandings Builds His Dream House* (1948). Reg gratefully accepted the part as architect Simms in the film directed by H. C. Potter. After learning of Reg's new film role, Whitley Collins called his business partner in for a meeting. Collins told Reg that, as their vice president, he was away too much and shouldn't be gone all the time with a second job working on films. He referenced the actor as "Remotely Reg" and threatened that if he took this film role, it would jeopardize his career at Radioplane. Reg laughed at the reference and said he didn't appreciate being told he couldn't continue working as an actor, nor how he should conduct his business. He left Collins' office and showed up on the RKO set for his first day of shooting with Cary Grant.

On the set of *Mr. Blandings Builds His Dream House*, Reg developed another close friendship with fellow Britisher Cary Grant, much like his friendship with Bob Montgomery. Both loved to read and Grant gifted Reg one of his favorite non-fiction books of the time. The two got along famously, both very intelligent with a kind indifference toward women who only amused them. Once Reg finished his work at the RKO studio, he showed up at the Radioplane plant to conduct his drone business there. Whitley Collins curtly entered Reg's office to advise him that he'd been fired from his "day job." He said that Reg would remain on the Board of Directors with the company he co-founded, of course, unless the businessmen with the dough were to vote him out. This time Reg stormed out of his own office, infuriated.

Reg and aviator colleagues John "Jack" Northrop and Moye Stephens had been in communication over the years while they respectively developed their game-changing aircraft. As he sensed a disconnect with his business partners and was now hearing rumors that they were selling the company to Northrop Aircraft Company, Reg invited Northrop over for dinner. He shared with Jack his vision of pilotless aircraft as well as his sensing of the Radioplane partners pushing him out of his interest of the company. Jack had been developing his innovative YB-35 "Flying Wing" and expressed he was having similar difficulties with his company. He said he also felt the government was trying to sabotage him. Both gentlemen shared their concerns of betrayal and sensed their business partners' agenda to oust the eccentric aviator artists. In the meantime, Whitley Collins had been warming up to top executives at Jack's Northrop Aircraft Company as they strategically worked to segue Radioplane into use with the larger aerospace company without either of the founders' involvement. When Reg told Northrop he was fired from working at his own company, Jack became even more concerned about his company's agenda and told him he'd keep in close touch.

Following the successful release of *Mr. Blandings Builds His Dream House*, Reg returned to the theater to star in *The First Mrs. Fraser* (1948) at the La Jolla Playhouse. This time, he brought Bubbles and the kids to the San Diego resort town for a summer vacation where they stayed at the Valencia Hotel overlooking the ocean. Reg took fourteen-year-old daughter Joan out for a swim in the ocean while Bubbles stayed on the shore with ten-year-old Debbie. Fifty yards out, circling sharks surrounded Reg and Joan without warning. Reg told Joanie to be very still, not to splash or panic, and to swim very slowly back to shore with the breaststroke he had taught her. When they both safely reached the sandy beach, they were relieved to be alive. When the family got back to the hotel room, Reg received another scare when he got a phone call from Barbara's husband with news that his wife was seriously ill.

During the month of August 1948, a freak infantile paralysis epidemic spread throughout Los Angeles County affecting over fifteen-hundred people, Barbara Denny Simmons being one of them. She had contracted the polio disease and was hospitalized. Reg left the stage production and rushed to the Los Angeles hospital where his daughter was in an iron lung. The epidemic killed over fifty-five people and, after two weeks in the hospital, Barbara became one of those fatalities at the young age of thirty-two. Reg was at her bedside, alongside Rene, their son-in-law Jim, and their four-year-old grandson Craig. The small family cried together at the loss of their precious angel. Reg was devastated.

After watching his daughter die, Reg hibernated for the rest of the year to recover from the loss while he spent time with Bubbles and his remaining two daughters. He was distraught that not only was he losing grip on his drone-baby, but he had lost the daughter with whom he hadn't spent the time he had wished, nor did he have a relationship with his little grandson. His world was falling apart and he continued to stay under the radar in more ways than one. When his deal with Radioplane began, Reg had turned the Reginald Denny Hobby Shop over to his operating manager, Martin "Pete" Veir. Veir had diligently managed the shop while Reg was focused on designing his Radioplane, for which Reg was extremely grateful. For his taking over responsibility of the model airplane business, Reg gifted his hobby shop to Pete Veir and asked him to carry it on as his own.

During the holidays, George Dodge of *American Magazine* contacted Reg. He had heard about how the military used his target drone during the war and wanted to run a story in his magazine about "Reggie's Robots." After his meeting with Reg, Dodge wrote a respectful story in *American Magazine* featuring a photo of Reg operating the controls while launching his Radioplane. "Almost any fairly frequent movie fan of the last twenty years knows Reginald Denny as the guy who plays those likable, but dim-witted Britisher roles; but relatively few know there is another and far more important side to the actor. He is the inventor of a midget robot plane—very hush-hush during the war—used extensively by both Army and Navy Air Forces as targets in the training of aerial and antiaircraft gunners. Denny is not a scientist nor unusually mechanically minded. It all started when he tried to help a youngster fly a model plane and it crashed. The actor sent for a new one, and before he knew it, he was making all sorts of models himself. Then, back in 1934, Denny had his idea of the radio-controlled target plane for gunnery training, and no one would listen to him; but when the war came on, the Government took interest, and had him manufacture them in quantities. They are named after the actor, being called Target Drone Dennys. The services still use them. Furthermore, Denny believes there are commercial uses of the plane, one of which is shown taking off in the photo and controlled by Denny. He says they could make crop-dusting safer and more efficient and be used in fighting forest fires. Denny's latest film role was in *Mr. Blandings Builds His Dream House.* He has three children, and his principal diversions, aside from the robots, are gardening, painting, and sailing."

Whitley Collins called Reg on the phone and again expressed his disapproval of the actor discussing the history of the company without his permission. This time Reg told Collins to go to hell and hung up the phone.

After taking much needed time off, Reg went back to the stage that summer and co-starred with Jessie Royce Landis in *Theatre* (1949) at the Laguna Playhouse. After a summer run, Reg returned to Los Angeles and made his first appearance on a television show called *Your Show Time* (1949) as guest star in its episode "The Invisible Wound" written by Robert Louis Stevenson. He then appeared in an independent film production, *The Iroquois Trail* (1950), with George Montgomery and Sheldon Leonard, before Leonard became a popular television writer, director, and producer of successful situation comedies.

The Iroquois Trail shot up at Big Bear Lake where Reg made one last visit to view his long-lost cabin with weeping eyes to the sky. He had lost his favorite sojourn and felt he was losing his grip on life. Reg's friend Bob Montgomery had gotten a divorce that same year and was on his way to New York to start his own television series, *Robert Montgomery Presents* (1950). The two buddies met outside at the cabin and reminisced about old times and their lost friendship over the course of their marriages, their involvement with the military, and life. When Bubbles found out Reg's friend was now divorced, she prohibited them from getting together. The world was closing in and Reg had nowhere to run to escape the madness in his mind from the unreasonable demands of his "partners."

The occasion to flee arose when Reg was contacted by the producers of *Theatre* with an offer to return to their production. They had changed the name of the play to *Larger Than Life* and were bringing the show to London. Reg jumped at the opportunity and left Hollywood, Radioplane, Bubbles, and his family far behind to make his way back to the motherland for some fresh air. He returned to London for the first time in twenty-three years, reunited with his sisters, and starred as Michael Gosselyn in *Larger Than Life* (1950) with Jessie Royce Landis at the Theatre Royal in Brighton. The play was based on Somerset Maugham's novel and directed by Jack Minster with its first British performance on January 23, 1950.

While he was in Brighton, Reg wrote a letter to Reggie Jr. from his room at the Royal Crescent Hotel. "My Dear Reg, At last I have a breathing spell and can sit down and write you. It is Sunday morning and am leaving for Cardiff at 3 o'clock this afternoon. We have been playing the show at night and rehearsing in the daytime, as new lines have been written every day and other changes made, but at last I think we are through with all this, and the play is finally set. It has been terribly hard work, and this morning is the first time I have been able to sleep late, and I feel much better, as I was getting really exhausted. What time I had in between rehearsals was taken up with newspaper interviews. Two days before leaving London I had to have the cyst on my shoulder cut out. It was so big and so deep I had to have a general anesthetic. It was quite a pleasant one however, injected in the vein and I just went off to sleep very happily. I had the stitches removed yesterday and there were ten of them. Had a wonderful flight across and very smooth. I became a little worried when we came in for a landing at Chicago. It was snowing heavily—and four times just when the pilot was levelling off to set the plane down, the control tower gave us a red light, and the pilot gained her and circled again. I was quite worried as I thought that the retractable landing gear may have stuck. However, the fifth approach was all right and we landed. I found out afterwards that the reason for the red warning was because there was about ½ inch of ice on the runway and the pilot had to come in shorter. As it was, he used up all the runway and had to do what felt like a ground drop to avoid running off. The flight across the Atlantic was very smooth at about 20,000 feet, but quite interesting. There was a heavy overcast, and only twice did I catch a glimpse of the ocean. It was raining and inky darkness when we arrived at Shannon in Ireland where we had an hours wait. I had breakfast at the airport, the waitress recognized me, and I had quite a session of autograph signing. After we took off the sun came up but all you could see was billowy clouds below. When we came down for a landing we were over Richmond and strangely enough the plane banked for the approach right over White Lodge which I recognized right away. The opening night of the play was very rough. So many changes had been made that we should have had at least another week's rehearsal added to which Royce Landis broke a small bone in her ankle and could not rehearse at all for 5 days. The two local papers did not give it a good notice, but everybody tells me that they seldom praise any new play that opens here that is at all light; they are very artistic and like the 'Heavy Stuff.' However, the audience liked it very much. We have had packed houses at every performance and now that the play is beginning to run smoothly, they seem to really enjoy it. We take Q&A curtain calls after the final curtain. The London Theatre papers—who came to see the show last Wednesday—gave it a great write up and said that it was a sure audience hit. Tell mummy I will get the notices and send to her. Gerry, Nora's young son, is quite a lad. He is not yet seventeen and is about 6 feet tall—quite good looking and is already what we call a man about town. He is having the same school trouble as you had so maybe it runs in the family. He likes clothes so am giving him my old tuxedo when my trunks arrive, and he is tickled to death. Nora does not want to have one made for him yet as he is still growing and when he fills out would have to have another one made. Apart from that it would cost about seventy-five pounds and even at that it is almost impossible to get silk facings. Well, am going to take my bath and then go for a walk. Strangely enough the sun is shining brightly, but it is quite cold. I certainly miss you Reg, and I know that while I am away you are going to take my place and look after mummy and your sisters. Fondest love. Your loving Dad. P.S. Who the hell do you find to argue with now that I've gone?"

Just after Reg Jr. received the letter from his distant dad, he followed his father's footsteps and enlisted in the U.S. Army. Reggie Jr. was soon transported to Japan, then onward to the frontline in South Korea. At the same time, Reg Sr. learned that Rene had passed away at the age of fifty-six, almost two years to the day of their daughter's death. A couple months later, George Bernard Shaw died at the age of ninety-four. Reg paid his respects and attended Bernard's funeral, wondering how different life would have been if he would have moved back to England after meeting with the playwright.

Reg had made Brighton his home for almost a year. When the long run of *Larger Than Life* came to an end, he decided it was time to get back to Los Angeles. After being unofficially separated from Bubbles, he returned home just in time to spend their twenty-second wedding anniversary together. Reg had changed and life had changed. He returned home to a more docile and less temperamental wife with two teenage daughters. Bubbles was remorseful about her behavior of the past promising that she would be a better wife and supporting partner. Reg apologized for running away and leaving her to manage the household alone. They both agreed they'd been through hell and would now work together to be supportive of each other with a new beginning.

Now back home in Los Angeles, Reg decided to make a visit to his Radioplane plant and get an update on the drone's progress. He met with the manager of contracts, Jules Plummer, and was impressed that the company had kept up with the evolution of the military's manned aircraft. The Army Air Corps had branched off to become the United States Air Force (USAF) and as the new aircraft were jet-powered, the Air Force issued a specification calling for a new type of high-speed target drone. Radioplane's RP-19 had evolved into the pulsejet-powered "RP-26" by the company, and "XQ-1" by the USAF. The RP-26 was a new high-wing, rocket sled launched aircraft. For air launching, the ground catapult rail launches were replaced with launching the drones from manned military aircraft, as an "aerial torpedo."

Reg Jr. was still in Korea and wrote letters to his father with weekly updates of how the military was using his target drones for use in the new war. Reg was further reminded what it was like to be on the frontline and thought of additional ways to help his son in practice, to protect their territory, and locate the enemy. Inspired by his night flights during WWI, Reg had an idea to illuminate enemy targets for surveillance and bombing, so pilots and ground forces could see in the dark, as well as friendly fire for target drone practice. As the original drones he designed for Radioplane had no lighting devices nor could they track enemies at night or when dark, they were limited to flying during the daylight hours. Reg designed a new drone which had remote lighting features so it could be flown at night and also accomplish reconnaissance and rescue missions by illuminating enemy targets when it was dark. He finally got wise and on June 9, 1951, Reg filed his own Patent #US 2636697 for the "Flareplane" (Appendix B). He was hesitant to share his vision with his business partners as he now knew they'd betray him and take it as their own. As it was, they were communicating with various companies and the military without consulting with him.

Reg got back to work into the new year and made appearances in television with two episodes of *Hollywood Theatre Time* (1951), "His Lordship Detects" and "New York Story," and *Personal Appearance Theatre* (1951), "He Woke Up Smiling." On Independence Day, the military put on a benefit show for the Korean War vets called *Cavalcade of Stars Show* at the Santa Monica Civic Auditorium in which Reg and a number of Hollywood entertainers performed. He did a comedic musical skit and the vets loved it. Several of them had operated his drone and expressed their gratitude for coming up with such a great soldier to help them on the frontlines. The Disabled American Veterans Beverly Hills Chapter 58 issued a certificate to Reg thanking him for his exceptional and meritorious service to the hundreds of amputee, paraplegic, and disabled veterans, including soldiers, sailors, marines, and those of the Air Force recently returned from Korea now hospitalized in Beverly Hills.

That fall, Reg hit the road again and toured with the stage production of T.S. Eliot's comedy hit, *Cocktail Party* (1951-1952). He played the role of Alexander MacColgie Gibbs with Vincent Price, Marsha Hunt, and Estelle Winwood. Reg had a great time and while in Chicago, he hosted a brunch with the Drama League and told them, "I'm having a very good time. Probably because I understand the play the least." The play had a good run and after touring throughout the country for six months, it was time to go home.

When he returned home, Reg was surprised to be contacted by the United States Secretary of Defense, Robert A. Lovett. Lovett told Reg in recognition of his services in developing the radio-controlled target plane, he had been nominated as a member of the Joint Civilian Defense Orientation Conference. The first Secretary of Defense James V. Forrestal had founded the Joint Civilian Orientation Course (JCOC) in 1948. The oldest and most prestigious public liaison program in the Department of Defense, it was the only outreach program sponsored by the Secretary of Defense. It dealt with national policy, problems confronting the United States in pursuing its policies, and the economic, political, and military means to carry out that policy. The mission of JCOC was to "increase public understanding of national defense by enabling American business and community leaders to directly observe and engage with the U.S. military." In his letter, Lovett asked if Reg would accept the election and be an honorary guest at their upcoming conference at the Pentagon. Reg accepted the invitation and made the trip to Washington, DC, for the week-long summit to discuss the future of unmanned aviation.

During the week of March 30, 1952, Reg attended restricted meetings at the Pentagon where he was honored by the Joint Chiefs of Staff and Secretary of Defense for his major contribution to pilotless aviation. Reg listened to important information regarding defense, given out by the Joint Chiefs of Staff, the Secretary of Defense, and other military leaders. He in turn shared his ideas about his proposed use of the Radioplane drones with the Army, Navy, Marines, and Air Force. He shared the same ideas he'd previously discussed with Colonel Holloman and his team almost fifteen years earlier about Radioplane, Radiotank, Radioship, and Radiorocket, as well as his new concept of the Flareplane. There, Reg also attended several Air Force Association dinners as guest speaker to tell the story of his early development of the "Robot Plane." His ideas were well received during the conference and he was invited to make visits with the country's leading colonels at various Army, Navy, Marine, and Air Force bases. A small booklet was issued by the Association which provided the names and address of all the participants. In it, Reg was listed as Reginald Denny, Founder T.D.D.

After his fifth day at the Pentagon, Reg got an urgent call from Jack Northrop who told him he'd better get back to Los Angeles. Reg advised Lovett that an emergency called him home whereby he'd regrettably have to interrupt his participation in the conference. He left Washington and returned to Los Angeles where negotiations for the sale of Radioplane to Northrop Aircraft Company were in progress. Collins and Powell were smart and savvy businessmen who had sabotaged their takeover of Reg's invention over the years. As Reg and Jack Northrop suspected, the company's businessmen maneuvered their way into management of their products with their own agenda to merge the two companies to form a bigger supplier for the military, without involvement of its founders.

Reg Jr. had been honorably discharged from the Army and had returned from his duty in the Korean War. When he found out his father was considering letting go of something he'd worked so hard in creating, he urged Reg not to give away his drone like he'd given away everything else. Reg told his son he didn't have a choice. Collins claimed to own Reg's idea due to the deal they made at the onset of forming the company, and he never patented his Radioplane. They had him by the balls and Reg was forced to sell his shares in an underhanded hostile takeover. That summer, Northrop Aircraft Company acquired the Radioplane Company without Reg's involvement in any capacity. Jack Northrop subsequently left his own company as Reg was segued out of his. Shortly after that, Whitley Collins took Jack's place and became president of Northrop Aircraft Company.

After he let go of his brainchild, Reg made a guest appearance on Robert Cummings' television series *My Hero* (1952) in an episode titled "Movie Star." Following the show, Reg was interviewed by the press. Now, when reporters asked about his robot plane, Reg didn't hold back about how he was victimized by this most recent form of buggery. "In 1936, I developed the radio-controlled target plane. Everyone thought I was crazy. I saw the future, however, and knew someday planes and missiles would be controlled from the ground. We had $82-million in back orders. Then I was squeezed out by legal maneuvers. I was forced to sell my interest in the radio-planes, worth millions, for $100,000."

17

FLAREPLANE AND
FAIR LADY

AFTER EVERYTHING SET IN, it broke the inventor's heart to realize he had lost the pet project he'd spent his life dreaming up, over twenty years developing, and finally seeing to fruition. The money he'd received from the sale of Radioplane was just enough to pay his overdue debts. Reg had been royally screwed by someone taking off with his baby. It had been a constant fight for dignity all his life; now that he had sacrificed so much time, money, and mental energy, he was tired. Bubbles was glad the drone thing was over and she demanded that no one talk about the hobby that made them broke.

After a brief hiatus and time spent with his family, Reg segued into the new medium of home entertainment that had become quite popular. He did a couple of television plays for *Cavalcade of America* (1952-1953), "All's Well with Lydia" and "The Stolen General." In 1953, Reg acted in "The Deauville Bracelet" for the popular teleplay series *Fireside Theatre.* He then returned to the big screen as Inspector Trevett in *Fort Vengeance* (1953) with James Craig and Rita Moreno; was another inspector in *Abbott and Costello Meet Dr. Jekyll and Mr. Hyde* (1953); and played Major Ian Bone in *World for Ransom* (1954) with Dan Duryea and British friend Nigel Bruce. Reg made television guest star appearances in *The George Burns and Gracie Allen Show* (1954) as Mr. Petrie in the episode "George Reading Play to Be Done in London" and as Roger Peabody in the *Ford Television Theatre's* "The Mason-Dixon Line" (1954) with Peter Lawford and Joanne Gilbert.

During this time, Reg received an official letter from the United States Government that his pending patent for the Flareplane had finally been approved. Although the Korean War had just ended, there was talk of continued war overseas. Reg wanted to pitch his newest idea to the Department of Defense and hired Yoh Engineering to work out the specifications. On February 8, 1954, he composed a letter to President Eisenhower's Secretary of Defense, Charles Erwin Wilson, and submitted a proposal accompanied by his Flareplane brochure (Appendix C): "Herewith is respectfully submitted for consideration a description of a plan believed to possess military value. Basically, this scheme embodies an improved technique for illuminating enemy target areas. Although the scheme presented herein may be employed for a number of military situations, it is considered most useful for support to ground forces located within striking distance of an enemy. The principle of the illumination technique is to employ an intensive light source whose altitude and position may be controlled to produce the maximum effectiveness. To accomplish this, a remotely-controlled, expendable drone is employed. The drone is equipped with flares, that burn during flight. The actual operation, therefore, involves launching the drone and directing it to the target area via a ground located radio control network. Once the drone is over the target area, the flares are ignited, and flight is continued as desired over points of interest. The flares are retained as an integral part of the airplane with burnout. It is strongly believed that many advantages are obtainable through the use of this method over current practices that involve free-fall flares. It is envisioned that a relatively small number of drones may be attached to ground troop operations and may be set up and operated by ground troop personnel. This is advantageous because minimum tactical liaison is required. Also, the cost of operation is reduced because the cost of the drone is actually less than the operational cost required for an airplane flight that is normally associated with dropping flares. Further, upon examination of information related to vulnerability, it is seen that a relatively low altitude drone flight presents a more difficult interception problem than high flying aircraft. The reason for this is vested in the fact that most anti-aircraft fire control systems are operated from radar information and are designed to function against high altitude flights, therefore, such systems are relatively ineffective against very low altitude operations. The validity of this situation is further confirmed by the effectiveness of low altitude operations during the Korean conflict. As previously stated, the position of an illumination flare may be controlled through the use of a drone aircraft. It is desired at this time to point out that such a drone has been conceived and a United States patent has been granted which covers the features indicated below. The drone, as presently conceived, is extremely simple and may be produced at a very low cost. This is true because the flight operational requirements are minimum and very little equipment is involved. The speed need only be in the order of one hundred miles per hour with flight duration of approximately one-half hour or one hour. Also, because it is expendable, no recovery equipment is necessary. The principal feature incorporated into the design pertains to the burning of the flares. This feature entails storing flares within the wing and burning individual flares at each wing tip. Continuous burning or intermittent burning is accomplished as desired by automatically bringing each flare to the wing tip and igniting it upon burnout of the previous flare. By so-doing, successive flares may be ignited as its predecessor ejects at burnout, or a delay between flares may be effected by the control system. The physical arrangement embodies the use of several tubes extending from the drone body to each wing tip. These tubes serve as structural members and also as containers for the flares. The automatic flare arming devices are located at each wing tip and also incorporated in the wing tips are reflector surfaces designed to focus the generated light. Beyond this the most simple construction is used throughout. An inexpensive, low horsepower, two cycle engine is used to power the drone, and a simple five-channel radio control receiver is used for control purposes. It should be noted that all equipment used is essentially identical to that presently utilized for the most simple type target drones. In order to assure low-cost production, it is considered desirable to obtain the services of an established organization. In this respect, I have contacted members of management of the Rheem Manufacturing Company. As you may know, this Company has a sizable Aircraft Division located in Downey, California. This facility is fully equipped and is producing major aircraft assemblies, and in addition, has a well-organized Research and Development Laboratory devoted to the engineering and development of pilotless aircraft. Those people contacted have given me their assurance that they are definitely interested in such a program and are willing to offer their support in any way desired. Therefore, in the event that the scheme presented herein is looked upon with favor, I would be most happy to make the necessary arrangements to have members of Rheem organization and myself to carry the matter further. Sincerely, Reginald Denny."

On March 8, 1954, the Secretary of Defense responded to Reg's Flareplane proposal with an encouraging note. "Dear Mr. Denny: Your letter to Mr. Wilson, Secretary of Defense, containing a proposal for illuminating enemy target areas, has been referred to this office. Copies of your letter have been furnished to the three military departments and, thus far, the Department of the Army has indicated an interest in your technique. That Service is currently evaluating your proposal and you may expect to hear from them in the near future. If you should have any questions concerning the current status of your proposal, please contact me directly. Sincerely yours, Kenneth S. Colmen, Staff Assistant, Resources Division."

Reg was grateful the Army had taken interest in his Flareplane. He responded to the Secretary of Defense with a note of appreciation and anticipation of the Army's order.

Playwright Tom McGowan phoned Reg and asked him if he'd be interested in doing a one-man show about his longtime experience as one of Hollywood's leading legacies. It was just what he needed. Reg shared highlights of his Hollywood lore with McGowan who wrote a number of sketches for a monolog he tagged *Tales from Hollywood*. Reg pegged his show on his long film career and used old clips from his own vast collection to share with the audience. On May 6, 1954, he hit the stage with his solo act beginning at Santa Barbara's Lobero Theater, with following performances at theaters in Salinas, Fresno, Carmel, Bakersfield, Santa Rosa, and San Luis Obispo, then back home for his final call in Hollywood.

Following a quiet time at home with the family over the holidays, Reg made a personal appearance on *The Jack Owens Show* (1954) where he openly discussed his drones and his daughter's death by making an appeal about polio. After the talk show aired, *Daily Newslife Beverly Hills* columnist Jerry Pam called Reg for an interview and featured an honorably respectful article. "Many remarks have been made about British actors taking over Hollywood and when one considers such names as Greer Garson, James Mason, Michael Wilding, Ronald Colman, Jean Simmons, George Sanders, Bob Hope, David Niven, Basil Rathbone, Edmund Purdom, Deborah Kerr, Edmund Gwenn, Rex Harrison, Richard Burton, Stewart Granger, Elizabeth Taylor, and many others, one considers that there is something to this statement. But then one always hears of these famous entities. What about some of the greats of yesteryear who are still great but are not seen so much on the silver screen for some unknown reasons. I would like to reintroduce Reginald Denny. His face is familiar to so many moviegoers yet casting directors do not seem interested in the fact that he as appeared with success in more than two hundred movies. When the war commenced, Reggie, a part-time inventor, felt that he had much to offer his new country. He developed the radio-controlled target plane which was in much demand by the U.S. Navy. Even now Reggie is working in close contact with the Department of Defense on some new inventions. But he still has time for acting and apart from appearing in many

TV shows he travels with theatrical groups around the country. We have too few talents that can match those of Reginald Denny—we all hope that we will see much more of him in the future."

After that, the former resident of India was pleased when he was offered two roles based around that country. Reg had the opportunity to return to Mysore for the first time in forty years in Frank Ferrin's *Sabaka* (1954) as Sir Cedric and reunite with Boris Karloff. The film was based around an elephant trainer and a maharajah, reminiscent of Reg's days spent at the palace. He was sorry to learn the real raja had died at the young age of fifty-six in 1940. While there, Reg was sentimentally reminded of what the king taught him; to sing with his eyes to the sky. When he returned from India, Reg played the commissioner in *Escape to Burma* (1955) filmed at Jungle Land in Thousand Oaks with Barbara Stanwyck and Robert Ryan.

Back home, Reg opened the following year with appearances in many popular television series and became a celebrity guest star as "Reggie the Butler" on *The Red Skelton Hour* (1955). In addition to his work with Skelton, Reg played Carrington on an episode of *The Whistler* (1955) titled "A Case for Mr. Carrington," and was in two *Eddie Cantor Comedy Theatres* (1955) as the lead guest star in "The Hypochondriac" and "Ten Thousand Years from Now." Reg appeared on Ann Sothern's *Private Secretary* (1955) in an episode titled "Anything Can Happen" and as Albert in "The Neighbors" episode of *Topper* (1955) with Anne Jeffreys and Robert Sterling. Reg starred in a teleplay on *Jane Wyman Presents the Fireside Theatre* (1955) as Thompson in "The Sport," followed by his performance on the *Colgate Comedy Hour* (1955) as Lord Henry Delves in "Roberta."

That spring Reg was asked by the United States Air Force to attend a special meeting in Long Beach and discuss his major contribution as inventor of the Robot Plane. Reg accepted the invitation and while at the meeting, the military leaders discussed the advancement of his Radioplane. Just as Reg had proposed seventeen years earlier, remotely piloted vehicles (RPVs) were now being designed and built to serve as small reconnaissance robot planes equipped with cameras that relayed or brought back photos of simulated enemy installations, as well as RPVs that could deliver bombs and other weapons during wartime situations. Reg mentioned that in addition to now using his drones as he had proposed, the Secretary of Defense had advised him that the Army was interested in his Flareplane. Reg asked the team if his Flareplane had been discussed with the Air Force, now that it was a separate unit. Representatives of the Air Force told him they had heard of the Flareplane, but they were uncertain if the government would utilize it. They then asked Reg if he would attend the California Wing Air Force Association Convention to act as their master of ceremony. He also would be given an award as pioneer of the Robot Plane. He graciously accepted the invitation.

On April 22, Reg attended the Air Force convention in Long Beach. Before hundreds of military personnel, he gave a warm-hearted speech about how he came to dream up the Radioplane with a chronological timeline of the drone's history. Afterwards, Reg was handed an award with the inscription, "For performing an outstanding service in bringing the message of air power to the public." He was surprised at the wording and afterwards asked the staff why the award didn't mention him as pioneer of the Robot Plane. No one could give him an answer. When Reg got home, he threw the award in the trash.

In the fall of 1955, Reg returned to the medium he loved so much and reunited with Mary Astor in George Bernard Shaw's *Don Juan in Hell* (1955). It had been thirty years since the two silent film stars had worked together and they were both elated at the opportunity to perform with each other again, this time on stage in one of Shaw's works. That September, the nostalgic team went on tour with *Don Juan* which opened in San Francisco, then continued throughout the Northwest and Canada for two reminiscent months. While in Minneapolis, Reg and Astor made a special appearance at the University of Minnesota where they spoke with the drama students and inspired them with their stories. The director of the University Theatre, Frank Whiting, sent a letter of appreciation and gratitude to the legendary actors: "Dear Mary Astor and Reginald Denny: We are deeply grateful to you for having appeared on our 'Theatre Hour.' The general feeling among our staff members was that never before had professionals who visited us been quite as genuine, friendly, and gracious. One of our more discerning students commented that people like you 'made him kind of proud to belong to this theater.' While I realize that such visits can be tiring and not particularly exciting to you, I hope you will find some satisfaction in the realization that they mean a great deal to our students—and many are very good students. Such friendly unaffected visits can do much toward bridging the gap that too often exists between the professional and the non-professional theater in America."

On November 1, 1955, the U.S. became involved in the Vietnam War. At that time, Reg was advised by Jules Plummer that his brainchild had evolved into Radioplane's "RP-71," the Army's first "SD-1 Surveillance Drone" and it had become the world's first reconnaissance Unmanned Aerial Vehicle (UAV). The drone was launched by a solid rocket booster with still picture and motion picture cameras mounted onboard and appropriately nicknamed "Falconer" as it tracked and hunted from the sky for its wing master on the ground. It had an autopilot system with radio-control backup, and could carry cameras, as well as illumination flares for night reconnaissance. Reg was confused to learn the Army and Air Force were using the illumination feature but hadn't contacted him about his patented Flareplane. Now, the military was not only using his drone for reconnaissance as he had proposed, but they were using his Flareplane patent. He was once again honored that the government was applying his proposition, but they took his Flareplane for their own and he was given no credit ... or payment. He asked himself what was he to do—sue both Radioplane and the government?

The same week, Reg listened to a radio broadcast called "Success Story." The show featured an interview with William Larrabee, who discussed the successful history of Radioplane's popular drone for use in the wars. In the interview, Larrabee talked about the new Falconer reconnaissance drone and also an experimental long-range anti-radar missile as a platform for reconnaissance, electronic countermeasures, and decoy roles. Larrabee boasted about the company's accomplishments and he proudly credited Whitley C. Collins for the invention but made no mention of Reg. Instead he stated, "In 1938 Whitley Collins invented the drone and secured the first government contract for the three experimental radio-controlled airplanes."

Reg was taken aback as he realized Whitley Collins had not only screwed him out of ownership of his company, but he had sabotaged the history of Radioplane while continuing to exploit it as his own. Reg's blood boiled at the realization his partners had wormed their way to ownership of his invention and they were expressing so publicly. He felt he should set the record straight and hired an attorney with the legal firm of Darling, Shattuck and Edmonds.

At the initial meeting with the legal team, Reg shared a brief history of his development of the target drone prior to Collins and Powell's financial involvement which led to the formation of the Radioplane Company. He expressed his concern about his ex-business partners' claims which conflicted with the truth. Reg told the legal team, "I think that all this proves definitely is that the credit taken by Mr. Larrabee on behalf of Radioplane Company and Mr. Collins on the 'Success Story' broadcast is false and does me a great deal of harm. I have given interviews for stories that have been published in magazines and newspapers, in which I have stated that I was the originator of the radio-controlled target plane, and that Reginald Denny Industries fulfilled the first government contract for any such type of plane, and that one of these three planes was (and still is I believe) on display in the museum at Wright Field and described as, 'The first successfully flown, non-man carrying, radio-controlled aircraft.' I feel that the statements made by Mr. Larrabee on the success story broadcast make me out to be a liar and a fraud and can do me considerable harm if, in the future, I should have a project I might submit to some aviation company."

Edward Shattuck didn't understand what Reg was after and questioned whether they had anything to pursue. Shattuck claimed their difficulty was that they were working on a negative proposition; Reg was seeking to establish damages not because of what was said but because of what was not said. Shattuck told Reg that unless he could provide clear-cut misrepresentations, it seemed unlikely they would be successful in a lawsuit. He advised Reg to write a chronological series of events leading to his invention of the drone, as well as provide copies of all written documents including the date of incorporation of Reginald Denny Industries, date of development of the first radio-controlled plane and who developed it, date of first negotiations with the government and who undertook them, securing letter of intent from the government and date, date of organization of the Radioplane Company and papers under which it was formed, what was transferred to Radioplane Company and on what date, date of incorporation of Radioplane Company, and what was transferred from the Trust or from Reginald Denny Industries direct to the new corporation and when.

Reg got to work on the items to prove the truth; however, he soon realized he hadn't kept any copies of the formal documents at his home as all the originals had been left at his office at the Radioplane plant twenty years earlier. On April 26, 1956, Reg wrote a letter to the Headquarters Commander of Air Material Command at Wright Patterson Air Force Base in Dayton, Ohio, in order to obtain the original letter of intent from Holloman, who was now deceased. "Dear Sir: In April or May of 1938 I was invited to Wright Field Dayton, Ohio, to discuss a contract for three experimental type radio-controlled target planes. The board appointed to evaluate this proposed contract decided in its favor and I (representing Reginald Denny Industries) was given a letter of intent for said contract. This contract was later drawn up and duly signed by both parties. Either after or during the fulfillment of this first contract, Radioplane Company was formed and bought out by the Reginald Denny Industries and all subsequent contracts for radio-controlled target planes were awarded by the Special Weapons Division of the A.A.F. to Radioplane Company. Would it be possible for you to give me the date of issuance of the letter of intent given me as the representative of Reginald Denny Industries and the date of the signing of the above mentioned first contract? I would also like to know the date of the fulfillment of this contract and also the date of changing the award of all contracts from Reginald Denny Industries to Radioplane Company. Circumstances have arisen which make it urgent for me to obtain this information in order to justify certain statements I have made so I would greatly appreciate your co-operation. Very sincerely yours, Reginald Denny."

On May 7, 1956, the Air Force Headquarters Air Material Command responded to Reg's request. "Reference your letter of 26 April wherein you requested information relative to a contract placed with Reginald Denny Industries in April or May of 1938. Records and contracts of that date have since been retired. In order to obtain these contracts and conduct the research requested, it will be necessary for you to furnish contract number or numbers involved. It is requested that your reply be forwarded to Commanding General, Headquarters, Air Material Command, Attention MCPSD by order of the Commander: Robert H. Denning, Deputy Chief Support Division, Directorate of Procurement and Production."

Reg didn't record a contract number let alone have the appropriate means to track down the contract, nor did he have the money to pursue a thorough investigation to legally retrieve the contracts or subpoena witnesses. Another smack in the jaw when he realized how foolish he'd been for not filing his own patent when he first began developing his Radioplane, nor had he kept copies of any of the written communications with the government, or Collins and Powell. All he had was his own timeline of the events which he typed up and promptly submitted to the inexpert legal firm. Shattuck told him they would review the matter and once they reached a conclusion, they would let him know what they recommended.

Reg realized he was screwed. He had made hasty decisions based on financial desperation and there was nothing he could legally do, as he had signed off on everything without protecting his interests at the onset of his invention. He also gave up the thought of pursuing legal action regarding his Flareplane, as it seemed a hopeless cause that would only bring disappointment and more pain to his family. Reg gave up on model making and returned to the only medium that kept him going to pay the bills as the minimal proceeds from the sale of his shares in Radioplane were all but long gone. "I've never went back to the drawing board since or built a model airplane. I was just too sick by what happened to me."

In 1956, he got back to work in television as Ronnie Pond in "The Hanging Judge" episode of the series *Climax!*; as Governor William Cosby in *Telephone Time's* "Grandpa Changes the World"; as George "The Professor" Thayer in the pilot *Alias Mike Hercules* starring Hugh Beaumont in the title role; in the episode "Edinburgh" on *Passport to Danger*; and on the *Matinee Theatre* teleplay "Perfect Alibi." He was happy to make his return to film and reunite with old friend Ronald Colman when they both performed cameo roles as Brits in India with Michael Todd's *Around the World in 80 Days* (1956). The film was a sensation and won several Oscars including Best Picture at the 29th Academy Awards ceremony.

Reg's daughter Joan had just graduated from the University of Southern California (USC) and she was dating the university's Trojan alumni football star, Ralph Pucci. She also had been studying drama with her good friend Elizabeth Montgomery under the teachings of accomplished actress and drama coach Agnes Moorhead. Joanie had auditioned for the lead role in Warner Bros.' *Marjorie Morningstar* (1958) at the same time Ralph proposed marriage to her. When she shared the news of both opportunities with her father, Reg advised her that marriage and being an actress didn't mix. He stressed that she'd have to choose between her acting career and being a wife if she wanted to be successful in either. He was hopeful she'd choose her career. A big slap in the face came to Bubbles and Reg when Joan took off to Las Vegas with the footballer. The *Los Angeles Times* featured a story about the elopement: "A reception Friday will officially welcome home newlyweds Joan Denny and Ralph Pucci, who eloped to Las Vegas on July 14, Actor Reginald Denny, father of the bride, said yesterday. 'Her mother wept, of course, but I really was not surprised,' said Denny in describing the family reaction to the elopement of his daughter and the onetime SC fullback." Bubbles and Reg weren't happy about their daughter's choice to elope with a known womanizer. They knew Ralph was an opportunist who wanted to advance his career in the entertainment and aerospace industries while playing up to his new wife's celebrity father. Months later, Joan announced she was pregnant.

The following year started out with more work in television which Reg was beginning to despise, but he had to earn a living. He played the role of Sir Bertram Cecil in "Cecil of Kabul" on *Tales of the 77th Bengal Lancers* and was in *The Joseph Cotten Show: On Trial's* "The Ghost of Devil's Island." Back again on *The Red Skelton Hour*, Reg made a guest appearance in the series' episode "Robinson Crusoe." Reg performed in two teleplays that year with *Playhouse 90*: In "The Last Tycoon," he played the role of Dean and appeared with a cast of pros that included Jack Palance, Keenan Wynn, Peter Lorre, and Lee Remick. Reg then portrayed theatrical and film producer and director George White in "The Helen Morgan Story" starring Polly Bergen and Hoagy Carmichael.

Reg got the big break he had been longing for when he received a phone call from Broadway producer Herman Levin. Alan Jay Lerner and Frederick Loewe had adapted George Bernard Shaw's *Pygmalion* into a musical called *My Fair Lady*. Levin had successfully opened the Lerner-Loewe production on March 15, 1956, at the Mark Hellinger Theater starring Rex Harrison and newcomer Julie Andrews. British actor Robert Coote played the role of Colonel Pickering; however, Levin needed a replacement when Coote left the production the following spring. When Reg got the call asking him if he would relocate to New York to replace Coote in the role of Pickering, he was skeptical. "When I first learned that they were adapting Shaw's *Pygmalion* for Broadway I had my doubts. I didn't see how they could ever produce it as a musical. When I heard the music and read the adaptation I was thrilled."

Reg accepted Levin's offer. He couldn't wait to return to the Broadway stage and get away from his obligatory work in television. He was all set to leave for New York when Bubbles told him that she would be joining him this time. Now that Reg Jr. and Joan had both married and they were out of the house, she asserted this time she wouldn't be left alone while he was away. Even though they had one infant granddaughter and another on the way, Bubbles insisted on joining her husband this time while on tour. That June, Reg brought Bubbles and daughter Debbie along on their first trip to New York where they settled in a small apartment near Mrs. Barnes' old boarding house.

On Broadway, Reg replaced Robert Coote as Colonel Pickering in the original stage production of *My Fair Lady* at the Mark Hellinger Theatre, first with Rex Harrison as Henry Higgins and Julie Andrews as Eliza Doolittle during the entire year of 1957, and then in 1958 into 1959 with Edward Mulhare as Higgins and Sally Ann Howes in the role of Eliza. The Broadway musical received some of the best reviews any stage production had ever garnered, being hailed as "the perfect musical."

Frank Hains of the *New York Times* wrote it best in his complimentary review: "The all but unprecedented reception of *My Fair Lady* has been wonderful for the show, of course, and it is a wonderful show, of course, but after having heard it praised to high so long one's reaction is simply that—of course. One goes expecting the moon, and one gets it, but there's no great thrill involved anymore … it was all to be. But, oh, how I envy those who saw *My Fair Lady* on opening night. Thrills must have been running out their ears. For it is magnificent and it leaves one wondering where the musical can go from here. At this point, it's pointless to review Lady—she's been more discussed than any musical since *Oklahoma*. She is, I'll say, a better show than *Oklahoma*, a better show than any I know by Rodgers and Hammerstein—and she may have sounded their knell as the unquestioned rulers of the American musical comedy stage. R & H hit it in *Oklahoma* and hit it big and deservedly for it is a great show. But, music-wise, they've been re-writing it ever since. And despite all the hoop-la about integration of music and dance and all elements into one unified whole (which *Oklahoma* unquestionably did) you can still smell a song cue a mile away in an R & H show, and chances are that when it comes it'll be a 'People Will Say We're In Love' type or a 'Many-a-New-Day' type song or whatever. The boys have found the formula and they're sticking to it; it becomes more obvious all the time—take the television of *Cinderella*. Perhaps that's what makes *My Fair Lady* great above all—no formula. In the first place, not many writers would have chosen *Pygmalion* for their vehicle. In the second place, the songs, in which invariably stick out like an extra arm in a book musical, don't in *Fair Lady*. They're suddenly on you—you don't realize they're coming and they're just right. The only exception is 'Street Where You Live' because of its great popularity one knows when Freddy gets on that street that he's going to sing that song. But even 'I Could Have Danced All Night,' which has been just as popular, caught me by surprise. If we must have a third place, I think the thing that actually impressed me most about *Fair Lady* is its staging, which is sheer magic in a number of spots. I shall not be convinced easily that there is not an alchemist-in-residence at the Mark Hellinger Theatre who is each night responsible for waving his wand and muttering the spells which create the grandest stage illusions imaginable. I was sorry to miss Rex Harrison of course, but Edward Mulhare is entirely commendable—in fact, some who have seen both have preferred him. Julie Andrews may perhaps be a bit on the mechanical side but whoever wound her wound her well and she's a delight to look at and sings prettily. Actually, in this show the stars are not the major element and mere competence on their parts would be sufficient to retain the greatness of the whole. Mr. Mulhare and Miss Andrews are of course far more than competent, and they work together exceptionally well. And Reginald Denny, who plays Colonel Pickering, is equally splendid—and possessed of a theatrical voice of the old school, which rings from the rafters and occasionally makes the stars smaller voices pale by comparison."

Reg's former employee Norma Jeane Mortenson, now Mrs. Arthur Miller and famous as Marilyn Monroe, attended *My Fair Lady*. After the show, she brought her husband backstage to meet her former boss. Marilyn complimented Reg's performance, congratulated him, and thanked him for giving her the job that launched her career in film twelve years prior. Reg shared news of the military's success with the drones she had helped assemble. Marilyn said she was honored to have been part of something so big. She laughed when she shared that people didn't believe her when she told them she had once worked on the drones. Reg said the same had happened to him but not to worry; he knew the truth, and then validated her claims to the actress's skeptical husband.

In addition to the stellar reviews of the successful Broadway musical, the press also acknowledged Reg's contribution to the military. World War II veteran and *Los Angeles Times* writer Bill "Mr. L.A." Kennedy was a big fan of Reg's. On September 2, 1958, Kennedy featured an article about Reg which he titled "The Many-Sided Man" and praised the actor-inventor. "When I was wearing Uncle Sam's khaki jumper in the first years of the late unpleasantness, our anti-aircraft battery used to haul the 40 mm guns out to the Mojave Desert for gunnery practice. The moving targets were radio-controlled drones, ingenious devices that revolutionized gunnery training. However, it came as rather a surprise to me to learn that they were developed from gas-powered model planes by Reginald Denny, who is usually associated with the silent-era films and the theater. Movie stars are notoriously about as active in the field of electronics as bird-watchers or maybe even car washers. As a matter of fact, Mr. Denny regards the drones as the forerunners of the guided missile. It is even possible that one day his name may become very large on the Moon. This all came out the other day as he sat across a table at Pucci's Restaurant and reminisced about his varied career. He was invited over by Ralph Pucci, the one-time USC fullback, who had the forethought to marry the actor's pretty daughter, Joan. 'I have been interested in aviation ever since I joined the Royal Flying corps in World War I,' he said stroking his jaunty moustache. 'I started to develop these gas-powered model planes about twenty-five years ago, and eventually they worked out fine in teaching gunners to shoot at moving targets.' Mr. Denny, who is currently essaying the role of Colonel Pickering in *My Fair Lady* on Broadway, came out here on a week's vacation. 'I keep in shape by swimming a couple of miles a day, using the underwater breast stroke. I actually find it less tiring than walking.' This is his 59th year in the theater. Now he's back with his first love, the stage, and it looks like Colonel Pickering will be around for years to come. He had credits in more than two hundred movies and was indeed a credit himself to the film and theater world." Kennedy thereafter continued to feature regular recurring stories paying tribute to the star's forgotten legacy.

While Reg was in New York, he received a letter from the United States Navy's Rear Admiral D. S. Fahrney as follow up of their ongoing correspondence. Fahrney had been promoted to the prestigious position of admiral and was in the process of writing a classified book about the official history of the drone entitled "From Muscles to Missiles" to be published by the Bureau of Aeronautics (BuAer). BuAer was the U.S. Navy's material-support organization for naval aviation from 1921 to 1959. The bureau oversaw all military aircraft development and had governmental responsibility for the design, procurement, and support of Naval aircraft and related systems. There was the question of "pilotless aircraft" as BuAer considered these to be aircraft, but the Navy's Bureau of Ordnance (BuOrd) saw them as guided missiles. Reg thought they were both, and more. The government eventually ended up merging the two organizations into one, the Bureau of Naval Weapons (BuWeps).

Fahrney had submitted his book proposal to BuAer with an entire chapter on Reg's Radioplane and he needed Reg's approval in order for it to be published that summer. Fahrney said he felt bad that Reg wasn't involved with the company which he formed, and also knew the Army used his ideas without giving him the proper and respectful acknowledgement. He said the Navy had always appreciated his invention and he felt Reg should be properly acknowledged for his historic accomplishments. Fahrney asked Reg to attend an event hosted by BuAer, where he'd be presented an award. On July 15, 1958, Reg took the train from New York City to Philadelphia where he attended the event given by the Naval Air Material Center. Rear Admiral Fahrney presented him with BuAer's Distinguished Civilian Award as pioneer of unmanned aviation. Fahrney provided Reg formal acknowledgement of his invention of the drone and its contribution to the military.

On May 11, 1959, the Veterans Administration in New York issued Reg a certificate for his duty as a war vet and for volunteering at their facility in the Bronx. When he returned to his apartment that night, Bubbles told Reg they got a call with news that Whitley Collins had died.

Although his business partners never acknowledged him while they continued to take all the glory—and money—of his invention for themselves, the military and the press provided him what he needed to prove he wasn't crazy and salvage some of his dignity. Even though his business partners had done everything to keep his important contribution as the real pioneer of unmanned aviation a secret, Reg was happy to finally receive the formal acknowledgement from those who used and benefited from his invention most. His heart was filled with joy to perform in Shaw's work as a musical with his new stage family, while being recognized in such an honorable fashion by the military and the press. He was at least gaining notoriety for his dreamchild and loved speaking about his hobby with those who chose to keep his legacy alive.

18

HIS REPRISE

REG'S SOUL REVIVED AS HE PERFORMED nightly to a full house with all his gusto in the extraordinary Broadway musical. The stage actor, however, was approaching seventy years old; all the knocks in the head from his boxing days, war injuries, and racing accidents had finally caught up with him. Reg was slowing down while Bubbles kept up her pace with extravagant shoe shopping, drinking, and dining in true Manhattan style draining what money he earned.

Back in Los Angeles, Reggie Jr. had a three-year-old daughter and was going through a divorce; Joan was home alone with two toddler girls while Ralph entertained business clients and cocktails till the wee hours. Bubbles and Reg felt it was time to go home and get to know their grandchildren. After a stellar couple of years in New York, Reg gave notice to Levin that he was leaving the show. The entire cast and crew of *My Fair Lady* threw him a glorious send off with gratitude for his outstanding performance as Colonel Pickering in the original historic production. They gifted him a silver port bottle necklace engraved with the inscription of one of his memorable lines in the musical, "Have some port, it'll quieten your nerves."

Upon his return to Southern California, Reg and Bubbles came to live with us at our home in Studio City. Once they settled in with the family, Reg was further acknowledged with a star on the newly created Hollywood Walk of Fame. On February 8, 1960, the Hollywood Chamber of Commerce and Hollywood Historic Trust held a special ceremony as the terrazzo marble star displaying the shiny brass letters of "Reginald Denny" was permanently laid in the cement sidewalk at 6657 Hollywood Boulevard, about a mile down the street from the hobby shop he'd opened twenty-six years earlier. On the way home, Reg stopped by the building which still displayed his name. When he walked inside, the shop's manager was surprised and greeted the actor with respectful hugs. Although Pete Veir had passed away, the Veir family had kept the business going for over twenty years while they kept Reg's legacy alive. Reg looked up to see one of his old Dennyplanes still hanging from the ceiling. When the manager got a ladder and brought the plane down as a gift to its creator, Reg handed it to a small boy and his father who eyed the model planes in the shop. He told them to keep the Dennyplane and enjoy flying it with their eyes to the sky. Shortly after, the business name was changed from the Reginald Denny Hobby Shop to California Hobby Distributors and moved to Alhambra where it's still proudly the original and oldest hobby shop in the world.

Reg came home and back to earth and during 1960 and '61 made several guest appearances on television shows. In *Dow's Hour of Great Mysteries*, he played the role of Inspector Ireland in the teleplay "The Dachet Diamonds" which also featured his *My Fair Lady's* castmates Rex Harrison and Melville Cooper. Reg played Chauvelin in "The Scarlet Pimpernel" on *The DuPont Show of the Month,* where he reunited with the host of that episode, Joan Fontaine. Although it was filmed in 1957, an unsold TV pilot Reg did, based on the newspaper comic strip *The Phantom,* finally aired in 1961. He portrayed Commissioner R.G. Mallory with Paulette Goddard, Roger Creed and Lon Chaney, Jr. heading the cast. Reg then made a guest appearance as Winston Harrow in "A Penny a Day" on the popular series *Adventures in Paradise.*

Although he enjoyed spending time with his family, Reg was getting bored with the redundancy of working in TV, along with sitting in front of the idle tube that was now America's popular pastime. He longed to fly again and wondered how his vintage British warplane was doing. Reg contacted the Los Angeles County Museum to whom he had loaned his Sopwith Snipe a lifetime ago. After an extensive excavation effort to locate the plane, he learned a museum curator had sent his Snipe to March Air Force Base during World War II. When Reg contacted the staff at March AFB, he was at first disturbed when they told him someone else had taken possession of the abandoned plane. Internationally known aeronautical engineer Jack Canary had been contracted by March AFB for aircraft maintenance during the Korean War. While working on military planes in the base's hangar, Canary noticed the 1920s biplane rusting away on the field. He was appalled that the historic plane had been left out to rot and then took the Snipe under his wing. Over the course of ten years, Canary invested the time and money to restore it to pristine operating condition.

When Reg finally got a hold of Canary the two made arrangements to meet at the March airfield. Reg cried tears of joy when he laid eyes on his Snipe. It looked better than it had when he first brought it over from England thirty-four years prior. Canary was not only thrilled to meet Reg and tell him his wife was a huge fan, but he was fascinated with the WWI vet's complete understanding of the warplane. They shared their love of the vintage craft, and they also shared their dire financial situations. Canary told Reg he had spent over $10,000 to refurbish the plane and he thought they could get a pretty penny for the restored aircraft. Reg appreciated Canary's work. In order to reimburse Canary for his debt, he agreed to take steps to sell the historic plane. With the help of Canary's attorney, they agreed Reg needed to first reclaim possession of the craft and officially register it with the Federal Aviation Authority (FAA) to obtain a certificate of airworthiness.

On July 25, Reg sent a letter to the Los Angeles County Museum. "Dear Sirs: Some years ago, I loaned to the Museum a Sopwith Snipe 7F-1 airplane (Serial No. E-6938) for the purpose of display with its aviation exhibit. At the time I loaned my aircraft to the Museum, it was my understanding that it would be properly cared for and would also be renovated. For reasons unknown to me, the Museum was unable to keep its commitment and the aircraft was never properly cared for and, in fact, at one time was turned over to the U.S. Army Air Force and stored in the open at March Air Force Base unprotected from the elements. Recently I have learned that my airplane has been skillfully and meticulously rebuilt from the wheels up by Mr. Jack Canary of El Segundo, California.

He has done an expert job and has devoted a tremendous amount of time and effort in restoring my plane to practically its original condition. Under the circumstances, I am constrained to cancel and terminate any agreement I may have had with the Los Angeles County Museum for the use and exhibit of my Sopwith effective upon receipt of this letter by you. I appreciate the museum's efforts in keeping this plane for me during the few years that you had it in your possession, but I feel that the proper use has not been made of it by the museum and I intend to make a more suitable disposition of it at this time. This letter will relieve the Los Angeles County Museum of any obligation or liability to me by reason of your possession or use of my airplane these past few years, and this letter will also acknowledge that I now have possession of the aircraft and the museum is hereby relieved of any further obligation in connection with it. You have my every good wish for your continued success in your most valuable efforts. Very truly yours, Reginald Denny."

Reg was gravely disappointed the museum and March AFB staff had let his plane go to hell and a civilian had spent his hard-earned money to restore it to pristine condition. While he waited for a qualified buyer, Reg made arrangements for the Air Force to transport the plane to Wright Field in Dayton where it would be kept safe inside their Air Force Museum near his original Radioplane prototype on display there.

Before the Snipe's departure, March AFB conducted a spectacular air show in which Reg's warbird was featured. He attended the show as an honorary guest where his full-scale plane was on display and where he had first demonstrated his smaller-scale aircraft twenty-five years earlier. For the first time in over thirty years, Reg sentimentally flew his Sopwith Snipe one last time before it departed for Dayton. It was an emotional moment for him to take the controls of the aircraft in which he'd learned to fly forty-three years prior, and last flown with Howard Hughes. His spirit was freed and he was no longer grounded as he operated his full-scale plane intimately rather than remotely. After the event, Jack Canary sent a letter to Reg with photographs of the historic day and to tell him the Air Force had picked up the Snipe and transported it to Wright Field parked alongside his first Radioplane prototype.

Following his soaring reunion with the Snipe, Reg felt great and wanted to perform. He left Los Angeles and went on a U.S. tour as Mr. Burgess in *Candida* (1961) at the Sombrero Playhouse in Phoenix, then on to Philadelphia and Algonquin as Sir Howard in *Captain Brassbound's Conversion* (1961), then to Dallas at the State Fair Musical Theatre in *Billion Dollar Baby* (1961). When he returned home, Reg closed out the year at the onset of the Christmas holidays on stage at the Pasadena Playhouse where he superbly appeared as Master Horner in a restoration comedy of *The Country Wife* (1961). On Christmas Eve, Ray Duncan of the *Independent Star News* wrote a respectful review of the legendary actor and his performance, as well as a respectful acknowledgement of his drone.

That following summer, Reg was asked to return to the television series *Adventures in Paradise* (1962) to play the role of Stewart in its episode titled "Policeman's Holiday." When he returned home after a day's work on the series, Reg was dismayed to learn disturbing news regarding one of his former employees. The brother of Reg's son-in-law Ralph was Frank Sinatra's bodyguard. Ed Pucci protected the famed performer and traveled with Sinatra wherever he went. Ed had accompanied his boss and Marilyn Monroe on Sinatra's private jet to Lake Tahoe to stay at the Cal Neva Lodge where they were to entertain the owners of the casino. When Uncle Ed returned from Tahoe that day, he shared with Reg and the family the terrible events that had taken place during that weekend. Reportedly, the owners of the casino had drugged and gang-raped the famously famous actress. There was nothing Ed could do, he said, and Marilyn was a complete mess. Reg felt bad for the sweet young lady whom he had hired to work at his Radioplane plant and felt guilty for exposing her to an industry that exploited her to such sickos. He had never understood the mentality of monkeys.

About a week later, Norma Jeane died of a drug overdose. The funeral services were on August 8 at the Westwood Memorial Cemetery in Los Angeles. Her death affected Reg in a profound way; he connected with her broken pain and inner turmoil that stemmed from childhood abandonment and was exploited by "industry." Two brilliant yet forsaken lambs thrown to the wolves and forced to fight their way through life with a sunny public persona for the screen and flashing cameras, only to have it all ripped away in the end by those with whom they had selflessly shared their magic. Reg found it ironic that the tragic beauty began her career with his company, and ended it with a member of his family. He was sick to his stomach and became ill, spending the rest of the year in isolation at our family home.

The following year, Reg was bemused when he received a call from Jules Plummer. Plummer had been manager of contracts for Radioplane since its inception and knew how hard Reg had worked on developing the drone while Whitley Collins snaked his way into its ownership. Now that Collins was gone, Plummer extended an invitation for Reg to meet him at the company's new headquarters. At first, he was apprehensive but decided to take Plummer up on the offer to see how far his dream had come.

Due to the incredible growth of its unmanned systems, Northrop Corporation had acquired a large parcel of land just northwest of Los Angeles in the Thousand Oaks community of Newbury Park. In July 1961, ground was broken and the Ventura Division of Northrop Corporation opened for business on January 7, 1963. When Reg arrived at the new offices in Newbury Park, he was awestruck to see the enormous production facility where the company manufactured improved versions of his drones, like clones in *Star Wars*. Plummer told Reg Radioplane had become the world leader in development and production of unmanned aerial targets and was now operating as Northrop Corporation's Unmanned Ventura Division. As he toured the facility, Reg witnessed the production of thousands of new anti-radar missiles, or "aerial torpedoes" as he had called them. He was amazed by the cigar-nosed turbo-jet targets, which Plummer told him acted as cruise missile simulators and traveled at speeds of up to 600 mph up to 40,000 feet above sea level.

Plummer took Reg to a huge warehouse where gigantic 130-foot orange and white parachutes were sewn by state-of-the-art sewing machines. Plummer imparted that the by-product of his drone recovery systems resulted in the Earth Landing Systems that returned every U.S. astronaut safely to earth, ensuring the lunar space craft and its astronauts floated to the sea, instead of crashing once they reentered Earth's atmosphere. By developing his parachute system, Reg's invention played a leading role in the U.S. space program for the Mercury, Gemini, and Apollo missions. Plummer added that in the Gemini Program, Radioplane drones were used for the Agena target vehicle to develop and practice orbital space rendezvous and docking techniques, which performed large orbital changes in preparation for the Apollo lunar missions. Reg thanked Plummer for his respectful invitation and for giving him the tour of Northrop's new facility, but silently questioned where the government was taking his invention.

Two days after Reg's seventy-second birthday on November 22, 1963, President John F. Kennedy was assassinated. As a family, we silently watched the black-and-white funeral procession on television. The world in which Reg had grown was shifting and he questioned the morality of humankind, disgusted with the monkey mentality of the coveting glare in the human stare.

The following year, Reg's spirit was lifted when he was contacted by theatrical producers Louis B. Robin and Allen Tinkley for a meeting. Robin and Tinkley advised Reg they were bringing *My Fair Lady* to the Los Angeles stage and asked if he would consider playing the role for which he had made famous on Broadway. He was elated by the opportunity and signed on to play Colonel Pickering in *My Fair Lady* (1964) once again, this time with the Westside Civic Light Opera Company in Southern California.

Reg and Bubbles had been living with us since their return. I had seen him perform with the original musical in New York, but I was barely two years old then. Now that I was turning seven, I could attend the play with Grandma and fully appreciate seeing my grandpa perform live on the stage. We were in his dressing room where he was getting ready to go on for the production's first performance at the Santa Monica Civic Auditorium. The call boy's knock came on the dressing room door.

"Half an hour, Mr. Denny!"

For Reg it meant thirty minutes to climb into his formal clothes for the opening scene. Grandpa changed into his black suit, put on his top hat, then looked in the mirror while he combed his iconic moustache. The final knock came at the door.

"Curtain, Mr. Denny!" said the callboy.

Grandpa smoothed his mustache, took a final look at the costume, and smiled at me. We all walked out the backstage doors. Reg reported onstage and we took our seats in the audience. I looked up at the beautifully decorated stage and my eyes widened as I watched my grandpa, Reginald Denny, come to life like a youthful child.

Los Angeles Times' staff writer George H. Jackson wrote a complimentary piece the day after a marvelous opening night on June 16, 1964. "A bright beginning to a new theatrical entry took place last night at Santa Monica Civic Auditorium as the Westside Civic Light Opera offered its initial production-in-the-round staging of the all-time winner, *My Fair Lady*. The auditorium has been cleverly converted to arena type staging for the season of six musical events all running two weeks with the exception of the current occupant, which is in for three weeks. It has been a massive undertaking to prepare both the theater and gather a competent staff for a season such as this, and so it was doubly astounding that last night's opening went off with so few miscues. The staging itself posed major problems for it is one of the first in the circle staging, and the intimacy and new outlook it gives are amazing. Also contributing heavily to the smoothness of the opening performance was the fact that two of the three leads are tried veterans in their roles. These are, of course, Edward Mulhare, who balanced nicely the sharp tongue but hidden softness of the character of Prof. Henry Higgins, and Reginald Denny, seen as Col. Pickering, whose dare sets the familiar story in motion. Third star of the production, and she is a star worthy of having her name above the title just as the other two, is Barbara Williams, who zestfully romps through the role of Eliza Doolittle—the flower girl whipped up from the gutter and turned into a 'duchess.' She is excellent in the part and it is sure to do wonders for her future in show business. Not only does her voice come across clear and sweet, but she manages to project convincingly the problems of heart and mind her new situation causes."

My grandpa sprang back to life before my eyes. To perform gave him pleasure and music made him feel alive. At home, he and I acted out musical numbers from the show; I'd rehearse with him as Eliza Doolittle, and he'd play all the other roles. I loved singing with him, especially when we performed "The Rain in Spain" and "Just You Wait." Grandpa also energetically taught me a dance he'd made up thirty-eight years before, the "Savannah Shuffle." My father scoffed at us, just like he had at The Beatles performance on *The Ed Sullivan Show*. We didn't care. Grandpa's resurrected youth made me giddy with delight in contrast to the familiar environment of my dad's yelling and demeaning of my mother, Joan. I'd look forward to rehearsing Grandpa's song-and-dance acts and enjoyed even more going to the theater with Mom and Grandma to see him perform.

Reg was filled with joy when old friends Bill Seiter and Marian Nixon showed up for one of his reprise performances at the Santa Monica Civic Auditorium. In 1960, Seiter had retired from his role as film and television director and the two had lost touch over the years. The next month, Seiter had a heart attack and on July 26, 1964, he died at his Beverly Hills home with wife Marian Nixon by his side. Reg was saddened to learn of Seiter's death, but glad to have been reunited with his old friend before he passed. He supported his co-star of the past and paid his respects to the beloved director at Forest Lawn Cemetery in Glendale.

The Los Angeles reprise of *My Fair Lady* did so well, that stage producers Nick Mayo and Randy Hale grabbed the opportunity and booked the musical at another venue. They contacted Reg and asked if he'd perform for their production, but switch him to the more comedic role of Alfred P. Doolittle. On August 18, 1964, the musical was once again reprised, this time at the Valley Music Theater in Woodland Hills. He was the only lead actor to move with the production. Actress Jane Powell replaced Barbara Williams as Eliza Doolittle, Michael Evans replaced Mulhare as Professor Henry Higgins, and Reginald Owen replaced Reg as Colonel Pickering, while Reg took over as Eliza's boozing father. Reg reveled in the role he had longed to play while on Broadway and it gave him a greater opportunity to expose his singing talents as a fun-loving character who made people laugh. He told the *Los Angeles Times*, "During that time, I used to watch the role of Doolittle and literally drool to play it. When Nick Mayo and Randy Hale offered me the role of Doolittle, I jumped to play it. I've grown my moustache a bit shaggier and put a bit of weight round my middle, practiced up me Cockney, and the illusion seems complete. I never had more fun in my life. It's fun and games from the word go."

On August 19, 1964, John G. Houser featured a story in the *Los Angeles Herald Examiner*: "That personal favorite, *My Fair Lady*, got all dressed up in lavish splendor again last night as it paraded the unique and brilliant talents of its star, Jane Powell, at the Valley Music Theater where it opened a three-week engagement and you haven't seen a 'lady' until you've seen it with lovely Jane. The radiant, scintillating vocal beauty of Miss Powell is ideally suited to the lilting, lyrical melodies of the great Lerner-Loewe musical and although it is (strangely) the first time the pretty lassie has played Eliza Doolittle, she seemed born to the part. There seems no limit to the little one's big talents. This is the second time she's played a 'rags-to-riches' role and made it into a personal, smashing success. Her first was as Molly Brown in *Unsinkable Molly Brown* at Melodyland last year and last night at the ultra-spacious Valley Theater, she warned her standing ovation and made it another personal triumph. The crystal clarity of Miss Powell's voice made even such durable tunes as 'Wouldn't It Be Loverly?' 'Just You Wait,' 'The Rain in Spain' and the hauntingly lovely 'I Could Have Danced All Night,' seem new again. Michael Evans, as the irascible Prof. Higgins, has played the role so often in his deft hands. His rendition of 'Why Can't the English?' was one of the best ever heard. The surprise of the evening, and happily so, was the bouncy, rambunctious Reginald Denny in the role of the boozing, crafty but likable Alfred P. Doolittle and he brought down the house with a soft shoe routine to the rollicking 'With a Little Bit O'Luck' number. Reginald Owen, as Col. Pickering, was another excellent choice and Russell Nype, as Freddy, is another stage veteran with a knowledge of timing and he capitalized on it several times. His 'On the Street Where You Live' vocal also was warmly, and rightly deserved. This 'Lady' is superbly directed by Oliver Cliff."

His two comic numbers in *My Fair Lady*, "With a Little Bit of Luck" and "Get Me to the Church on Time," Reg sang with proper Cockney gusto and even danced to them. From the audience, I cheered him on as he joyously sang on stage and then danced down the steps to roam the aisles of the audience and wink as he passed me by. Performing lifted Grandpa's spirit and it felt like heaven to bask in his animated aura.

Reg considered it a privilege to end his stage career starring in one of George Barnard Shaw's works which would pave the way to the Academy Award-winning film of the same title that year. Neither he nor Julie Andrews were asked to star in the film version of the Broadway hit, but Ms. Andrews outrivaled all the other actresses with her come-out film role in *Mary Poppins* (1964). She received the Oscar for Best Actress as the magical nanny against Audrey Hepburn who took her original role in *My Fair Lady* (1964).

After the play's run, British author Kevin Brownlow contacted Reg while doing research for a book he was writing about the long-lost medium of silent films. Brownlow wanted to dedicate a chapter of his book to the silent film star and asked if they could meet. In his book *The Parade's Gone By …*, Brownlow wrote about the day they met: "His career in silent pictures was forgotten, not only by movie audiences but by Denny himself. When I met him in Hollywood, he admitted he had not seen one of his silent films for over twenty years. He clearly had little idea of how good he was, and it took some persuasion before he agreed to see *Skinner's Dress Suit*. He and his family gathered in the Hollywood home of collector David Bradley, awaiting the film with a trace of nervousness. First in the program was an episode of *The Leather Pushers*, the boxing series which brought Denny to Hollywood. This two-reeler showed Denny as a likable but rather flat character; what humor there was came from other members of the cast. *Skinner's Dress Suit*, however, was a revelation. Smoothly and expertly directed by William A. Seiter, it showed Denny at his best—as a comedian whose polish and technical brilliance matched, but never outshone, his genuine warmth. As the Denny family watched this 1926 comedy, the atmosphere noticeably changed. The picture's gags at first received restrained, relieved chuckles. But as the story took hold, the audience, which included Sennett comedienne Minta Durfee, roared with laughter, giving the film their wholehearted approval. Mrs. Denny spotted herself as an extra and identified Janet Gaynor as another. At the end, Denny was assailed with congratulations. Grinning shyly, he confessed that he had expected the picture to creak. 'It certainly stands up a lot better than I thought it would,' he said."

It dawned on Reg he had fought so hard to prove that he was a serious actor and drone inventor only to find his true purpose in life was simply to make people laugh, just as Uncle Carl had said so many years before. He had kept the happy boy remotely hidden and realized the robbery of his youth had nothing to do with him. Instead of battling against the smile that knocked him out, he'd join in on the fun and laugh along with those in his world. With his new outlook of gratitude for the nine lives he'd been given, Reg decided to revel in each glorious moment of his charmed life. He spent the next year swimming his two miles a day in the cement pond rather than ten miles in a mountain lake, taking our fat beagle, Bogey, out for daily walks, cooking delicious curry dishes, and playing Solitaire at our kitchen table while sharing his tales and making me laugh.

Following his stage reprise and now into his seventies, Reg returned to the screen and played the role of villain Sir Harry Percival in the Western comedy *Cat Ballou* (1965) with Jane Fonda and Lee Marvin. He also gratefully continued work in television in an episode called "The Timothy Heist" for *Bob Hope Presents the Chrysler Theatre* (1964), then as George in the episode "Somewhere George Is Calling" of the sitcom *Please Don't Eat the Daisies* (1965) with Pat Crowley.

Following his sitcom appearances, Reg guest-starred as King Boris on two episodes of the new comic-book series *Batman* (1966) in which he was rescued by Caped Crusader Adam West. His back-to-back episodes were "A Riddle a Day Keeps the Riddler Away" and "When the Rat's Away, the Mice Will Play." The action-packed comedic series was so successful that there was a motion picture version, *Batman: The Movie* (1966). The producers asked Reg to play a cameo role as Commodore Schmidlapp, with Adam West once again rescuing him from the cast of sinister villains. That same year, Reg played the part of Master-at-Arms with Frank Sinatra in *Assault on a Queen* (1966). After work on the film, Reg and Sinatra attended a party together. While they smoked cigarettes and shared stories about the business, the two performers got into a heated conversation when Reg reproved Sinatra on what he knew about Marilyn's death. Uncle Ed was fired from his job soon after.

While he had been making his reappearance in film and television, Reg's spirit was again lifted when he was contacted by Wing Commander Ralph Manning of Canada's Department of National Defense. Commander Manning expressed to Reg that the Canada Aviation and Space Museum badly wanted his historical warbird for display at their hangar in Ottawa. Due to the Snipe's war service flown by Canadian Major Barker, they made an offer to purchase Reg's biplane in its pristine museum quality condition. Even though they offered less than half of what he wanted, Reg sold the Snipe to the museum who made arrangements to pick it up from Wright Field and transport it to Ottawa. Manning sent Reg a letter of gratitude and told him that the beautifully restored biplane was now at its new home. In honor of the plane's history and Reg's service in both World Wars, the Snipe was flown by Wing Commander David P. Wightman of the Royal Canadian Air Force on Canada's National Air Force Day in 1965. Manning sent Reg a photograph taken of his plane flying on that memorable day before it took its place inside the museum. Reg paid Jack Canary and was contented knowing the last pieces of his past had been restored, now in its permanent home with the care it had always deserved. The aircraft still sits pretty at the Canada Aviation and Space Museum in their First World War Exhibition as the only Sopwith Snipe in existence that flies.

19 LEAVING A LEGACY ON WINGS HOME

THE 38TH ACADEMY AWARDS was the last memorable Hollywood event Reg would attend. The ceremony took place on April 18, 1966, at the Santa Monica Civic Auditorium, the same venue where he'd performed *My Fair Lady*. *Cat Ballou* was up for five Oscars that night with Lee Marvin taking the win for Best Actor due to his dual performance as drunken cowboy hero Kid Shelleen and criminal Tim Strawn. Reg's Broadway co-star and previous year's Best Actress winner, Julie Andrews, was nominated for her performance as Maria von Trapp in *The Sound of Music* (1965). She didn't win that year, but the musical garnered several Oscars. Reg was happy to reunite with Ms. Andrews at the Oscar's after-party, but his spirit was fading and his health declining. It got to the point he couldn't attend public functions with his co-stars any longer nor act out musical scenes with me from *My Fair Lady* and *The Sound of Music*.

I eventually spent time with Grandpa during our visits to the Motion Picture Hospital in Woodland Hills instead of in our family den. I felt bad watching his condition worsen, so I'd create greeting cards with happy stories of my own that I'd bring to his cottage and hand to him with a reassuring smile. I just wanted to see him sing and dance again, not confined to a hospital bed. While he was ailing, old friends also came for bedside visits, including Bette Davis, Cary Grant, and Jack Northrop. As we were leaving the hospital one evening, a man donning a vintage military uniform stepped into the room. He held a wooden propeller with "Radioplane" engraved on it. The soldier said he'd just returned from duty in Vietnam and came to thank Grandpa for saving his life as he handed the Falconer drone remnant to Reg. A slow smile came to Grandpa's face as he recognized the Naval officer who'd helped him test the drones during WWII then gone off to the Pacific over twenty years earlier. Instead of keeping the propeller, Reg signed the iconic relic and handed it back to the soldier with gratitude for the war vet's service in making his own dreams come true.

The next night, Grandpa claimed a woman stood at the foot of his bed and told him his time hadn't come yet, that he needed to return to his homeland one last time. My mom thought he was hallucinating while he conversed with "the Virgin Mary," but I knew it was his mother beckoning him home.

Shortly after that last hospital visit and just before my tenth birthday, we went to the airport to see my grandparents off for a trip to London. Wishing I could go, I hugged

277

them and watched as they stepped up that stairway to the sky. Grandpa looked out the oval window of the plane and smiled at me as they pulled away from the terminal. I waved goodbye as the TWA jet lifted off the runway, not knowing this would be the last time I'd see him. Grandma sent me postcards of the beautiful gardens in Richmond and the castles of Great Britain. I drew pictures from the postcards and sent them back. I looked forward to their return, when Grandpa could once again share stories of adventures in the faraway land. After his reunion with sisters Nora, Mona, and Madge, Reg was admitted to a hospital in Teddington on the Thames near his childhood home and right next door to the studio where Jack Warner had wanted him to work so long ago.

Bubbles and Nora made their daily visits with Reg in his room with a view of the river. One sunny day, they walked into the hospital room. Reg lay in his bed watching the boats sail on the Thames outside his window. He turned to Bubbles, reached out his hand, and strained to speak.

"I'm sorry, my dear, for leaving you with not a penny to my name."

Bubbles took Reg's hand. "Don't worry, sweetheart. You're the most wonderful man I've ever known and I'm the richest girl in the world."

Reg smiled his crooked smile. "I love you, darling." He turned to Nora, "You will make sure she's taken care of, won't you?"

Nora smiled at her brother. "My darling, don't you know that all great actors and artists die penniless? You're an extraordinary actor who entertained the world and the most incredible artist who protected it. Trust all will be taken care of as you fly high in the sky."

Reg smiled. "When do I stop fighting?"

Nora replied, "Never, my darling, never."

On June 16, 1967, Reg made his final bow as the curtain went down with Bubbles and Nora at his bedside. True to his declaration, he died without a penny to his name, but with a wealth of love in his heart. The next day, the Royal Air Force made an honorary fly by over White Lodge at Richmond Park. When Wing Commander Ralph Manning learned the news of Reg's death, the Royal Canadian Air Force made one last flight with his Sopwith Snipe at Rockliffe in honor of the WWI veteran.

I came home from the last day of school to start summer vacation when my mom told me the news of Grandpa's death. She was distraught by the loss of her dear father. When the press learned of his passing, several major national and worldwide newspapers and magazines honored him and expressed their condolences by saying, "That true-blue red-blooded go-getter leather-pushing American, with the improbable name of Reginald is gone. Denny's greatest role was playing himself, an imposter from England who fooled and pleased America for a half century. Handsome and debonair, Denny appeared in more than 200 screenplays—among them *Around the World in Eighty Days* and *Mr. Blandings Builds His Dream House*. The debonair actor also was a designer and manufacturer of model airplanes and developed a radio-controlled target aircraft used by the armed forces in World War II. Mr. Denny, standing six feet tall and weighing about 175 pounds, presented a tall and trim figure with a debonair mustache and an infectious grin. He maintained his sense of humor on and off the stage and the screen. Mr. Denny, whose stage and screen appearances usually won the approval of both critics and audiences, was hailed in a *New York Times* movie review as 'a mature player, getting his laughs without once being hit by a pie or being mistaken for somebody else's aunt.' Although his career encompassed the full range of parts, from straight drama to farce, most filmgoers remember him as the comedy Englishman with the infectious smile."

When Bubbles returned from England with Grandpa's casket, she told me how much he loved his Little Princess with whom he so cherished sharing his stories and acting out musicals. I was devastated when I realized he was really gone.

Now who's going to tell me the stories?

After the solemn funeral at Forest Lawn Cemetery in the Hollywood Hills, Grandma took me to the upstairs room of her sister's home and unlocked its door with an antique key. As she opened the creaky door, I noticed several stacked boxes in the otherwise empty room. Just boxes to the rest of the family, but treasure chests filled with gold to me. I peeked inside to find an *Around the World in Eighty Days* music box and a Regency transistor radio personally embossed by Michael Todd as a gift for Grandpa's work on the film; a bound *Rebecca* script with stills of Grandpa inserted and a personal note of thanks from David O. Selznick; a *Book of Naturalists* as a gift from Cary Grant with a personal note from the friend who got him "fired." Grandma opened a large cedar chest and showed me hundreds of letters, documents, and vintage movie stills featuring Grandpa in scenes with various movie stars. I also noticed photos of him standing with his large biplanes. Then, I came across photos of him with smaller toy planes; pictures caught in time of Reg building model airplanes, testing them, and flying them by holding a black box with what looked like a telephone and antenna on it.

The Drone Tales and his magical box!

It was like having him right there in the room with me as his stories came to life, in the palms of my hands. Grandma told me those were nothing, just a hobby and a bunch of dizzy dreams; she instead pulled out glamourous studio portraits of she and Grandpa for me to view. Afterwards, those in the model plane and aviation industries made several attempts to speak with Bubbles about her husband's legacy, but she never responded. One letter in particular really maddened her when I read it aloud.

"Dear Mrs. Denny, Your husband was a pioneer in the model airplane field, back during the thirties and forties. He designed and manufactured his own model engine—the Dennymite—and his own airplanes. He was also a pioneer and a leader in the Radio Control field. His contributions to Aviation and Modeling in this country are immeasurable and perhaps exceed even his place in the Acting field. Yet when Reginald died not a single Model Magazine or periodical of Aviation Science paid homage to this fine gentleman. One reason for this, I believe, is because he died in England while visiting his sister, and few people heard of it. I have proposed a long article in America's largest Model Magazine, *Model Airplane News*, about Reginald Denny. I need a few additional facts and I need to borrow some pictures from you—if you have any—about his activities concerning modeling. Here is what I am hoping for: Pictures or negatives of Reginald with one of his engines, his models, and/or his factory during the thirties, Pictures or negatives of Reginald and his Target Drone Dennys (Reggie's Robot), and a few brief dates of when he started these projects. Also, did Mr. Denny ever play any Shakespearian Roles? Any pictures you could send me would be reproduced and returned to you within three days. He may someday be forgotten as an actor, but he will never be forgotten as an Aviation

Pioneer. Any help you could give me on this would be greatly appreciated. Thank you for your courtesy, Jim McNeill."

When Bubbles didn't reply, McNeill sent her another letter which I again recited.

"Dear Mrs. Denny, While waiting for your reply I have done a great amount of research on Reginald and I have nearly enough now for my article. All I really need now is five or six good pictures of Reggie during his modeling activities in the thirties and one or two of him about his Hollywood career. Of course, if I knew—Are you the same girl he married in India before World War I? What airplanes did he fly in the Royal Flying Corps in World War I? and, How did Reggie get into making model airplanes in the first place? All this would be a help … I greatly fear that if I do not hear from you, my editor of *Model Airplane News* will pass this article by and go on to the next one in historical sequence. I have very strong feelings about Mr. Denny because I remember the enormous impact he made on the hobby all during the thirties and the envy that all of us kids had that a glittering movie star was so deeply involved with model airplanes. Also, when he died in Middlesex the other day while visiting his sister not ONE word was mentioned of his passing in the model industry. One reason for this was his death in another country not being circulated by the news media. What I want to do, Mrs. Denny, is to say good-by to Reggie in the same magazine wherein he used to run full page ads back in the thirties, and in behalf of all of the many thousands of his friends and admirers who considered him to be first of all an aerodynamicist, and to say it in a manner that they will not soon forget. To do this I need your help my dear. You've just got to loan me some pictures and fill in a few blank spots in his background. Thank you, James E. McNeill."

Bubbles was disturbed with McNeill's questions, especially the one about his first marriage and his war service which she knew nothing about. She told me it was all hogwash and she never responded to McNeill nor anyone else who inquired about his hobby. I was asked never to bring it up again, so I didn't. In the years that followed, Bubbles and other members of the family wouldn't speak of Reg's hobby or his Radioplane. In fact, they were all rather bitter about events of the past, which carried through time like a shameful family curse festered with judgmental betrayal rather than that of loving support.

As I became an adult, Bubbles and I developed more of a sisterly relationship and she did her best to continue with Grandpa's story-telling legacy, although her versions focused more on their adventures during the Roaring Twenties, while she held an Early Times cocktail in hand. She edited her stories only focusing on the good times; however, her ugly tantrums frequently came out in the form of nightmares that scared the crap out of my family members and me. She was angry about the past and couldn't let go of the robbery of her youth. Bubbles got into therapy, but didn't discuss her inner turmoil until my mother Joanie died of ALS at the young age of fifty-five in 1989. Bubbles said the loss of her daughter broke her heart to the point she couldn't bear living. It was unthinkable, she said, to lose her child before her time, and she now understood how her husband felt when he lost his first-born baby. She was forever a changed woman and said she knew that Reg, Joanie, and Barbara were all together in heaven smiling upon us.

When Bubbles approached the age of ninety, Uncle Reggie, Aunt Diane, and I decided it was time for her to live at the Motion Picture Hospital near my home in Woodland Hills where she would receive the care she required. One Saturday, I made my daily visit to the convalescent unit of the hospital. The nurse had placed Grandma in a wheelchair alongside another elderly woman who was seated in the hallway in front of their rooms. I approached the two elderly ladies and gave Grandma a gentle hug. The other woman motioned for me to hug her as she couldn't speak. I looked across the hall to see the nameplate above her at the entrance of her room. It read "Laura La Plante."

I cried with joy and hugged Ms. La Plante, reminding her of the actress's handsome co-star in their silent film days at Universal. She was happy with tears of joy that we had been brought together at this point of her life. The next day, I returned to Ms. La Plante's room with nostalgic photos frozen in time. She smiled when I showed her a photo of herself as a beautiful young movie star on her wedding day, with Reggie as best man standing proudly next to Bill Seiter. I also showed Ms. La Plante movie stills from films which she and her handsome leading man had starred in together seventy years earlier and then taped them to the mirror in her room. One was from a scene of *Skinner's Dress Suit* with the image of a much younger Betsy Lee smiling in the background. Ms. La Plante couldn't have been happier and in silent laughter she slowly mouthed to me "Thank You."

A couple months later, dear Ms. La Plante joined her husband Irving Asher along with Bill Seiter, Reg, Barbara, and Joanie when she too took her place up and away. A few months later, I was three months pregnant when Bubbles' health took a steep decline. The week before she passed, she motioned for me to come close and whispered.

"You were always his Little Princess, Kimmy. Your son will be his Great Grand-Prince. Fly high, my angel and he will too."

On December 19, 1996, Grandma Bubbles joined Grandpa, Joanie, Ms. La Plante, and all the other attendees at their Hollywood party in the sky. I officiated at her private memorial service alongside Grandpa's grave at Forest Lawn Cemetery just over the hill from their original home of Universal City Studios with the spirit of my baby inside and hope of new life to come.

My prince was born that next year and I'd smile inside as I'd watch Grandma's prophecy come true at each milestone of his life. When Jeremy was only a year old, he'd excitedly notice airplanes in the sky. At two, he would draw pictures of aircraft, play with small models, and pretend he was flying. He'd make models from kits at age four and won first place for building a B-1 Lancer military jet at the Ventura County Fair. He started flying remote control park flyers at age five and then joined the Channel Island Condors at their Camarillo flying field to graduate to large gas-powered scale models, much like the ones his great-grandpa first designed. On his tenth birthday, Jeremy's dream came true when he took the controls of a Beaver float plane as Captain Brooks guided him on a beautiful maiden voyage over Lake Coeur d'Alene. A few years later at Condor Field, Jeremy met Jason Rohr and Greg Banas of AeroVironment, the largest military supplier of small unmanned aircraft systems (UAS). Jason and Greg were Air Force men training soldiers how to operate the devices for the war in the Middle East. During a celebration for Jeremy at the model plane field, Jason was testing drones and told us they had to leave on a special mission in the Afghanistan. Before he left, Jason gifted Jeremy one of the drones as a birthday present. The mission, we later found out, was to train the Seals how to expertly use their devices to locate Osama bin Laden and bring the notorious terrorist down.

Through my son's passion, I was once again inspired to delve into our rich heritage as well as honor my legendary grandfather with the writing of this book. My interest in unmanned aviation had been revived because of my wonderful son and it has touched my heart to watch him build and fly scale model planes and fly real aircraft, living his great-grandpa's dream while bringing my memories to life. Maybe Jeremy is the boy who Reg so colorfully described in his not so crazy "Drone Tales."

20 REMOTE POSSIBILITIES

ALTHOUGH HE'S MOST REMEMBERED as the debonair British movie star who entertained the world with his infectious grin, Reggie's greatest legacy is being responsible for leading unmanned aviation into the role with which UAVs are most strongly associated today. With a passion for aviation, a love for whittling, and a dream, this child-hearted actor planted a seed that Northrop Corporation continued to grow in building the future.

In 1990, Northrop Corporation closed its Newbury Park facility and relocated the entire unmanned systems program to their aerospace headquarters in Redondo Beach, California. In 1994, Northrop Corporation acquired Grumman Corporation to become known as today's Northrop Grumman Corporation (NG) which has been and continues to be the premier producer of global security and recognized leader of unmanned systems today. The stellar team at Northrop Grumman have developed an ever-growing fleet of craft used worldwide by businesses, the government, the military, and NASA that enables souls "to boldly go where no man has gone before."

From Radioplane's Falconer reconnaissance drone evolved their earth-scoping autonomous Global Hawk with a wing span the size of a 737 jet that can fly up to altitudes of 65,000 feet with the most advanced in technology to govern environmental pirates and global terrorists. On April 24, 2001, NG made history when its Global Hawk became the first pilotless aircraft to cross the Pacific Ocean; it flew non-stop from Edwards Air Force Base to the Royal Australian Air Force (RAAF) base in Edinburgh Australia.

Modeled after the Global Hawk, NG's MQ-4C Triton unmanned aircraft system provides real-time intelligence, surveillance, and reconnaissance (ISR) over vast ocean and coastal regions for the U.S. Navy. Triton can fly over twenty-four hours at a time in altitudes higher than ten miles with an operational range of 8,200 nautical miles and will support a wide range of missions including maritime ISR patrol, signals intelligence, search and rescue, and communications relay. We sure could have used Triton in 2014 when Malaysia Airlines flight 370 "disappeared" from the sky into oblivion. NG's MQ-8C Fire Scout is the Navy's next generation autonomous helicopter designed to provide reconnaissance, situational awareness, aerial fire support, and precision targeting support for ground, air, and sea forces. Their environmental surveillance "Polar Eye" monitors climate change and glacial ice melting, in addition to tracking stranded Arctic polar bears for rescue. "Bat" is NG's family of affordable, medium altitude, multi-mission unmanned aircraft systems used for ever-changing tactical missions including ISR, target acquisition, and communications relay. It has a blended body design, enabling a much larger payload volume that allows it to carry more payload than other UAVs of its size. Currently the Bat family product line features both 12-foot and 14-foot wingspan aircraft, similar in size to Reg's original Radioplane.

Not only did his vision become a reality in the form of target drones, but Reg's dream has taken off in the form of reconnaissance craft, fighter jets, and even with the space program. His proposal for the radio plane to take the place of manned warbirds has evolved into the autonomous X-47B unmanned combat air vehicle similar to the futuristic craft with a mind of its own from his "Drone Tales." Now, NG is in the completion stages of building NASA's James Webb Space Telescope which is scheduled to launch in 2021 to record the history of our Universe. Who knows what we'll learn when NASA launches that unmanned device into the wild blue yonder. Northrop Grumman is an innovative company who's accomplishing amazing feats for our survival, flying higher with their eyes to the sky, just as their Unmanned Systems' founder dreamed of and did.

Descendants of "Reggie's Robots" have not only evolved for use in the military, but drones have become a commonplace word for civilian use on land, in the sea, and sky-high into space just as Reg envisioned. Aerial drones are now used for filmmaking, real estate marketing, package delivery, search and rescue, environmental protection, agriculture, weather forecasting, wildfire fighting, and even for human transportation. Remotely piloted craft cannot only assist humans, but they can help fellow creatures with whom we share this planet by monitoring elephant poachers, whalers, and pirates of nature by going where man can't go but where frigatebirds and dolphins can. The University of Hawaii, Air Shepherd and Sea Shepherd have recently incorporated drones in their programs to protect endangered species from poachers on land and in oceanic locations that were previously difficult or impossible to reach by humans. In the field of science and medicine, various robotic devices are used to transport medicine in treating infectious diseases which would otherwise contaminate humans, as we witnessed with the Ebola outbreaks. In addition to being used by Homeland Security, border patrol agents and law enforcement officers more effectively monitor and seek out terrorists and criminals with surveillance drones in their selfless service for our safety. Unmanned systems can assist us with exploration to unreachable lands in the highest mountains on earth to the deepest leagues of the sea, and even into outer space as in the Rover on Mars to Elon Musk's Falcon 9.

There's been a lot of discussion in the media with much controversy about these "flying robots" which now seem to have a bad rap concerning privacy with use in surveillance, as well as artificial intelligence (AI) proposed for use in their operation. It's understandable that there's apprehension regarding the future of our technology, especially with the use of drones. As typical with any powerful technology, there has been and always will be positive and negative aspects warranting concerns of its use. I'm especially concerned about the AI factor, applied to any technological device. The notion of a computer thinking for itself, like HAL in *2001: A Space Odyssey* (1968), is unsettling but seems to be an interesting part of our evolution. It's up to us to figure out how to use these devices in a constructive manner for the good of mankind, by creating laws, and to enforce them by carefully monitored distribution of technology so that those who might abuse it in a destructive manner, won't.

As in *Raiders of the Lost Ark*, the ark of the covenant was a "radio for speaking to God," but in the wrong hands it could destroy. As in *Star Wars*, the Jedi worked alongside droids to help them bring order to the Galaxy, but when in the wrong hands of the Dark Side they were used for destruction and dominance. Perhaps if the drones that evolved from Reg's invention were in use when he fought the Dark Side one hundred years ago, the holocaust wouldn't have happened and he wouldn't have been shot across the stomach in combat, which caused the circulatory problems that ultimately led to his death. This technology, as he said, "can be of inestimable value" in the right hands. In the right hands, any technology can enhance life on this planet and in space; but in the wrong hands it can destroy. It's all up to whose minds and hands they're in, and we've got the thumb to operate the joystick. Reg had a trusting spirit that instead of acting like monkeys, we'd use our minds to evolve into a more compassionate species, with hands to save lives rather than abolish, while keeping our eyes to the skies.

Due to Reg's historic contribution to unmanned aviation and knowing I was working to bring his legacy back to life, the folks at Northrop Grumman invited me to meet with the staff at their Space Park in Redondo Beach. Tom Vice and Cynthia Curiel's team were wonderfully gracious when they greeted Jeremy and me at the NG Southern California campus, as though we were royalty. They told us they wanted to share how far the company had come with a tribute to Reg and gave us an honorary tour of the expansive facility, including a peek at the beginning stages of the dynamic James Webb Space Telescope. They had just completed designing their NGenuity in Motion museum which features the rich history of Northrop Grumman from its beginnings to the future of its unmanned systems. We were in awe of the work they had put into the historic exhibition where they featured Grandpa's noteworthy accomplishments in naming him the Father of Unmanned Aviation and Founder of Northrop Grumman's Unmanned Systems.

After that special day, I was filled with hope and thought it would be enlightening for other members of my family to see what the company had created in Grandpa's honor. I planned a special reunion party to celebrate Uncle Reggie's eighty-fourth birthday at Northrop Grumman. The same NG team met me along with Uncle Reggie, Aunt Diane, Cousin DeDe, her husband Roger, and sister Jill in the lobby of the Northrop Grumman Aerospace Systems' Space Park. As we entered the museum doors, everyone looked above the entrance and noticed the vintage Radioplane logo. We walked inside where various types of model planes flew from the ceiling. On the wall to the left was a large fresco, which the company referred to as their "Founders Wall." Painted on the plaster canvas above the clouds was the larger-than-life face of Reginald Denny, alongside aerospace pioneers Jack Northrop, Roy Grumman, T. Claude Ryan, Simon Ramo, and Burt Rutan.

From his wheelchair, Uncle Reggie looked up to the sky mural at the image of his father looking down on him. He smiled, then paused, and broke down with tears of exultation. His reaction touched us all and brought tears to our own eyes. It reminded me of the final closing scene in *Star Wars: Episode VI - Return of the Jedi (1983)*, in which Luke Skywalker puts Darth Vader's body to rest. As the galaxy celebrates its freedom from the Dark Empire, Luke looks up to see the ghosts of Obi-Wan Kenobi, Yoda, and his Jedi knight father, Anakin, smiling upon him.

I looked up at Grandpa's image on the wall and gave him a knowing smile back.

Reginald Denny's star sits near Harrison Ford's in front of Musso & Frank Grill on the Hollywood Walk of Fame. Possibly there's a pilotless starship that will bear Reggie's name in honor of his contribution to unmanned aviation someday in a galaxy not so far, far away....

With his Radioplane (1936). Courtesy of Reginald Denny Collection.

With his Radioplane RP-2 and smaller drone (1937). Courtesy of Reginald Denny Collection.

With Paul Whittier and the RP-2 (1937). Courtesy of Marc Wanamaker/Bison Archives.

Showing one of his military model float planes to Ida Lupino and Walter Connolly
on set of *Let's Get Married* (1937). Courtesy of the Everett Collection.

With son Reggie Jr. on Paramount set of *Bulldog Drummond* (1937).
Courtesy of Marc Wanamaker/Bison Archives.

Radioplane RP-3 parachute test at March AFB (1938). Courtesy of Reginald Denny Collection.

With Captain Holloman at U.S. Army Air Corps' Wright Field (1938).
Courtesy of Reginald Denny Collection.

As Captain Douglas Loveland in *Four Men and a Prayer* (1938).
Courtesy of Marc Wanamaker/Bison Archives.

Showing miniature model boats to Heather Angel on Paramount set of *Bulldog Drummond* (1938).
Courtesy of Marc Wanamaker/Bison Archives.

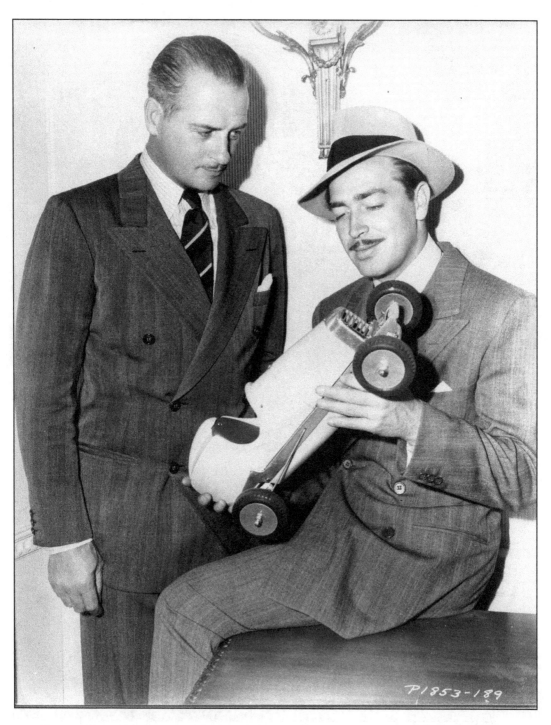

Showing his model racecar to John Howard on Paramount set of *Bulldog Drummond* (1938). Courtesy of Marc Wanamaker/Bison Archives.

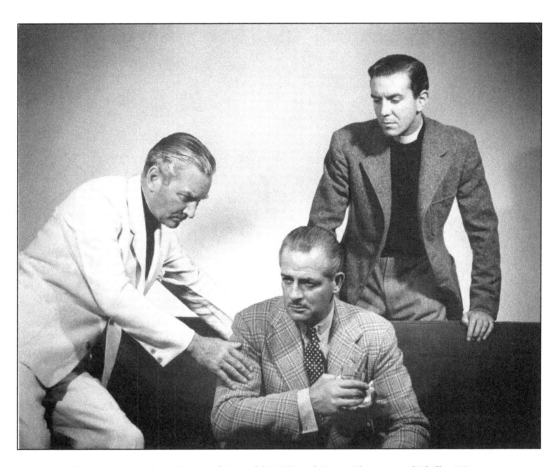

As depressed drunk in *Outward Bound* (1939) with Evan Thomas and Phillip Winter at Biltmore Theatre Los Angeles. Courtesy of Marc Wanamaker/Bison Archives.

With Academy Award winning cinematographer George Barnes, Alfred Hitchcock, and
Joan Fontaine during birthday celebration break on set of *Rebecca* (1939).
Courtesy of Marc Wanamaker/Bison Archives.

As Frank Crawley with Laurence Olivier, Joan Fontaine, and others while they watch burning Manderley in Academy Award winning *Rebecca* (1939). Courtesy of Reginald Denny Collection.

With Paul Whittier, Walter Righter, and Kenny Case unloading RP-4 at Muroc Dry Lake for U.S. Army Air Corps experimental target drone tests (1940). Courtesy of Reginald Denny collection.

Attaching RP-4 to the "trimming frame" of Righter's 1929 La Salle sedan prior to test flight at Muroc Dry Lake (1940). Courtesy of Reginald Denny collection.

Getting the La Salle up to simulated flight speed with RP-4 nose to the wind (1940).
Courtesy of Reginald Denny Collection.

Trimming the RP-4 for speed test prior to actual flight for the U.S. Army Air Corps. Notice
spinning propeller and uplifted wings (1940). Courtesy of Reginald of Denny Collection.

Reg in the backseat of La Salle viewing RP-4 as Walter Righter drives for wind tunnel speed test prior to flight (1940). Courtesy of U.S. Air Force Flight Test Nation Edwards Air Force Base.

Three experimental RP-4 drone prototypes, one on the original rail launching apparatus at Muroc Dry Lake (1940). Courtesy of Reginald Denny Collection.

The first RP-4 target drones ready for flight before the U.S. Army Air Corps at Muroc Dry Lake (1940). Courtesy of Reginald Denny Collection.

The three original RP-4 prototype experimental drones (1940).
Courtesy of Reginald Denny Collection.

All smiles at Muroc Dry Lake on the historic day in April (1940).
Courtesy of Reginald Denny Collection.

Testing the RP-5 with Walter Righter's stripped Packard 12 limousine for an increased flight
speed of 95 mph, Reg as backseat driver (1941). Courtesy of U.S. Air Force Flight Test
Nation Edwards Air Force Base.

Rehearsing with Lilian Bond for *All Men Are Alike* at Hudson Theatre on Broadway (1941). Courtesy of Marc Wanamaker/Bison Archives.

As Alfred J. Bandle with Bobby Clark, Velma Rayton, and Jeraldine Dvorak in *All Men Are Alike* (1941). Courtesy of Marc Wanamaker/Bison Archives.

As Stephen Lawry with Ann Harding, Edward Arnold, and Donna Reed in *Eyes In The Night* (1942). Courtesy of AF archive/Alamy Stock Photo.

As Charles Condomine with Lillian Harvey and Mona Barrie in *Blithe Spirit* (1945).
Courtesy of Marc Wanamaker/Bison Archives.

With Radioplane's RP-5A, U.S. Navy's TDD-2/U.S. Army's OQ3 at Van Nuys Metropolitan Airport (1945). Courtesy of Marc Wanamaker/Bison Archives.

With Farmers and Merchants Delegation owners in front of "aerial torpedo" at Pt. Mugu
NAS (1947). Courtesy of Reginald Denny collection with photo credit to U.S. Navy.

As the Colonel with Danny Kaye in *The Secret Life of Walter Mitty* (1947).
Courtesy of Marc Wanamaker/Bison Archives.

As Henry Simms with Myrna Loy and Cary Grant in *Mr. Blandings Builds His Dream House* (1948).
Courtesy of Marc Wanamaker Bison Archives.

ALMOST ANY fairly frequent movie fan of the last 20 years knows Reginald Denny as the guy who plays those likable, but dim-witted Britisher roles; but relatively few know there is another and far more important side to the actor. He is the inventor of a midget robot plane—very, very hush-hush during the war—used extensively by both Army and Navy Air Forces as targets in the training of aerial and antiaircraft gunners. Denny is not a scientist nor unusually mechanically minded. It all started when he tried to help a youngster fly a model plane and it crashed. The actor sent for a new one, and before he knew it he was making all sorts of models himself. Then, back in 1934, Denny had his idea of the radio-controlled target plane for gunnery training, and no one would listen to him; but when the war came on, the Government took interest, and had him manufacture them in quantities. They are named after the actor, being called Target Drone Dennys. The services still use them. Furthermore, Denny believes there are commercial uses of the plane, one of which is shown taking off in the photo and controlled by Denny. He says they could make crop-dusting safer and more efficient and be used in fighting forest fires. Denny's latest film role was in *Mr. Blandings Builds His Dream House.* He has 3 children, and his principal diversions, aside from the robots, are gardening, painting, and sailing.

PHOTOGRAPHS BY GEORGE DODGE FOR THE AMERICAN MAGAZINE

Reggie's robot

INTERESTING PEOPLE

From February issue of THE AMERICAN MAGAZINE

American Magazine piece by George Dodge (Feb 1949). Courtesy of Reginald Denny Collection.

Lt. Reginald Denny (Ret) in Royal Air Force uniform with RAF pilot during stay in England (1950).
Courtesy of Reginald Denny Collection.

Boarding Marine helicopter at Joint Civilian Orientation Conference (1952).
Courtesy of Reginald Denny Collection with photo credit to U.S. Army.

In flight demonstration stands at Joint Civilian Orientation Conference (1952). Courtesy of Reginald Denny Collection with photo credit to U.S. Army.

M.C. at U.S. Air Force Convention Long Beach (1956). Courtesy of Reginald Denny Collection with photo credit to Wm. W. Walker.

As Bombay Police Inspector with Robert Newton in *Around The World In Eighty Days* (1956).
Courtesy of Marc Wanamaker/Bison Archives.

As Dean with Viveca Lindfors, Jack Palance, Lee Remick, John Hudson, Peter Lorre, and
Keenan Wynn in "The Last Tycoon" teleplay of *Playhouse 90* (1957).
Courtesy of Reginald Denny Collection.

As George White with Polly Bergen, Silvia Sydney, Lili Gentle, Benay Venuta, Hoagy Carmichael, Robert Lowery, and Ronnie Burns in "The Helen Morgan Story" teleplay of *Playhouse 90* (1957). Courtesy of Reginald Denny Collection.

Bubbles' favorite publicity photo (1956). Courtesy of Reginald Denny Collection
with photo credit to Amos Carr Hollywood.

As Colonel Pickering with Julie Andrews, Prime Minister of Pakistan Huseyn Shaheed Suhrawardy,
and Rex Harrison on set of *My Fair Lady* at Mark Hellinger Theatre (July 25, 1957).
Courtesy of Getty Images.

As Colonel Pickering with Philippa Bevans, Edward Mulhare, and Sally Ann Howes in *My Fair Lady* (1958) at Mark Hellinger Theatre. Courtesy of Marc Wanamaker/Bison Archives.

With Charles Wilkes, Helen Christen, George Garman, Paul Tomaine, William Lipton and Jack Jason for U.S. Army and U.S. Air Force nationwide radio broadcast *Stars On Parade* episode of "Mickey and The Judge" by New York City Radio Station WMGM (1959). Courtesy of Reginald Denny Collection with photo credit to U.S. Army.

Sopwith Snipe reunion with Jack Canary and Reginald Denny Jr. at March AFB. (1961).
Courtesy of Reginald Denny Collection.

Restored Sopwith Snipe at U.S. Air Force Museum Wright Field, Dayton, Ohio (1961).
Courtesy of Reginald Denny Collection.

As Master Horner in *The Country Wife* at the Pasadena Playhouse (1961).
Courtesy of Reginald Denny Collection.

As Alfred P. Doolittle in *My Fair Lady* (1964) at the Valley Music Theater.
Courtesy of Everett Collection.

Bubbles and Reg at LAX boarding flight to England (1967). Courtesy of Reginald Denny Collection.

Reggie's star on the Hollywood Walk of Fame. Courtesy of Kimberly Pucci/
Reginald Denny Collection.

EPILOGUE

Dear Grandpa,

Thank you for teaching me to keep my eyes to the sky. I believed your stories then, and now the world will know they're true.

Eternally,
Your Little Princess

Appendix

RADIOPLANE BROCHURE 1945

NOTICE

This document contains information affecting the national defense of the United States within the meaning of the Espionage Act (U. S. C. 50:31:32). The transmission of this document or the revelation of its contents in any manner to an unauthorized person is prohibited.

RADIOPLANE COMPANY ❖ METROPOLITAN AIRPORT ❖ VAN NUYS ❖ CALIFORNIA

COPYRIGHT 1945 -- RADIOPLANE COMPANY

EARLY DEVELOPMENT ★ ★ ★

In 1935, after nearly five years of preliminary experiments Reginald Denny, in collaboration with N. Paul Whittier, designed and constructed a gas-driven model airplane that incorporated a semblance of radio control.

Their belief that it might be adapted to use as a military target stimulated Army interest. A test flight at Fort MacArthur before Army observers was of brief duration, but sufficient to result in the award of an experimental contract for three units. These were to become the first non mancarrying, radio-controlled aerial gunnery targets ever built. Specifications exceeded by far the accomplishments of the prototype, and indicated the need for extensive engineering to develop a target possessing positive response to radio control under all conditions, a catapult launching mechanism, and a parachute release permitting recovery of the target with a minimum of damage.

The association of Whitley C. Collins and Harold H. Powell was sought in creating the nucleus of a manufacturing organization which was expanded, after Army tests of the three experimental models, into the RADIOPLANE COMPANY, now located at Metropolitan Airport, Van Nuys, California.

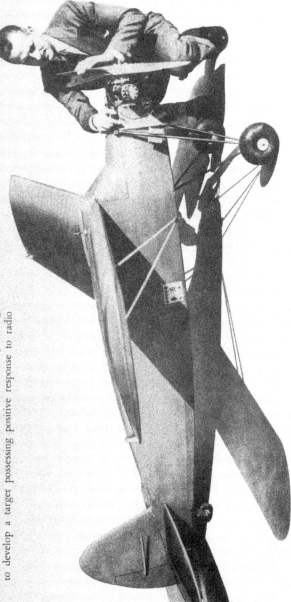

WHITLEY C. COLLINS
President

HAROLD H. POWELL
Executive Vice President

WILLIAM LARRABEE
General Manager-Treasurer

FERRIS M. SMITH
Vice President-Engineering

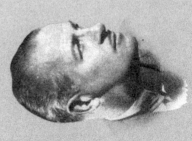

REGINALD DENNY
Secretary

RADIOPLANE ADMINISTRATION

WHITLEY C. COLLINS — Bachelor of Science degree in economics, University of Pennsylvania. Wharton School of Banking and Finance. Eight years with Continental Illinois National Bank and Trust Company, Chicago. General manager, treasurer and director of the original Lockheed Airplane Company. Vice-president and director of Elastic Stop Nut Corporation of America. Director of Menasco Manufacturing Company.

HAROLD H. POWELL — Degree in engineering from Sheffield Scientific School of Yale University. Engineer for General Electric Company and H. M. Byllesby Engineering and Management Corporation. One of the organizers of National Air Transport Company. Partner, Collins-Powell Company.

WILLIAM LARRABEE — Bachelor of Arts and Doctor of Jurisprudence degrees, University of Iowa. Fifteen years practice of law, Los Angeles, engaging primarily in corporate and banking fields.

FERRIS M. SMITH — Graduate aeronautical engineer, University of Michigan. Influential in the design and development of Douglas Aircraft Company's DC-1 DC-2 and DC-3 transport aircraft. Project engineer for the production of Lockheed Aircraft Corporation's XC-35 sub-stratosphere airplane and XP-38 "Lightning" interceptor pursuit.

REGINALD DENNY — With the R. A. F. during World War I. Sportsman pilot. Model manufacturer. President of Reginald Denny Industries, Inc.

120 MPH OPEN AIR WIND TUNNEL

Persistant ingenuity in RADIOPLANE COMPANY'S engineering research was evidenced when the company was confronted with its first, and rigid, Army specifications.

Solution of the problem of longitudinal balance was necessary to assure the stability of production models to come, but at the time when one was most needed, no wind tunnel was available for the controlled testing of an engineering model under simulated flight conditions.

RADIOPLANE engineers met the situation in a manner typical of American industry.

To the stripped-down chassis of a Packard V-12 limousine was attached a steel tube framework extending ahead of the automobile and terminating in supporting brackets for the mounting of the test model plane.

Racing over the table-smooth surface of Muroc Dry Lake, this "blue sky wind tunnel" subjected the model to true flying speeds up to 120 miles per hour, showing quickly the airplane's characteristics of balance.

Design changes to eliminate the balance "bug" were made

possible with a minimum expenditure of time. This was accomplished without trial-and-error crash losses of costly engineering models each of which represented a heavy investment in design and production manhours.

RADIOPLANE'S high standard of engineering resourcefulness was indicated by the creation of this apparatus. So successful was it in determining the sensitivity required in target controls that after testing the first three models, no further use of it was necessary.

★ DESIGN EVOLUTION ★

Development of the RADIOPLANE target is interesting from the standpoint of improvements realized through a succession of models perfected for use by both the Army and Navy. From the time of the completion of the first demonstration model bearing the manufacturer's designation "RP-1", the target has shown the result of aggressive work in the perfection of design, control, durability and ease of maintenance—all representing advancement in the target's military utility. Throughout the course of development RADIOPLANE COMPANY engineers had the benefit of close collaboration from the Special Weapons Branch of Wright Field's Equipment Laboratory and more recently from the Special Designs Section of the Navy Bureau of Aeronautics. Without the cooperation of those military engineering agencies, the design advancements would not have been possible.

A speed of approximately 50 mph was maximum for the prototype RP-1, a high-wing monoplane with a nine-foot wing span and conventional landing gear.

1939
MODEL RP-3
50 MPH

1940
MODEL RP-4
60 MPH

RP4
I

1942
ARMY OQ-2A
NAVY TDD-1
88 MPH

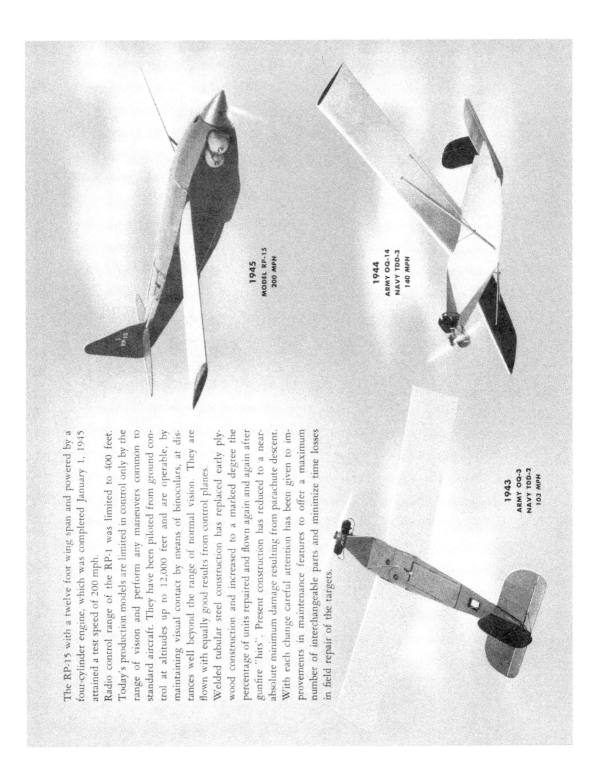

The RP-15 with a twelve foot wing span and powered by a four-cylinder engine, which was completed January 1, 1945 attained a test speed of 200 mph.

Radio control range of the RP-1 was limited to 400 feet. Today's production models are limited in control only by the range of vision and perform any maneuvers common to standard aircraft. They have been piloted from ground control at altitudes up to 12,000 feet and are operable, by maintaining visual contact by means of binoculars, at distances well beyond the range of normal vision. They are flown with equally good results from control planes.

Welded tubular steel construction has replaced early plywood construction and increased to a marked degree the percentage of units repaired and flown again and again after gunfire "hits". Present construction has reduced to a near-absolute minimum damage resulting from parachute descent. With each change careful attention has been given to improvements in maintenance features to offer a maximum number of interchangeable parts and minimize time losses in field repair of the targets.

1945
MODEL RP-15
200 MPH

1944
ARMY OQ-14
NAVY TDD-3
140 MPH

1943
ARMY OQ-3
NAVY TDD-2
103 MPH

PARACHUTE RELEASED!

The fact that the RADIOPLANE target had been developed and was in use by the Army Air Forces before Dunkirk, established the wartime importance that was to be attached to RADIOPLANE COMPANY.

When the United States was forced into the war, operational tests of early production models had proved their tactical usefulness. All that was necessary to obtain production, geared to the demands of extended combat training, was the physical expansion of the company's plant facilities. The bulk of engineering research already had been accomplished. Air warfare had gained such headway by the time Japan attacked Pearl Harbor that the benefits of training both surface and flying gun crews with "live" and lively targets were obvious to military authorities.

RADIOPLANES proved ideal in simulating every conceivable type of air attack, and the improvement of the morale of gunners as well as their accuracy was notable wherever they were used as training equipment.

It is probable that familiarization of gun crews with such actual conditions of air attack has resulted in the saving of thousands of lives.

RADIOPLANES have been used successfully in the training of gunners manning weapons ranging from the Garand rifle to 90mm. anti-aircraft guns employing unseen firing technique.

MORE ALLIED T...

ESCAPE FLAND

War May Engulf World, Says Roosevelt Defense Message

First Photo

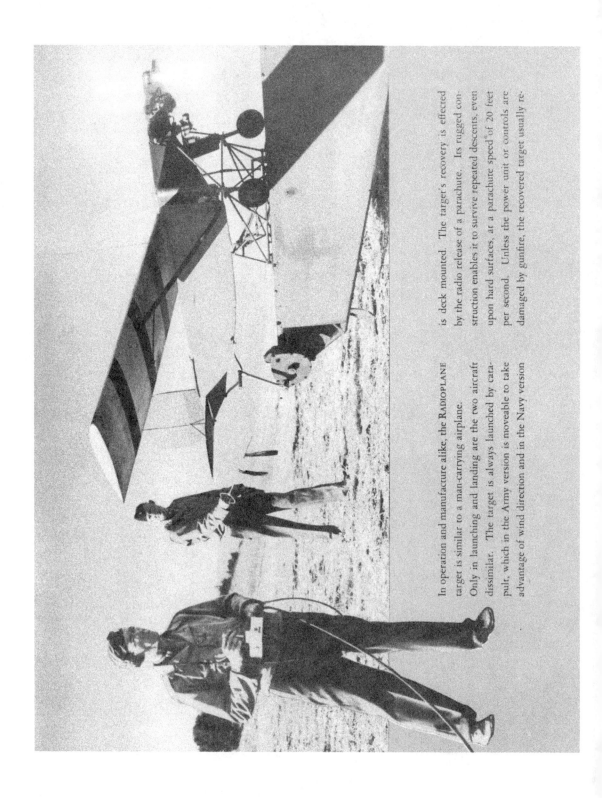

In operation and manufacture alike, the RADIOPLANE target is similar to a man-carrying airplane. Only in launching and landing are the two aircraft dissimilar. The target is always launched by catapult, which in the Army version is moveable to take advantage of wind direction and in the Navy version is deck mounted. The target's recovery is effected by the radio release of a parachute. Its rugged construction enables it to survive repeated descents, even upon hard surfaces, at a parachute speed* of 20 feet per second. Unless the power unit or controls are damaged by gunfire, the recovered target usually re-

quires only refueling and the installation of a freshly packed parachute to prepare it for another flight. As is the case in the manufacture of combat aircraft, target plane assembly has advanced from unit to mass production. At the Metropolitan Airport plant of RADIOPLANE COMPANY, production line methods are employed and full use is made of jigs and fixtures to insure both uniformity of the product and a minimum expenditure of manhours per unit. Noteable too, in the RADIOPLANE target, is the attention given to easy replacement of the parts and accessibility of engine, radio and servo control installations.

OFF ON ANOTHER MISSION

MISSION OVER—FLOATING TO EARTH   JEEP CREW RETRIEVING TARGET PLANE

LIKE BIG BROTHERS — BULLET DAMAGED TAIL DIRECT HIT THRU ENGINE — PLANE UNDAMAGED

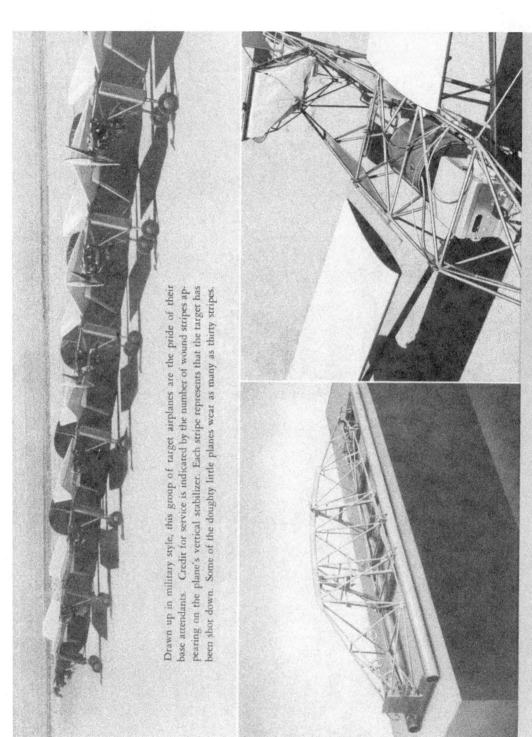

Drawn up in military style, this group of target airplanes are the pride of their base attendants. Credit for service is indicated by the number of wound stripes appearing on the plane's vertical stabilizer. Each stripe represents that the target has been shot down. Some of the doughty little planes wear as many as thirty stripes.

FIELD JIG—FOR ALIGNING DAMAGED FUSELAGE   RADIO, FUEL AND PARACHUTE INSTALLATION

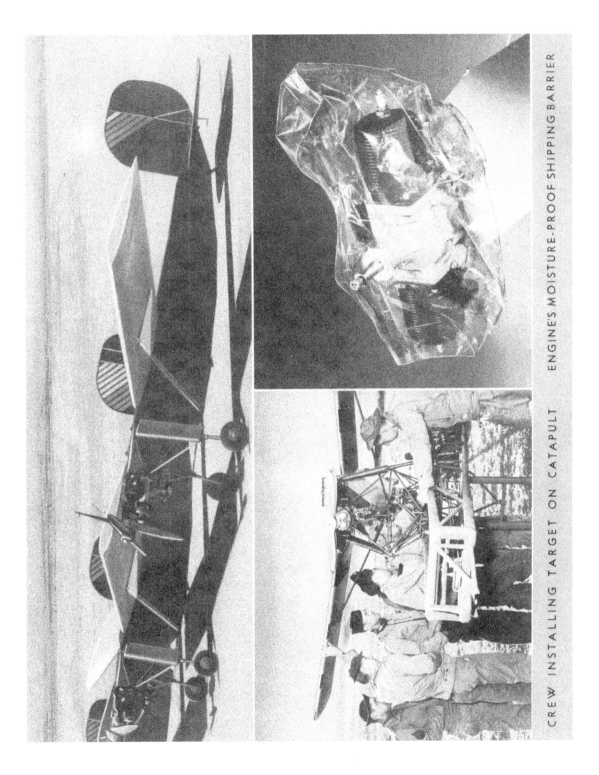

ENGINE'S MOISTURE-PROOF SHIPPING BARRIER

CREW INSTALLING TARGET ON CATAPULT

RADIOPLANE COMPANY is the owner of patent No. 2257277, covering radio-controlled parachute release mechanisms that give a distinctive measure of utility to the target. The 24-foot canopy is packed in the hatch in the upper portion of the fuselage between the wing and empennage. Its release mechanism is held in place by the radio transmitter carrier. If this carrier wave is interrupted intentionally by the "pilot" or by gunfire, the parachute is released instantly.

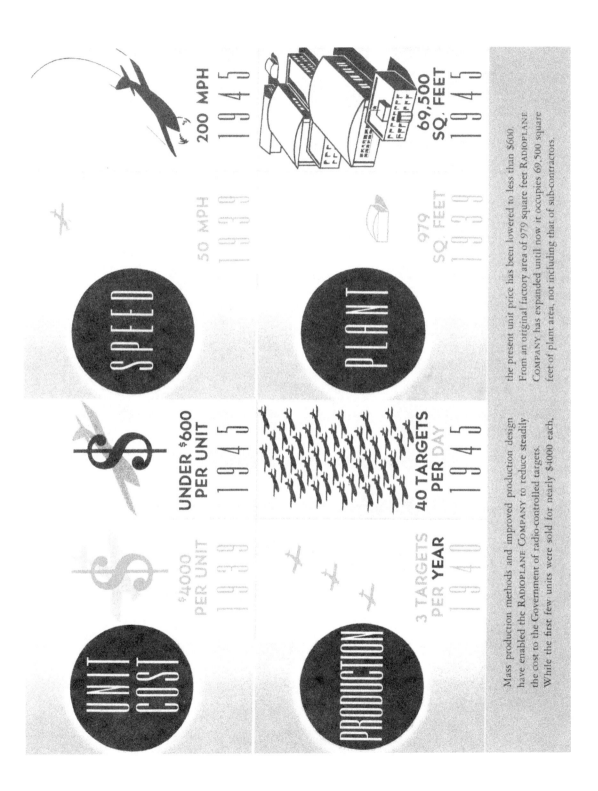

SPEED
200 MPH
1945
50 MPH
1939

PLANT
69,500 SQ. FEET
1945
979 SQ. FEET
1939

UNIT COST
UNDER $600 PER UNIT
1945
$4000 PER UNIT
1939

PRODUCTION
40 TARGETS PER DAY
1945
3 TARGETS PER YEAR
1940

Mass production methods and improved production design have enabled the RADIOPLANE COMPANY to reduce steadily the cost to the Government of radio-controlled targets. While the first few units were sold for nearly $4000 each, the present unit price has been lowered to less than $600. From an original factory area of 979 square feet RADIOPLANE COMPANY has expanded until now it occupies 69,500 square feet of plant area, not including that of sub-contractors.

PRODUCTION LINE WELDING METHODS

DEFT HANDS COVER FUSELAGE FRAMES

FABRIC CUTTING AND SEWING GROUP

LARGE AIRPLANE TECHNIQUES IN MINIATURE

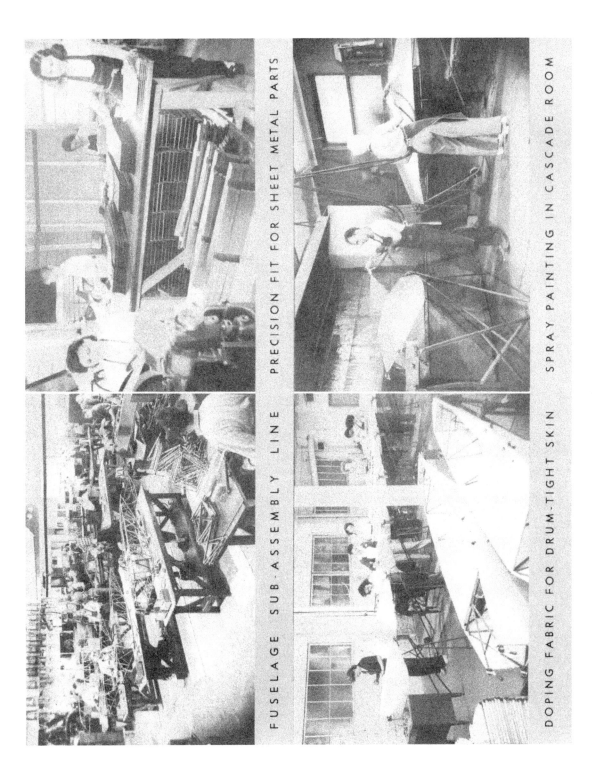

PRECISION FIT FOR SHEET METAL PARTS

SPRAY PAINTING IN CASCADE ROOM

FUSELAGE SUB-ASSEMBLY LINE

DOPING FABRIC FOR DRUM-TIGHT SKIN

FUSELAGE STORAGE PREPARATORY TO DELIVERY

"KEEP 'EM FLYING"—"SPARES" IS THE ANSWER

PARACHUTE-LIFE PRESERVER OF THE TARGET

CAREFUL INSPECTION—PERFECT PARTS ASSURED

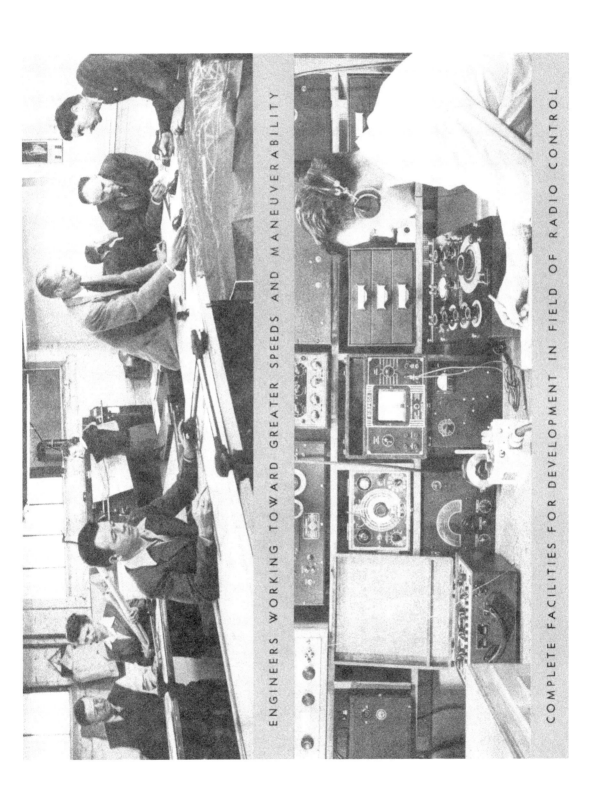

ENGINEERS WORKING TOWARD GREATER SPEEDS AND MANEUVERABILITY

COMPLETE FACILITIES FOR DEVELOPMENT IN FIELD OF RADIO CONTROL

Thousands of radio-controlled airplane targets built by RADIOPLANE COMPANY are being used for training purposes by the Army and Navy throughout the Unitel States and in all theaters of war.

RADIOPLANE'S present production at the rate of 40 units per day gives only a small indication of the extensive use of the target. A single target plane may be good for hundreds of runs over firing range during the period of its useful life.

Utilization of the device has gone well beyond the training of gunnery crews for defense against common attack maneuvers. Control of the target plane has proved so positive that it is being used to simulate every new maneuver observed in combat, with the result that gunners trained in repelling target planes are seldom at loss when under attack by an actual enemy.

RADIOPLANE COMPANY has aimed its ten years of engineering experience at producing a radio-controlled target that will match, in ratio to size, the performance of the most modern fighters. Its engineers are keeping abreast with these developments and are working today upon new experimental models offering greater speed and maneuverability.

There is ample indication, too, that experiments now being conducted by the armed services will require the production of specially designed RADIOPLANE equipment.

Today the expanding utility of the radio-controlled target is such that the Radioplane Company feels amply justified in its possession of manufacturing facilities which will permit an increase of at least 50 percent over current production.

★
★
★

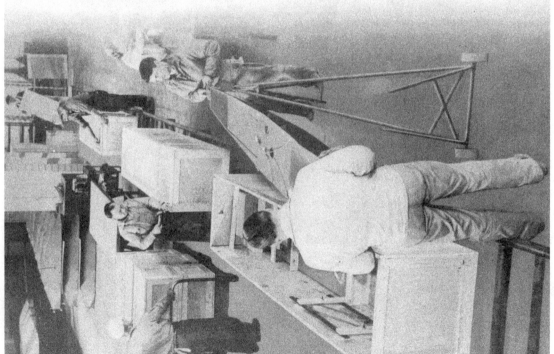

RADIOPLANE COMPANY
METROPOLITAN AIRPORT
Van Nuys, California

KEMMERRER INC. - LITHO ART - U.S.A.

Appendix

B

FLAREPLANE PATENT

April 28, 1953   R. L. DENNY   2,636,697

FLARE PLANE

Filed June 9, 1951   2 SHEETS—SHEET 1

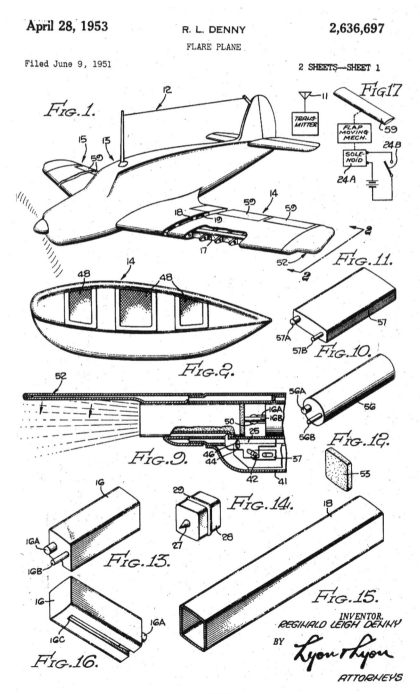

359

April 28, 1953

R. L. DENNY

FLARE PLANE

2,636,697

Filed June 9, 1951

2 SHEETS—SHEET 2

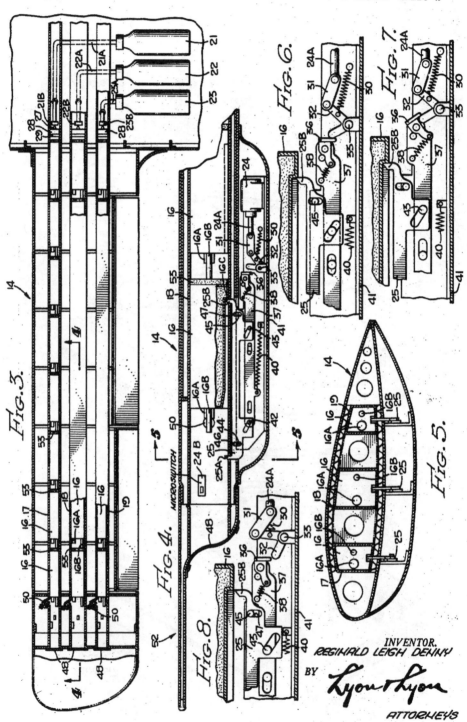

INVENTOR.
REGINALD LEIGH DENNY

BY

Lyon & Lyon

ATTORNEYS

Patented Apr. 28, 1953

2,636,697

UNITED STATES PATENT OFFICE

2,636,697

FLARE PLANE

Reginald Leigh Denny, North Hollywood, Calif.

Application June 9, 1951, Serial No. 230,756

10 Claims. (Cl. 244—1)

1

The present invention relates to an improved arrangement and technique for producing controlled illumination using flares disposed in a novel manner in radio controlled aircraft.

It is desirable, under certain conditions, to produce a controlled illuminating source located at an optimum distance from the area which is to be illuminated. Thus, in certain instances it may be desirable to illuminate effectively desired portions of a battlefield so as to observe infiltration movements of the enemy, and in naval warfare to illuminate selected portions of harbor or sea for purposes of observing enemy craft such as, for example, submarines.

Heretofore for these general purposes different techniques have been proposed, and the one commonly employed involves the idea of dropping flares from aircraft or shooting the flares from guns located on the ground. In such cases the flare is most effective when located a certain distance above the ground, but of course, due to its flight, the flare occupies its most effective position for a rather limited period of time. For that reason it has heretofore been proposed to slow up the speed of descent of the flare, as for example, by use of parachutes.

With the aforementioned prior art techniques and arrangements in mind, it is an object of the present invention to provide an improved arrangement and technique whereby the aforementioned desirable results may be obtained most effectively.

A specific object of the present invention is to provide an improved arrangement and technique which includes the use of an aircraft having flares mounted thereon, with provisions for burning the flare during its complete burning life while on the aircraft.

Another specific object of the present is to provide an improved arrangement of this type mentioned in the preceding paragraph associated with means for controlling the flight of the aircraft and for dispensing the different flares into burning position from a remote location while the aircraft is in flight.

Another specific object of the present invention is to provide an improved arrangement of this type in which a portion of the aircraft provides a reflector for the burning flare.

Another specific object of the present invention is to provide an improved arrangement of this character in which a novel wing structure is provided for storing the unburned flares, including associated means for dispensing successively the burned flares into a burning area.

2

Another specific object of the present invention is to provide an improved arrangement of this character which includes a plurality of hollow wing spars within which flares are stored and from which such flares are dispensed to an area adjacent the outer tips of the wing structure, such wing tips serving as reflectors for the burning flares.

Another specific object of the present invention is to provide an improved arrangement of this character in which a plurality of individual flares may be burned simultaneously to thereby provide a greater illumination intensity per unit weight of flare material.

The features of the present invention which are believed to be novel are set forth with particularity in the appended claims. This invention itself, both as to its organization and manner of operation, together with further objects and advantages thereof, may be best understood by reference to the following description taken in connection with the accompanying drawings in which:

Figure 1 represents a radio controlled system embodying features of the present invention;

Figure 2 is a view taken substantially in the direction indicated by the line 2—2 in Figure 1;

Figure 3 is a top plan view of one of the wing structures of the aircraft shown in Figure 1, with portions of the structure fragmented to disclose internal constructional features, it being noted that while the left wing is shown in Figure 3, the right wing is of identical construction as shown in this Figure 3;

Figure 4 is a sectional view taken substantially on the line 4—4 of Figure 3;

Figure 5 is a sectional view taken substantially on the line 5—5 of Figure 4;

Figures 6, 7 and 8 show in enlarged form a portion of the mechanism shown in Figure 4 but in different operating positions;

Figure 9 shows one of the flares in the position it assumes while burning;

Figure 10 is a perspective view showing in modified form an unburned flare;

Figure 11 shows another form which the flare may take;

Figure 12 is a perspective view showing one of the heat insulating elements used to separate the flares stored in the aircraft wing;

Figure 13 is a perspective view showing one of the unburned flares used in the aircraft wing shown in the previous figures;

Figure 14 is a perspective view showing the

2,636,697

3

gas seal puncturing element used in the arrangement shown in Figure 3;

Figure 15 is a perspective view showing the rectangular cross sectional features of the wing spars shown in Figure 5 for storing the individual flares;

Figure 16 is a perspective view showing the underside of the flare shown in Figure 13.

Figure 17 shows the manner in which the flap may be controlled by a solenoid.

The present invention contemplates the use of a radio controlled plane as shown in Figure 1, the radio controls for the plane being essentially conventional and forming, per se, no part of the present invention. The radio control system includes a ground based transmitter with antenna 11 for radiating five different types of signals for reception on the antenna system 12 of the plane 13. A pair of such signals is used conventionally to control up and down movement of the plane; a second pair of control signals provides so-called "left" and "right" flight control; while the fifth signal heretofore conventionally transmitted in a so-called "parachute" channel is used to control the flares which are stored in the wing structures 14, 15 of the plane.

The wing structures 14, 15 are essentially of identical construction, and for that reason a detailed description of the wing structure 14 suffices as a description for the other wing structure 15.

The wing structure 14 is designed not only for its normal useful purposes of providing lift and control for flight of the aircraft, but is designed, in accordance with the present invention, for storing a plurality of flares 16 which are burned in succession in an area in proximity to the wing tips.

For this purpose the wing 14, as shown in Figures 3 and 5, includes three hollow spars 17, 18, 19, each of different cross-sectional shape, for storing the series of correspondingly different shaped flares 16. The flare 16 in the center spar 18, as observed in Figure 5, is of greater cross-sectional area than the flares in the adjacent spars 17, 19, so that the intensity of illumination developed upon burning of the flare in the center tube or spar 18 is greater than that produced by the flares 16 in the tubes or spars 17, 19.

It will be observed, as seen from Figures 13 and 16, that each one of the flares 16 includes a fuse 16A and a mechanical spacing element 16B which is longer than the fuse 16A so as to provide some protection for the fuse or detonator 16A when the fuses are stored in position as shown in Figure 3.

Preferably, the flares 16 are ejected in succession under the influence of high pressure gas from a corresponding one of the pressure tanks 21, 22, 23 (Figure 3) upon operation of the mechanism shown in Figure 4, such mechanism normally serving to maintain the string of flares 16 in stored position but, upon actuation of the solenoid 24, allowing the escape of only one flare, i. e., the outermost flare 16, to a burning position shown in Figure 9.

With reference to Figure 4, the string of flares 16 in each tube or spar 17, 18, 19 is controlled by a separate mechanism of the character shown in this particular figure. This mechanism includes a vertically movable plate 25, having a pair of dogs or hooks 25A, 25B on opposite upper ends thereof, for engaging the outermost flare 16, so as to prevent its ejectment under the influence of the aforementioned pressure. This pressure developed by the pressure of the gas in tanks 21, 22,

4

23 is automatically made available for purposes of ejecting the flares when and as the string of flares 16 is originally stored in the corresponding tube or spar 17, 18, 19.

For this purpose each of the tanks 21, 22, and 23 is connected through suitable conduits 21A, 22A, 23A to a closure member 21B, 22B, 23B, each of such closure members having a frangible surface which may be punctured by the conical spike 27 on the member 28 (Figures 3 and 14). This member 28 is slidable in the corresponding tube or spar 17, 18, 19 and carries an annular gasket 29 which cooperates with the internal wall of such tubes or spars to provide a pressure-tight seal preventing the escape of gas. It is clear that when a sufficient number of flares 16 are loaded, the member 28 carrying the spike 27 punctures the frangible wall in the closure member 21B to automatically allow the escape of gas under pressure from the corresponding tank 21, 22, 23, as the case may be, such pressure acting to normally eject the flares outwardly; but the mechanism as mentioned previously with reference to Figure 4 prevents such ejectment.

More specifically, with reference to Figure 4, the dog 25B engages the shoulder 16C (Figures 4 and 16) to prevent dispensing or ejectment of the flare 16 from its normally stored position shown in Figure 4 to its burning position shown in Figure 9. Upon downward movement of the plate 25, by means described later, the dog 25B is no longer effective; however, subsequently, when the plate 25 moves upwardly to its normal position the other dog 25A engages the same shoulder 16A so as to maintain such flare 16 in its burning position. The mechanism for actuating the plate 25 is now described in detail.

As alluded to previously, the plate 25 is operated in accordance with signals transmitted over the conventional so-called "parachute" channel, such signal being continuously transmitted and the control apparatus being actuated upon interruption of such signal. Thus, the solenoid 24 in Figure 4 is shown in its normally energized position wherein its armature 24A is maintained in a retracted position against the action of the coil compression spring 30. Upon deenergization of the solenoid 24, i. e., upon interruption of the received control signal, the actuated parts assume in succession the positions shown in Figures 6, 8 and 7. It is observed that the armature 24A is pin connected to one end of a link 31 which has its other end pin connected to a bell crank 32. The bell crank 32 is pivoted on the axle 33 with a free end thereof adapted to engage and move the pivoted spring biased dog 36, such dog 36 being pivotally mounted on the horizontally moving plate 37. The dog 36 is normally maintained in its position shown in Figure 4 by the coil tension spring 38, having one of its ends connected to the pawl 36 and the other one of its ends connected to the plate 37. The plate 37 is normally biased to the right in Figure 4 by the coil tension spring 40, having one of its ends attached to the stationary wing portion 41 and the other one of its ends attached to the plate 37. A cam mechanism interconnects the horizontally movable plate 37 with the vertically movable plate 25, so that upon horizontal movement of the plate 37 the plate 25 moves vertically. For purposes of achieving this result the plate 37 is interconnected with the plate 25 through pins 42, 43, and the plate 25 is constrained to move vertically by the pins 44, 45 cooperating with the walls of the corresponding lost

2,636,697

5

motion slots 46, 47 in the plate 25. Thus, it is clear, upon deenergization of solenoid 24, the outermost flare 16 is allowed to move to its burning position and be arrested in such burning position shown in Figure 9.

Preferably, after the flares are stored and before burning, the outermost open ends of such tubes or spars 17, 18, 19 are closed by frangible, burnable material 48 for protection against weather and other elements. At the same time the solenoid 24 is actuated, i. e., deenergized, the flare igniting means 50 (Figure 3), which is preferably a spark plug, is energized for purposes of producing burning of the fuse or detonator 16A. Thus, initially the flare is lit while in the retracted position shown in Figure 4, and the resulting burning flare in its movement outwardly to its position shown in Figure 9 causes the barrier 48 to disappear, i. e., be burned or broken.

Another feature of the wing structures shown herein resides in the provision of a reflector for the burning flare. This reflector, having the general reference numeral 52, comprises the wing tips and is preferably of light reflecting material which likewise is capable of withstanding high temperatures. Preferably, the wing tips 52 are stainless steel.

Also preferably, to prevent heating of the flares which remain still unburned, small layers of heat insulating material 53 (Figures 3 and 12) are disposed between adjacent flares.

While the drawings show the flares and corresponding tubes or spars of square or rectangular cross section, the flares and corresponding spars may take the general shapes as indicated by the modified flares shown in Figures 10 and 11, Figure 10 showing a cylindrical flare 56 and Figure 11 showing a relatively flat flare 57, each having a corresponding detonator 56A, 57A and corresponding spacer 56B, 57B.

While the drawings show the use of gas pressure to urge the flares outwardly and to eject the same, it is clearly within the province of the present invention to provide other means for this purpose and, for example, springs either of the tension or compression type may be used for this purpose, i. e., of urging, moving and ejecting the flares.

Preferably, the aircraft shown in Figure 1 includes gyro stabilizers, thereby avoiding the use of ailerons. However, it is desired that the speed of the aircraft be relatively high so that it may be maneuvered into position quickly, but it is likewise desired to slow the flight of the aircraft while the flare is burning. For this purpose automatic means are provided for lowering the flaps 59 of the aircraft while the flare is burning. For that purpose a flap moving mechanism may be coupled to the solenoid armature 24A as shown in Figure 17. This automatic control of the flap, however, is optional although desired. The flap actuating mechanism is such that so long as a flare assumes a burning position shown in Figure 9, the flaps remain in a lowered position. To achieve this condition a microswitch controlling such flap moving mechanism may be disposed for engagement with a flare in its burning position. Thus, the flap moving mechanism may cause the speed of the plane to be reduced from 90 miles per hour to a speed of, for example, 50 miles per hour.

In operation of the arrangement the flares are first loaded in the hollow spars, a sufficient number being loaded so that the frangible diaphragm of the closure member 21B, 22B, 23B, as the

6

case may be, is broken to allow the escape of gas under pressure from the corresponding tank 21, 22, 23. Upon such loading, the plate 25 (Figure 4) is cammed downwardly but the dog 25B thereon prevents outward movement of the flares even when gas under pressure is liberated. Thus, in the loaded condition, the flares assume the position shown in Figures 3 and 4, and the openings to such flares or tubes may be closed by frangible burnable closure member 48. The plane is then placed in flight by conventional means and directed to an optimum distance above the area which is desired to be illuminated. When the aircraft is in the desired position the control signal transmitted from the transmitter 10 (Figure 1) is momentarily interrupted to cause deenergization of the solenoid 24 and energization of the spark plug 50, to in turn cause ignition of the flare. Upon deenergization of the solenoid 24 the flare moves from its normal retracted position shown in Figure 4 to its burning position shown in Figure 9, breaking and/or burning the frangible closure member 48 in its movement. In its burning position in Figure 9 the stainless steel wing tip 52, serving as a reflector, directs a concentrated beam of light downwardly. After the flare has burned, the burning time of each flare being for example 2 minutes, the control signal from the transmitter 10 is again momentarily interrupted, causing ejectment of the expended flare and ignition and movement of the adjacent flare into burning position. In the meantime, the aircraft is flying at a reduced speed of, for example, 50 miles per hour, since at this time the flare is in burning position, causing actuation of the flap moving mechanism to in turn cause the flaps to be lowered.

In general, the burning time of each flare is determined by the length of the flare, while the intensity of illumination, i. e., the candle power developed, is determined by the cross-sectional area of the flare. These two variables, i. e., the length and cross section, may assume different proportions and, as shown in the drawings, the flare 16 in the central tube 18 develops a greater amount of candle power than the flares in the outside tubes 17 and 19.

While the particular embodiments of the present invention have been shown and described, it will be obvious to those skilled in the art that changes and modifications may be made without departing from this invention in its broader aspects and, therefore, the aim in the appended claims is to cover all such changes and modifications as fall within the true spirit and scope of this invention.

I claim:

1. In an arrangement of the character described, an aircraft having a wing structure, said wing structure including a plurality of parallel extending open-ended hollow spars, the open ends of said hollow spars being adjacent and beneath the tip of said wing structure, at least one flare in each of said spars, and said tip serving as a reflector for the flare while burning.

2. In an arrangement of the character described, an aircraft having a wing structure, said wing structure including a plurality of parallel extending open-ended hollow tubes, the open ends of said hollow tubes being adjacent and beneath the tip of said wing structure, at least one flare in each of said tubes, said tip providing means which serve as a reflector for the flare while burning, means normally urging said flare outwardly toward said tip, and controllable latching

2,636,697

7

means preventing movement of said flare by said urging means.

3. In an arrangement of the character described, an aircraft having a wing structure, said wing structure including an open-ended hollow tube, the open end of said hollow tube being adjacent and beneath the tip of said wing structure, at least one flare in said tube, and said tip providing means which serve as a reflector for the flare while burning.

4. In an arrangement of the character described, an aircraft having a wing structure, said wing structure including a plurality of parallel extending open-ended hollow spars, said wing structure including a tip of light reflecting material disposed adjacent and above the open ends of said spars, a string of flares in each of said spars, means normally urging said string of flares outwardly towards the open ends of said spars, and controllable locking means for dispensing said flares in succession to a burning position adjacent the open ends of said spars.

5. In an arrangement of the character described, an aircraft having a wing structure, said wing structure including a plurality of parallel extending open-ended hollow tubes, said wing structure including a tip of light reflecting material disposed adjacent and above the open ends of said tubes, a string of flares in each of said tubes, means normally urging said string of flares outwardly towards the open ends of said tubes, and means for dispensing said flares in succession to a burning position adjacent the open ends of said tubes.

6. In an arrangement of the character described, an aircraft having a wing structure, said wing structure including at least one parallel extending open-ended hollow tube, said wing structure including a tip of light reflecting material disposed adjacent and above the open ends of said tube, a string of flares in said tube, and means for dispensing said flares in succession to a burning position adjacent the open end of said tube.

8

7. The arrangement in claim 6 in which said dispensing means includes radio controlled means.

8. The arrangement in claim 6 in which said aircraft includes at least one speed reducing member normally maintained in inoperative condition, and means rendering said speed reducing member effective upon actuation of said dispensing means.

9. In an arrangement of the character described, a radio controlled aircraft incorporating means for controlling the flight thereof from a ground position, said aircraft having a wing structure which includes at least one open-ended hollow tube extending longitudinally of said wing structure, said wing structure including a tip of light reflecting material disposed adjacent and above the open end of said tube, a string of flares in said tube, radio controlled means for dispensing said flares in succession to a burning position adjacent the open end of said tube, and radio controlled means for igniting said flares prior to movement to said burning position.

10. The arrangement set forth in claim 9 in which said aircraft includes at least one speed reducing member normally maintained in inoperative condition, and means rendering said speed reducing member effective upon actuation of said dispensing means.

REGINALD LEIGH DENNY.

References Cited in the file of this patent

UNITED STATES PATENTS

Number	Name	Date
1,304,314	Hill	May 20, 1919
2,019,652	Brookley	Nov. 5, 1935
2,381,332	Boldt	Aug. 7, 1945

FOREIGN PATENTS

Number	Country	Date
328,847	Italy	Aug. 22, 1935
445,813	France	Sept. 13, 1912
865,600	France	Mar. 3, 1941

Appendix
C FLAREPLANE PROPOSAL

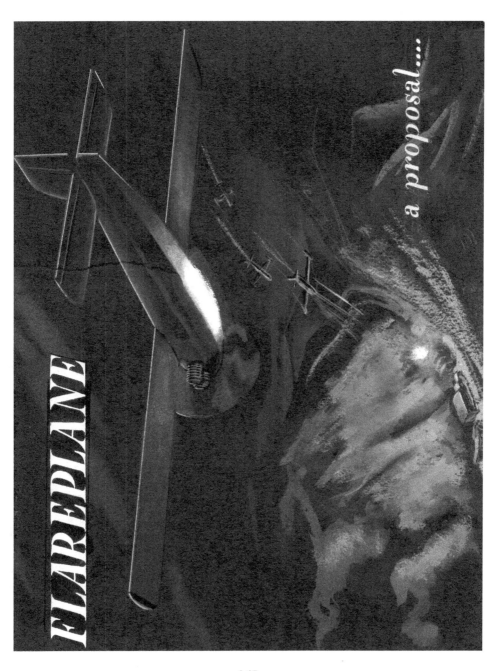

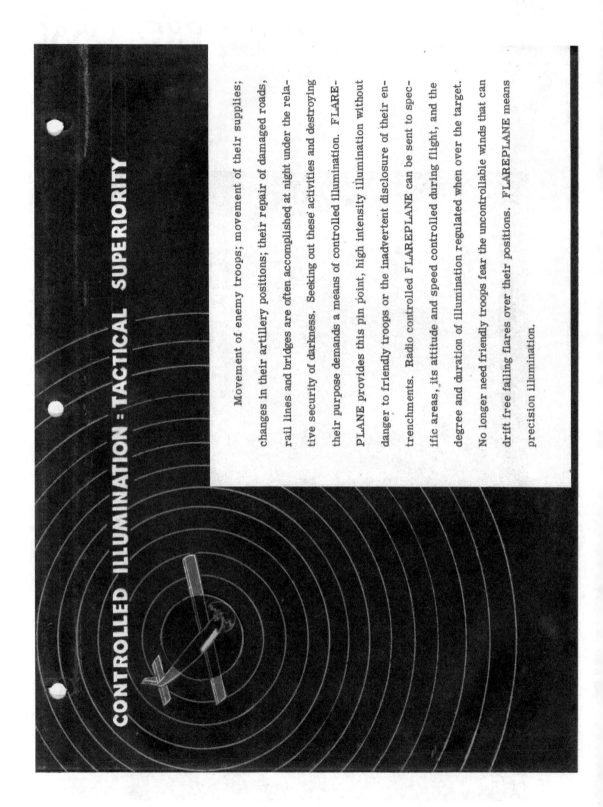

CONTROLLED ILLUMINATION = TACTICAL SUPERIORITY

Movement of enemy troops; movement of their supplies; changes in their artillery positions; their repair of damaged roads, rail lines and bridges are often accomplished at night under the relative security of darkness. Seeking out these activities and destroying their purpose demands a means of controlled illumination. FLARE-PLANE provides this pin point, high intensity illumination without danger to friendly troops or the inadvertent disclosure of their entrenchments. Radio controlled FLAREPLANE can be sent to specific areas, its attitude and speed controlled during flight, and the degree and duration of illumination regulated when over the target. No longer need friendly troops fear the uncontrollable winds that can drift free falling flares over their positions. FLAREPLANE means precision illumination.

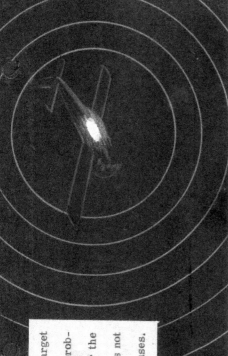

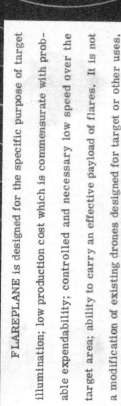

FLAREPLANE is designed for the specific purpose of target illumination; low production cost which is commensurate with probable expendability; controlled and necessary low speed over the target area; ability to carry an effective payload of flares. It is not a modification of existing drones designed for target or other uses.

Through one of its four radio control channels, the illumination intensity produced by FLAREPLANE over selected areas may be varied from 75,000 to 500,000 cp and the light duration from one to thirty minutes. CONTROLLED ILLUMINATION results in TACTICAL SUPERIORITY.

Utilizing existing and proven remote control mechanisms, FLAREPLANE can be radio controlled from a mother ship or command post position. Either radar or visual tracking by means of a small marker light may be employed for guidance. FLAREPLANE'S 100 mile flight range makes it effective over large areas. Control of long-range operations may be maintained by radio control relay stations on the perimeter or approaches to the target.

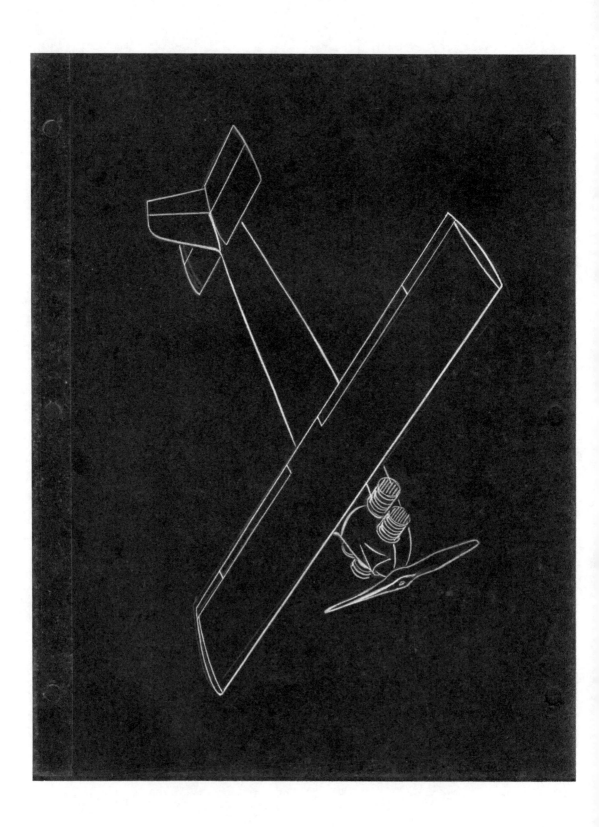

GENERAL ARRANGEMENT

AIR FRAME

FLAREPLANE will be a conventional, high wing, cantilever monoplane, designed to hold production costs at a minimum. The fuselage will be of monocoque or semi-monocoque construction utilizing moulded fiber-glass or plywood for the structure. Field erection of FLAREPLANE will be simplified by using a three or four point attaching method for the two piece wing and similar attaching methods for the components of the empennage section.

ENGINE

A two-cycle, four cylinder, air-cooled engine, developing 58 horsepower will provide power for FLAREPLANE and enable it to attain a maximum speed of 100 miles per hour enroute to target areas.

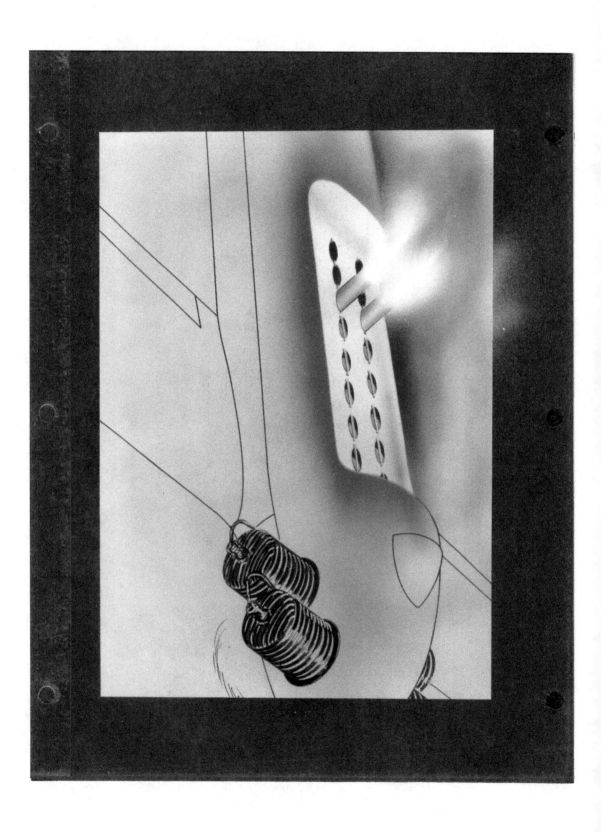

FLARES A flare package, installed in the fuselage aft of the fire-wall bulkhead, provides socket-type mounts to accommodate eight to twenty-four flares having a total weight of 144 pounds. Flares may be selected and ignited singly or in combinations through one of the four radio control channels. Aft mounted flares are ignited first to prevent pre-ignition of the remaining flares. A fuseable link which retains the flare candles in their sockets burns away when flares are ignited and allows the candle to drop downward to the burning position. The concave surface of the flare package serves as a reflector, thereby increasing effective illumination of the target area.

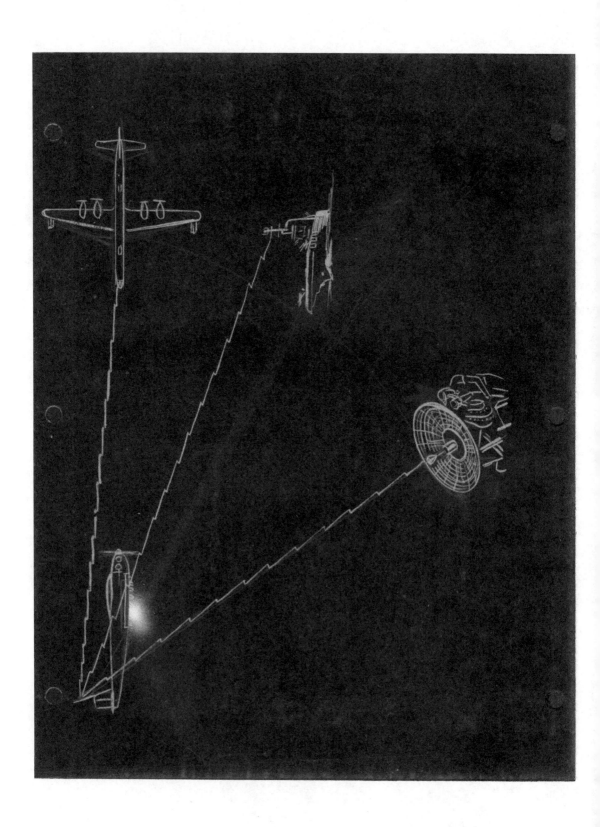

CONTROL   FLAREPLANE is radio controlled through four channels. A separate channel is provided for throttle-flap control, aileron-rudder control, elevator control and flare selection-ignition control. Flight is gyro stabilized and FLARE-PLANE will maintain a given roll or pitch attitude until a subsequent command is received through the radio receiver-selector. Servo control of aileron, rudder and elevator movement is integrated to provide flat turns when FLAREPLANE is maneuvered over the target area. FLAREPLANE may also be throttled back by radio control from its 100 miles per hour maximum speed to 40 miles per hour cruising speed when over the target area. Automatic lowering of flaps at low cruising speeds may be provided to obtain better control and stall characteristics for increased low speed flight stability.

PITOT TUBE

A unique arrangement which uses pitot tube pressure may be used to prevent stall conditions when operating at cruising speed. A pressure relay switch and throttle servo is connected to the pitot tube. When pitot tube pressure indications sense airspeed near stalling speed, the switch and throttle servo would be engaged to advance the throttle and prevent stalling. This sensitive device will compensate for sudden changes in pitch attitude and the resultant possibility of stalling caused by shell or missile bursts.

LAUNCH-ING

FLAREPLANE may be launched from a mother ship, from a ground catapult utilizing rocket power for the take-off, or from rotary launching facilities. Launching techniques are similar to those used for existing drones.

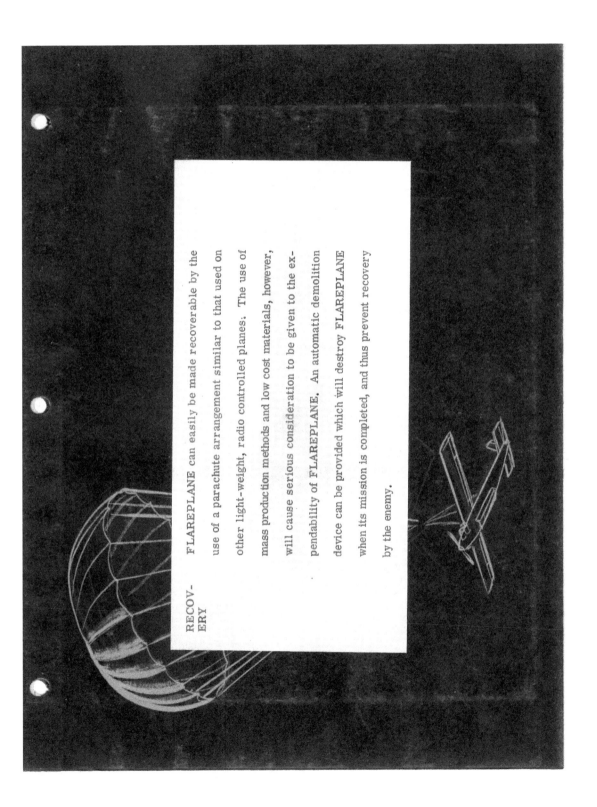

RECOV-
ERY

FLAREPLANE can easily be made recoverable by the use of a parachute arrangement similar to that used on other light-weight, radio controlled planes. The use of mass production methods and low cost materials, however, will cause serious consideration to be given to the expendability of FLAREPLANE. An automatic demolition device can be provided which will destroy FLAREPLANE when its mission is completed, and thus prevent recovery by the enemy.

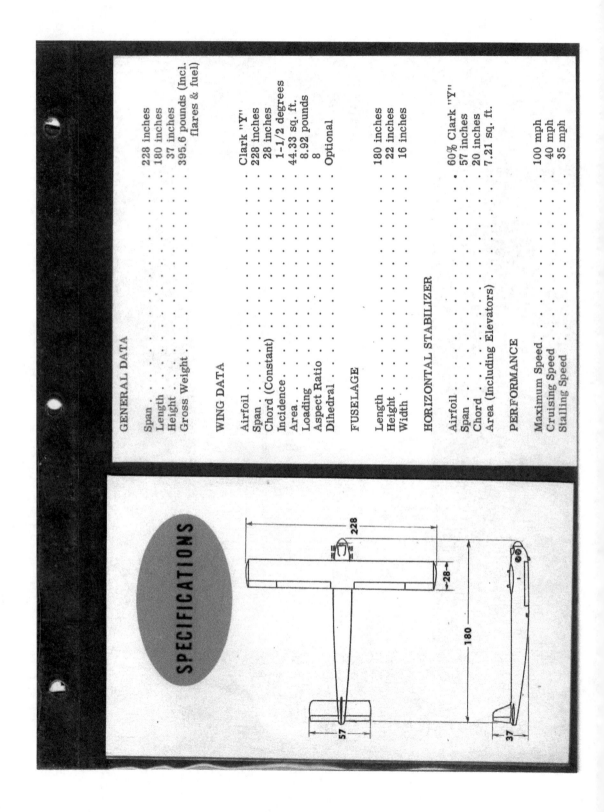

SPECIFICATIONS

GENERAL DATA

Span	228 inches
Length	180 inches
Height	37 inches
Gross Weight	395.6 pounds (Incl. flares & fuel)

WING DATA

Airfoil	Clark "Y"
Span	228 inches
Chord (Constant)	28 inches
Incidence	1-1/2 degrees
Area	44.33 sq. ft.
Loading	8.92 pounds
Aspect Ratio	8
Dihedral	Optional

FUSELAGE

Length	180 inches
Height	22 inches
Width	16 inches

HORIZONTAL STABILIZER

Airfoil	60% Clark "Y"
Span	57 inches
Chord	20 inches
Area (Including Elevators)	7.21 sq. ft.

PERFORMANCE

Maximum Speed	100 mph
Cruising Speed	40 mph
Stalling Speed	35 mph

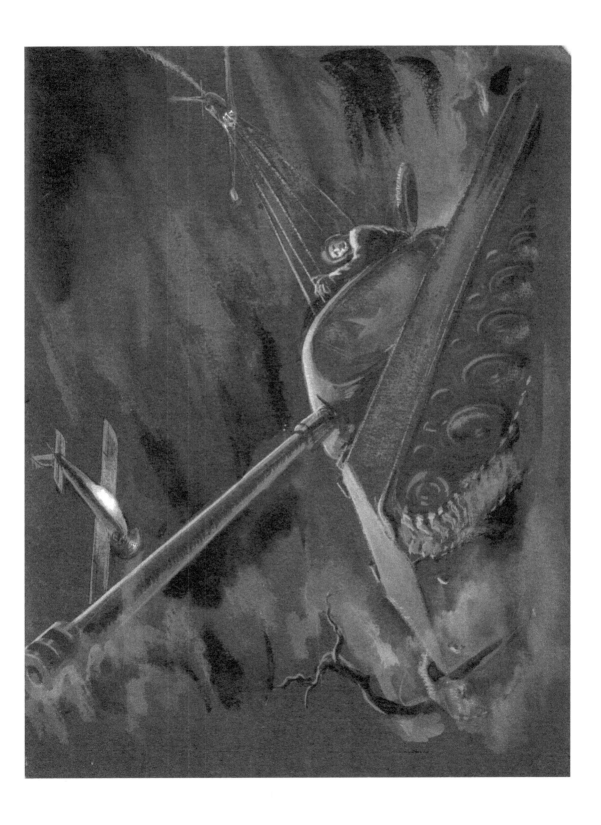

BIBLIOGRAPHY

Armstrong, Alice Catt, *Who's Who in Los Angeles County 1950-1951*, Who's Who Historical Society, Los Angeles, California, 1950

Botzum, Richard A., *50 Years of Target Drone Aircraft*, Northrop Corporation, 1985

Brownlow, Kevin, *The Parade's Gone By ...*, University of California Press, 1968

Denny, Reginald, *Autobiography,* Reginald Denny, 1966, *Correspondence, Journals, Letters, Screenplays, and Statements,* 1913-1967

Eames, John Douglas, *The MGM Story: The Complete History of Fifty Roaring Years*, Crown Publishers, 1985

Eames, John Douglas and Abele, Robert, *The Paramount Story*, Simon & Schuster, 1985, 2002 by Paramount Pictures Corporation

Higham, Charles, *Bette: The Life of Bette Davis*, Dell Publishing, 1981

Hirschhorn, Clive, *The Columbia Story*, Hamlyn, 2001

Hirschhorn, Clive, *The Universal Story*, Octopus Books Limited, 1983

Hirschhorn, Clive, *The Warner Bros. Story*, Crown Publishers, 1979

Hurlburt, Roger, *Monroe: An Exhibit of the Early Days of Marilyn Monroe—Before She Became A Legend—Brings The Star's History in Focus, South Florida Sun Sentinel*, Jan 6, 1991

Jewel, Richard B., *The RKO Story*, Arlington House, 1985

Naughton, Dr. Russell, *Hargrave Aviation and Aeromodelling Interdependent Evolutions and Histories, The Pioneers: Fathers of Today's UAV Industry*, Monash University Australia, www.ctie.monash.edu.au/hargrave/denny, 2005

Newcombe, Laurence R "Nuke," *Unmanned Aviation: A Brief History of Unmanned Aerial Vehicles*, American Institute of Aeronautics and Astronautics, Inc., 2004

Orriss, Bruce W., *When Hollywood Ruled the Skies*, Aero Associates, 2013

Sims, George R. *Living London, Vol. III*, Cassell and Company, Limited, London, Paris, New York & Melbourne, 1903

Solomon, Aubrey and Thomas, Tony, *The Films of 20th Century-Fox*, Citadel Press, 1989

Witwer, H.C., *The Leather Pushers*, Grosset & Dunlap, 1921

Magazines 1920 - 1967: *Universal Weekly, Life, Picture Play, Photoplay, Motion Picture Magazine, Movie Weekly, Screenland, The Film Daily, Model Aviation, Model Airplane News, Air and Space Magazine, American Magazine, Flying Magazine*

Newspapers 1899-1989: *Los Angeles Herald Examiner, Los Angeles Times, Hollywood Variety, Hollywood Reporter, Los Angeles Herald Express, The New York Times, Variety, Citizen-News, San Bernardino Sun, The Evening Herald and Express, The Times, News Chronicle of Thousand Oaks, The Harvard Advocate, Birmingham Mail, Birmingham Gazette, Birmingham Post, Bolton News, Bristol News, Cinema, Daily Mail, Daily News, Daily Chronicle, Daily Herald, Daily Sketch, Daily Express, Daily Film Renter, Daily Mirror, Daily Telegraph, Evening News, Eastern Press, Film Renter, Glasgow Citizen, Glasgow Evening Times, Illustrated Sun, Liverpool Echo, Liverpool Post, Lloyds Weekly News, Leeds Mercury, Manchester Evening News, Manchester Dispatch, Middlesex Times, Morning Post, Nottingham Evening Post, Northern Echo, Newcastle Chronicle, Newcastle Journal, People, Picturegoers, Paisley Express, Southern Daily Echo, Star (London), Sphere, Sunday Express, South Wales Express, Shields News, Sheffield Independent, Scotsman, Westminster Gazette, Weekly Scotsman, World's Fair, Worcester Times, Yorkshire Evening News, Yorkshire Post*

Northrop Grumman Corporation, www.northropgrumman.com, 2019

Canada Aviation and Space Museum, https://ingeniumcanada.org/aviation/collection-research/artifact-sopwith-7f-1-snipe.php, 2019

Academy of Model Aeronautics (AMA), www.modelaircraft.org, 2019

California Hobby Distributors, www.calhobbydist.com/history, 2019

Internet Movie Data Base, www.IMDB.com, 2019

INDEX

#

39 East 24

A

A Bedtime Story 167
A Dark Lantern 24, 67
A Lady's Morals 155
A Royal Family 5, 6, 62
Abbott and Costello Meet Dr. Jekyll and Mr. Hyde 255
Abbott, George 16
Abysmal Brute, The 30, 31, 32, 38, 89, 90
Academy Awards 148, 163, 170, 171, 175, 196, 239, 246, 261, 273, 277
Academy of Model Aeronautics (AMA) 166
Actor's Equity Strike 22, 23
Actor's Orphanage 8
Adelphi Hotel 132
Adelphi Theatre 9
Adventures in Paradise 268, 269
Air Adventures of Jimmie Allen, The 166
Albertini, Bill 230
Albertini, Gerry 251
Alcazar Theatre 16, 157, 244
Alhambra Theatre 148
Alias Mike Hercules 261
All Men Are Alike 240, 306, 307
All Quiet on the Western Front 159
All Women Have Secrets 238
Allen, Frederick Lewis 159
Allen, Judith 160

Anderson, Will 52
Andrews, Julie 262, 263, 273, 277, 323
Angel, Heather 176, 295
Angelus Productions 158
Angelus, The 25
Anna Karenina 173, 228
Apfel, Oscar 23, 25, 176
Apollo space program 270, 271
Appointment for Love 240
Arden, Doris 163
Arliss, George 16, 24
Army Aeronautical Museum 179
Arnold, Edward 158, 173, 241, 308
Around the World in 80 Days 261, 279, 319
Arrest Bulldog Drummond 180
Arthur, Jean 175
Ascot Speedway 34, 37
Asher, Irving 167, 168
Assault on a Queen 274
Astor, Gertrude 29, 53, 54
Astor, Mary 25, 34, 35, 259
Ayres, Lew 173

B

Baby Peggy 33, 137
Bad Sister, The 151
Baggot, King 29
Bandmann Opera Company 11, 12
Bandmann, Maurice 11
Barbarian, The 158, 218

Barker, Major William George 19

Barnes, Eleanor 52

Barnes, George 298

Barnes, Mrs. 10, 15, 49, 263

Barrie, J. M. 8, 16

Barrie, Mona 309

Barrow, Tracy 24

Barrymore, John 24, 27, 34, 157, 161, 175, 176, 180, 233, 234, 241

Bartholomew, Freddie 166

Batman 274

Batman: The Movie 274

Baxter, Warren 241

Be Yourself 139

Beach, Mayor Albert 49

Beal, John 171

Beau Brummel 34

Beerbohm Tree, Sir Herbert 6, 168

Beery, Wallace 155

Beg, Borrow or Steal 176

Beggar Maid, The 25

Bellamy, George 5, 132

Bellamy, Ralph 176

Benjamin, Joe 35

Bennett, Joan 174, 248

Bennett, Richard 16

Bergen, Polly 262, 321

Berle, Milton 241

Bevans, Philippa 324

Beverly Hills Hotel 29, 32

Big Bluff, The 158, 160, 163

Biggers, Earl Derr 32

Billion Dollar Baby 269

Biltmore Theatre 236, 239, 297

Binney, Constance 24

Birth of a Nation, The 146

Blache, Herbert 25

Black Cats, The 42, 43, 44, 55, 104, 105, 149

Blackley Palaise-de-Danse Theatre 131

Blackstone Theatre 21

Blake, Judge Samuel R. 147

Blandy, Admiral William H. P. 242

Blessed Event 157

Blithe Spirit 244, 245, 309

Blockade 179

Blue Bird, The 10

Bob Hope Presents the Chrysler Theatre 274

Bogart, Humphrey 151

Boles, John 159, 160

Bond, Lilian 306

Booth Theatre 17, 65

Booth, John Hunter 48

Boris, M. I. 118, 119

Borum, Major F. M. 178

Bosworth, Hobart 235

Boucicault, Dion 5, 6

Bow, Clara 33

Boyer, Charles 240

Bradley, David 273

Brady, Alice 24, 67

Braham, Lionel 47

Brahm, John 248

Brennan, Walter 148

Brent, George 175

Brian, Mary 159

Brick, Elizabeth 10

Bringing Up Betty 23

Brisbane, Walter 234

Brisson, Carl 132

Broad, Captain Hubert 133, 185

Broadhurst, George 46

Broadway Melody, The 154

Brown, Clarence 173

Brown, Melville 39, 46, 56, 57, 58, 61

Browne, K. R. G. 53

Brownlow, Kevin 136, 273

Bruce, Nigel 161, 241, 255

Bryson, James 26, 128, 129, 131, 182

Buck, Frank 176

Bulldog Drummond 176, 291, 295, 296

Bulldog Drummond Comes Back 176

Bulldog Drummond Escapes 176

Bulldog Drummond in Africa 180

Bulldog Drummond's Bride 180

Bulldog Drummond's Peril 176

Bulldog Drummond's Revenge 176

Bulldog Drummond's Secret Police 180

Burdett Airport 42, 104

Bureau of Aeronautics (BuAer) 264, 265
Bureau of Naval Weapons (BuWeps) 265
Bureau of Ordinance (BuOrd) 265
Burke, Billie 158, 159, 160, 166, 169, 240
Burne-Jones, Edward 25
Burns, Ronnie 321
Bush, James 229

C
Caddo Field 149
Cagney, James 240
California Hobby Distributors 267
California Straight Ahead 37, 38, 41
Campbell, Louise 176
Canada Aviation and Space Museum 274, 275
Canary, Jack 268, 269, 275, 326
Candida 269
Capitol Theatre 35, 36
Captain Brassbound's Conversion 269
Captain of the Clouds 240
Carey Players, The 15
Carmichael, Hoagy 262, 321
Carroll, Madeleine 161, 179, 240
Carthay Circle Theatre 175
Case, Kenneth "Kenny" 174, 175, 176, 177, 179, 236, 237, 300
Cashel Byron's Profession 130, 132, 140, 167
Cat Ballou 274, 277
Cavalcade of America 255
Cavalcade of Stars Show 253
Chadwick, Cyril 158
Chandler, Harry 30
Chaney, Lon Jr. 248, 268
Chaplin, Charlie 45
Charley's Aunt 14
Cheerful Fraud, The 53, 54, 123, 132
Chevalier, Maurice 167
Chickasha Bone Crusher, The 30, 80
Christen, Helen 325
Chute, Margaret 49, 51
Cinderella Man, The 16
Circle Theatre 35
Claire, Ina 10

Clark, Bobby 240, 307
Clayton, Ethel 24, 69
Clear the Decks 147, 148, 191
Clifford, Ruth 25, 26, 71
Climax! 261
Cline, Edward "Eddie" F. 148
Clover Field 42, 46, 55, 133, 134, 149, 166
Cobham, Sir Alan 138, 132
Cockney Kid, The 167
Cocktail Party 253
Colbert, Claudette 170
Colgate Comedy Hour 258
Colling, Bill 39
Collins, Whitley 236, 237, 238, 239, 242, 243, 247, 248, 249, 250, 254, 259, 260, 265, 270
Colman, Ronald 43, 261
Colonial Theatre 60
Colony Theatre 37, 39, 47, 49, 135, 145
Columbia Pictures 159, 175, 176, 241
Columbia Theatre 35, 95
Columbia, The Gem, and the Ocean 88
Compassionate Troubles 151
Connelly, Edward 217
Connolly, Walter 290
Conover, David 245, 246
Coogan, Jackie 137
Cook, Donald 159
Coolidge, President Calvin 51
Cooper, Jackie 166
Cooper, Melville 268
Cooper, Merian 157, 159
Coote, Robert 262, 263
Cornelius Griffin 16
Corning, John P. 37
Cotten, Joseph 246
Country Wife, The 269, 328
Court Theatre 6
Coward, Noel 244
Crabbe, Larry 169
Craft, William James 148, 151
Craig, James 255
Crane, James 24, 67
Crawford, Joan 173, 227

Creed, Roger 268
Crime Doctor's Strangest Case, The 241
Crisp, Donald 157
Criterion Theatre 6, 16
Crittenden, T. D. 94
Cromwell, John 161, 170
Crone, George, 154
Crowley, Pat 274
Cukor, George 173, 175, 234
Cummings, Constance 173
Cummings, Robert 238, 254
Cunningham, Earl 60
Curtiz, Michael 240

D
D'Orsay, Fifi 155
Dancing Man 160, 163
Dangerous Age, The 21
Davidson, Captain J. W. 242, 243
Davies, Marion 138
Davis, Bette 151, 161, 162, 170, 220, 277
Davis, Elmer 35
Dawn, Hazel 15
Day, Alice 146, 190
Day, Laraine 248
De Havilland Aircraft Company 133, 183, 184
Declaration of Independence 50, 51
Del Monte Racetrack 56
Del Rio, Dolores 142
Dell, Claudia 158, 173, 175, 221, 229
Dembow, Sam Jr. 54
DeMille, Cecil B. 154, 155
Denny Jr. model plane 166, 178
Denny, Barbara 30, 41, 46, 58, 59, 61, 102, 110, 127, 132, 138, 141, 167, 168, 169, 170, 173, 230, 238, 249, 280
Denny, Bubbles 138, 141, 142, 143, 147, 149, 150, 152, 154, 155, 156, 158, 160, 161, 162, 164, 165, 167, 168, 169, 174, 179, 192, 193, 197, 199, 201, 202, 206, 221, 231, 243, 244, 249, 250, 252, 255, 262, 262, 263, 265, 267, 271, 272, 274, 278, 279, 280, 281, 330

Denny, Deborah 176, 244, 249, 263
Denny, Diane 280, 285
Denny, Joan 160, 179, 231, 244, 249, 262, 267, 272, 280
Denny, Reginald Jr. 155, 156, 157, 164, 165, 176, 177, 179, 231, 243, 251, 252, 254, 262, 267, 280, 285, 291, 326
Denny, W. H. 5, 6, 9, 10, 64
Dennymite 166, 171
Dennyplane 171, 174, 225, 226
Dennywheels 166
Desmond, William 109
Dickson, Dorothy 24
Dieterle, William 179, 246
Dietrich, Marlene 238
Dillon, Franc 168
Disney, Walt 155
Disraeli 24
Dodge, George 249, 314
Don Coyote 86
Don Juan in Hell 259
Dougherty, James 245
Douglas, Melvyn 160
Dow's Hour of Great Mysteries 268
Dr. Jekyll and Mr. Hyde 24, 255
Dracula 155, 158
Du Maurier, Daphne 236
Dugmore, Georgina Pike 5, 6, 63
Dugmore, Nora 6, 16, 61, 127, 128, 132, 167, 168, 173, 230, 238, 240, 251, 278
Duke of York's Theatre 8, 9
DuPont Show of the Month 268
Durbin, Deanna 238
Durfee, Minta 274
Duryea, Dan 255
Duval, Lorayne 148, 194
Dvorak, Jeraldine 307
Dwyer, Ruth 32, 93

E
Ed Sullivan Show, The 272
Eddie Cantor Comedy Theatre 258
Edwards Air Force Base 236
El Capitan Theatre 157

Electrozone 58
Elliot, T. S. 253
Elliott, Gertrude 6
Embarrassing Moments 151, 152, 204
Ephraim, Lee 240
Erwin Wilson, Secretary of Defense Charles 255
Erwin, Stuart 217
Escape Me Never 248
Escape to Burma 258
Essanay Studios 24
European Motion Picture Company 128, 130, 132, 181, 182
Evans, Michael 272
Everybody's Baby 180
Experience 24
Eyes in the Night 241, 308

F
Fahrney, Admiral and Captain D. S. 239, 240, 247, 264, 265
Fairbanks, Douglas 129, 148, 155, 214
Famous Players Film Company 15, 16
Famous Players Lasky Company 24, 25
Farmers and Merchants Delegation 311
Fast and Furious 57, 58, 59, 60, 124, 125, 132
Fast Worker, The 33, 94
Fears, Peggy 173
Fejos, Paul 145, 146
Fellowes, Rockcliffe 24
Ferguson, Elsie 24, 70
Ferrin, Frank 258
Ferry, Norman 109
Fildes, Harry 131
Film Booking Offices of America 26
Findlay, Hal 207
Fireside Theatre 255
First Mrs. Fraser, The 249
First National Pictures 130
Fischer, Margarita 31
Fitzmaurice, George 24
Fitzroy, Emily 53, 107
Flareplane 252, 255, 256, 257, 258, 259, 261
Flirt, The 151

Florence Theater 36
Florey, Robert 174
Flynn, Errol 248
Fog 159, 160
Following Ann 53
Fonda, Henry 179
Fonda, Jane 274
Fontaine, Joan 236, 268, 298, 299
Footlights 24, 70
Ford Television Theatre 255
Ford, Edsel 106
Ford, Hugh 15, 24
Ford, John 159, 161, 163, 179
Ford, Wallace 159, 219
Forde, Eugene J 241
Fort MacArthur 175
Fort Vengeance 255
Fort, Garrett 159
Forum Theatre 37, 38
Foster, Preston 241
Four Men and a Prayer 179, 294
Fox, Sidney 151
Frankenstein 158
Franklin, Chester 157
Franklin, Edgar 39
Franklin, Sidney 155, 214
Fraser, Harry L. 176
Freulich, Roman 121, 213
Friars Club 23
Friend Martha 17, 65
Frohman, Charles 8, 9
Frye, Jack 42
Fugitive Lovers 161

G
Gable, Clark 170
Galsworthy, John 9, 167, 170
Garbo, Greta 151, 173, 228
Garman, George 325
Gates, Harvey 153
Gay, Maisie 50
Gaynor, Janet 274
Gebhart, Myrtle 139, 154
Gentle, Lili 321

Gentlemen: The King! 11
George Burns and Gracie Allen Show, The 255
Georgie 59, 141, 157, 179
Gerrard, Charles 53
Gest Morris 22, 49, 50, 155
Gibson, Hoot 29, 43, 109, 167
Gilbert, Joanne 255
Gilbert, W.S. 5
Gillaspey, A. Fulton 146
Gipsy Love 11
Gleason, Jimmy 217
Goddard, Paulette 268
Goebel, Arthur 42, 55, 104
Golden Gate Theatre 163
Goldwyn, Samuel 248
Gondoliers, The 5
Good Morning, Judge 141
Goodrich, Jack 32
Goodrich, Major Dan 238, 239
Gordon, Huntley 71
Goss, Gregory 60
Granby Cinema 131
Grant, Cary 248, 277, 279, 313
Great Catherine 16
Great Gambini, The 176
Great Millionaire, The 8
Greeley, Evelyn 23
Green, Alfred E. 173, 176
Greene, Major 178
Greenwald, Sam 42, 104
Greenwood, Charlotte 155
Griffith, Edward H. 173, 240
Grumman, Roy 285
Guillow, Paul 164
Gulick, Paul 56
Gulliver, Dorothy 141
Gulliver's Travels 45

H
Hains, Frank 263
Haisman, Irene "Rene" 11, 12, 13, 14, 15, 21,
      22, 30, 41, 46, 54, 58, 61, 102, 110,
      127, 132, 137, 138, 156, 168, 182,
      252

Hale, Alan 159, 161, 179
Hale, Randy 272
Hale, Wanda 169
Hamlet 157, 159
Hangover Murders 173
Harding, Ann 308
Harlan, Otis 34, 39, 46, 47, 53, 54, 107, 108,
      141, 147, 148, 194
Harland-Edgecumbe, F. W. 130, 132, 133, 183
Harris Theatre 15
Harris, Henry B. 9
Harris, Mildred 146
Harris, William Jr. 15
Harrison, Rex 262, 263, 268, 323
Harvey, Lillian 309
Hatton, Frederick and Fanny 142
Hayes, Helen 157
Haymarket Theatre 9
Hays, Will H. 48, 50
He Raised Kane 79
Hearst, William Randolph 138, 166
Heath, Arch 146
Hell's Angels 134, 148, 149
Hemmingway, Ernest 248
Henabery, Joseph 146, 147
Hendricks, Ben Jr. 32, 46, 47, 48, 59
Henley, Hobart 30, 31, 38, 151, 152
Henry Miller Theatre 21
Hepburn, Audrey 273
Hepburn, Katharine 171
Her Royal Highness 5
Here's To Romance 173
Hersholt, Jean 109
Herzog, Dorothy 35
Hewitson, E. 128
Higham, Charles 151
Hill, George 43
Hiller, Lejaren a 25
Hilliard, Ernest 71
Hilton, James 234
His Lucky Day 148, 194
Hitchcock, Alfred 153, 236, 239, 298
Hitchcock, Patricia 236
Hobhouse, Adam 173

Hodgins, Eric 248
Hodkinson, William Wadsworth 25
Hogan, James P. 176, 180
Holloman, Colonel and Captain George V.
    177, 178, 179, 236, 237, 247, 253,
    293
Holloway, Sterling 173
Hollywood Athletic Club 139, 147
Hollywood Walk of Fame 267, 286, 331
Holmes, Taylor 140
Hoover, President Herbert 155
Hope, Bob 248
Hopkins, Arthur 23
Hopkins, Miriam 169
Hopper, Harold 160
Hopper, Hedda 47, 158
Horton, Edward Everett 55, 167
Hotel Astor 50
Hotel Buckingham 49
Hottentot, The 61
Houser, John G. 272
Howard, John 176, 296
Howard, Leslie 155, 161, 162, 170, 175, 220,
    234
Howes, Sally Ann 263, 324
Hoxie, Jack 109
Hubbard, Harold N. 60
Hudson Theatre 306
Hudson, John 320
Hughes, Howard 134, 148, 149, 238
Hunt, Marsha 253
Hurn, Philip 139
Hurrell, George 198, 199, 200, 201
Huston, Walter 157
Hymer, John 148

I

I'll Show You the Town 35, 36, 37, 96, 97
Ince, Ralph 25
Independent Moving Pictures Company 26
Ingle, Gladys 42
International Squadron 240, 245
Invisible Ray, The 26
Iron Master, The 157

Iron Trail, The 24
Iroquois Trail, The 250
Irving, Sir Henry 6
It Couldn't Have Happened (But It Did) 174,
    240
It Happened One Night 170

J

Jack Owens Show, The 257
Jackson, George H. 271
James Webb Space Telescope 284, 285
Jane Wyman Presents the Fireside Theatre
    258
Jason, Jack 325
Jaws of Steel 29
Jazz Singer, The 141
Jeffreys, Anne 258
Jensen, Eulalie 10, 24
Joan of Newark 30, 83
John Westley 15
Johnson, Albert 42, 104
Johnson, Emory 55
Johnson, Kay 154, 161, 170, 207, 208
Johnstone, Will B. 52
Join the Marines 176
Joint Civilian Defense Orientation Confer-
    ence (JCOC) 253, 316, 317
Jones, Colonel 13, 14
Jones, E. X. 58
Jones, Jennifer 246
Jones, Robert Edmond 157
Joseph Cotten Show: On Trial, The 262
Jungle Menace 176

K

Kaliz, Armand 125
Karloff, Boris 159, 163, 248, 258
Kaye, Danny 248, 312
Keaton, Buster 155
Keith, Donald 158
Kendrick, Mayor W. Freeland 51
Kennedy, Bill 264
Kennedy, Edgar 136
Kennedy, John F. 271

Kennedy, Madge 15
Kennedy, Myrna 151
Kent, Barbara 136, 137, 145, 186
Kentucky Derby, The 29
Kentucky Jockey Club 49
Kerrigan, J. M. 219
Kiki 155, 211, 212
King Edward VII 6
King George V 19
King, Louis 176, 180
Kingsley, Grace 47, 147, 149
Kitty MacKay 15
Knickerbocker Theatre 16
Kolker, Henry 24
Koster, Henry 238

L
La Jolla Playhouse 249
La Plante, Laura 31, 33, 47, 48, 54, 59, 91,
    109, 111, 112, 124, 167, 168, 281
La Rocque, Rod 24, 164, 174
La Verne, Jane 136, 137, 186
Lady Huntsworth's Experiment 6
Lady in Scarlet, The 173, 229
Laemmle, Carl 26, 29, 30, 32, 36, 38, 39, 44,
    45, 46, 51, 52, 53, 55, 56, 57, 59, 61,
    115, 116, 129, 130, 131, 132, 133,
    135, 136, 137, 138, 140, 141, 145,
    146, 148, 152, 154, 175, 235, 274
Laemmle, Carl Jr. 53, 140, 151, 152, 158,
    167, 175, 235
Laemmle, Edward 55
Laguna Playhouse 250
Lake Arrowhead 43, 141, 165, 169, 170
Lake, Arthur 39, 47, 109, 138
Lamont, Charles 173
Lamour, Dorothy 248
Landis, Jesse Royce 250, 251
Lane, Nora 148
Lane, Tamar 51
Larger Than Life 250, 251, 252
Larrabee, William 237, 259, 260
Lawford, Peter 255
Lawton, Frank 167

Leather Pushers, The 26, 27, 29, 72, 135,
    154, 273
Lee, Betsy 109, 119, 138, 142, 143, 189,
    281
Lee, Jocelyn 142, 143
Lehman, Gladys 59, 135, 147, 148
Leigh, Mrs. Henry 5, 8
Leonard, Sheldon 250
Lerner, Alan Jay 262
Let's Get Married 176, 290
Levin, Herman 262, 267
Lewis, Ted "Kid" 53, 122
Liberty Theatre 47
Lind, Wild Billy 42
Lindbergh, Charles 55
Lindfors, Viveca 320
Lipton, William 325
Little Minister, The 171
Littlefield, Lucien 147
Lloyd, "Hub" 46
Lloyd, Harold 35, 54, 135, 136
Locket, The 248
Loewe, Frederick 262
Loftus, Cissie 236
Lone Eagle, The 55
Lonesome 145, 146
Lorre, Peter 248, 262, 320
Los Angeles Coliseum 43
Los Angeles County Museum 149, 268,
    269
Los Angeles High School 149
Los Angeles International Airport (LAX)
    166, 330
Lost Patrol, The 159, 163, 219
Lottery Lover 173
Love Insurance 32
Love Letters 246
Lovett, Robert A. 253, 254
Lowery, Robert 321
Lowther, Hugh 8
Loy, Myrna 158, 218, 248, 313
Lubitsch, Ernest 167
Ludlam, Helen 151
Lugosi, Bela 155

Lupino, Ida 176, 248, 290
Lyric Theatre 155

M

M. H. Whittier Company 165, 235
M'Gowen, Roscoe 54
Mabel Brownell-Clifford Stock Company 16
MacArthur, General Douglas 243, 246
MacDonald, Jeanette 155, 167
MacDonald, Philip 159
MacDougall, Bon 31, 41, 42, 43, 104
MacLean, Douglas 61
MacMurray, Fred 240
Macomber Affair, The 248
Madam Satan 154, 155, 161, 207, 208, 209
Madame X 8
Maharajah of Mysore Krishna Raja Wadiyar
  IV 13, 14, 33, 164, 258
Maharani Pratapa Kumari Ammani 13
Mahatma Gandhi 13, 14
Major Mosley's Aircraft Industries 166
Malone, Pat 9
Mann Waddel Woodrow, Nancy 173
Manning, Art 138, 139, 150, 162, 174
Manning, Wing Commander Ralph 274,
  278
Marble Arch Pavillion 132
March Air Force Base 177, 268, 269, 292
March, Frederic 173, 217
Margetson, Arthur 50
Mark Hellinger Theater 262, 263, 323, 324
Marmont, Percy 10
Marquess of Donegall 128
Marsh, Joan 169
Marshall, Captain Robert 5
Martin, William 133
Martini, Nino 173
Marvin, Lee 274, 277
Mary Poppins 273
Matinee Theatre 261
Matlock, Spider 42, 43, 104
Maugham, Somerset 170, 250
Maxine Elliott Theatre 16
May, Edna 227

Mayer, Louis B. 146, 155
Mayo, Nick 272
Mayo, Virginia 248
McClellan, Herb 42, 104
McComb, Judge Marshall 142
McCoy, T. F. 36, 37
McCrea, Joel 169, 174
McCutcheon, George Barr 33
McGowan, Tom 257
McGrail, Walter 29
McLaglen, Leopold 12, 13, 159
McLaglen, Victor 159, 219
McNeile, H. C. "Sapper" 176
McNeill, Jim 280
Mehaffey, Blanche 52
Melford, George 176
Melody of Love 145, 146
Merry Widow, The 9, 11, 167
Metro-Goldwyn-Mayer (MGM) 146, 154,
  155, 158, 167, 173, 175, 176, 241
Metropolitan Studios 153
Metropolitan Theater 47
Midland and Royal Theatres 37
Midland Hotel 131
Midnight Phantom 173
Milestone, Louis 94
Milland, Ray 176
Miller, Arthur 264
Miller, Eddie 23
Miller, Mayor Victor J. 49
Millet, Jean-Francois 25
Million Dollar Madrid Theatre 49
Milne, Peter 139
Mines Field 166, 171
Minster, Jack 250
Miracle, The 155
Mis' Nelly of N'Orleans 21
Mitchell, Grant 169
Mitchum, Robert 248
Model Airplane News 166, 171, 279
Monroe, Marilyn 246, 264, 269, 270, 274
Montana, Bull 141
Montgomery Ward 165, 171
Montgomery, Elizabeth 161, 262

Montgomery, George 250

Montgomery, Robert 155, 161, 166, 168, 173, 214, 217, 226, 227, 250

Moore, Grace 155

Moorhouse, H. D. 131

Moran, Lee 94, 98

More Than a Secretary 175

Moreno, Rita 255

Morgan, Byron 31, 37

Mortenson, Norma Jeane 245, 246, 264, 270

Motion Picture Hospital 277, 280

Movietone 148

Mr. Blandings Builds His Dream House 248, 249, 250, 313

Mulhare, Edward 263, 271, 324

My Fair Lady 262, 263, 264, 267, 268, 271, 272, 273, 277, 323, 324, 329

My Favorite Brunette 248

My Hero 254

N

Nagel, Conrad 151

National Sporting Club 8

National Theatre 32

Neill, Roy William 24

Neilson, Julia 6

Nelsen, Mayor Charles Clarence 36

Never Let Go 29

Newhouse Hotel 36

Newmeyer, Fred 135, 136, 139, 140, 142, 146

Newport Beach Yacht Club 34

Newton, Robert 319

Nichols, Fronty 43, 104

Nigh, William 173

Night Bird, The 141, 142, 147, 187, 188, 189

Niobe 16

Niven, David 179

Nixon, Marian 35, 36, 39, 46, 48, 59, 97, 98, 166, 167, 169, 272

No More Ladies 173, 227

No! No! Napoleon 148

Nolan, Mary 141

Northrop Aircraft Company 248, 249, 254

Northrop Corporation 270, 283

Northrop Grumman Bat 283

Northrop Grumman Corporation 283, 285

Northrop Grumman Global Hawk 283

Northrop Grumman MQ-4C Triton 283

Northrop Grumman MQ-8C Fire Scout 283

Northrop Grumman X-47B 284

Northrop, John "Jack" 248, 249, 254, 277

Novarro, Ramon 158, 218

Now I'll Tell One 136

O

O'Brien, Tom 136, 137, 194

O'Connell, Jack 133

Oakdale Affair, The 23

Ochs, Lee 34, 35

Of Human Bondage 161, 162, 163, 170, 220

Oh, Doctor! 34, 41, 95

Oh, For a Man! 155

Oliver, Edna May 169

Olivier, Laurence 236, 299

Olmstead, Gertrude 37, 53

Olympia Irlams-o'-th'-Height 132

On Your Toes 135, 141

One Hysterical Night 148, 195

One More River 167, 168, 170

One Night in Lisbon 240

Only Yesterday 158, 159

Out All Night 59, 60, 133, 126

Outward Bound 236, 297

Over My Dead Body 241

Owen, Reginald 161, 173, 272

Oxford Theatre 132

P

Paganini 16

Palance, Jack 262, 320

Pam, Jerry 257

Pantages Theater 170, 146, 159

Parade's Gone By... The 136, 273

Paramount Pictures 16, 24, 25, 47, 53, 54, 134, 135, 146, 149, 158, 167, 174, 176, 180, 240, 246, 248, 291, 295, 296

Park Hall 132
Park Theatre 9
Parker, Eleanor, 248
Parliament 129
Parlor, Bedroom and Bath 155
Parsons, Louella 35, 163
Pasadena Playhouse 269, 328
Passing Show of 1919, The 22, 23
Passport to Danger 261
Pasternak, Joe 238
Paterson, Pat 173
Patriot Theatre 133
Patrol 159
Paying the Piper 24
Peaks of Gold 25
Peck, Gregory 248
Pentagon, The 253, 254
Peple, Edward 17
Personal Appearance Theatre 253
Phantom of the Opera, The 34
Phantom, The 268
Philbin, Mary 109
Phillips, Eddie 148, 194
Piccadilly Theatre 34, 35, 128
Pichel, Irving 157
Pickford, Mary 155, 211, 212
Pidgeon, Walter 146
Playhouse 90 262, 320, 321
Please Don't Eat the Daisies 274
Plummer, Jules 252, 259, 270
Plunge Creek Fire 139
Plymouth Theatre 24
Polar Eye 283
Pollard, Harry 26, 29, 31, 32, 34, 35, 37, 38, 135, 136
Potter, H. C. 248
Powell, Harold 236, 237, 238, 254, 260
Powell, Jane 241, 272
Powell, William 27
Power, Tyrone Sr. 39
Powers Studio 26
Powers, Pat 26
President, The 6
Preston, Harry Sir 8, 18, 23, 30, 167

Preston, Robert 248
Preview Murder Mystery, The 174
Price of Possession, The 24, 68, 69
Price, Bridgett 152
Price, Guy 47
Price, Vincent 253
Prince of Wales Theatre 6
Private Lives 155, 214
Private Secretary 258
Professor's Love Story, The 16
Prouty, Jed 158, 161
Pt. Mugu Naval Air Station 311
Pucci, Ed 269, 270, 274
Pucci, Ralph 262, 267, 269
Puffy, Charles 109
Pursell, Roni 67
Pygmalion 262

Q

Quaker Girl, The 9, 10, 11
Queen of Angels Hospital 160
Queen Victoria 6
Queen's Enemies, The 16
Quimby, Margaret 109

R

Racket, The 148
Radio Pictures (RKO) 157, 159, 160, 161, 162, 163, 166, 169, 171, 248
Radioplane 1 (RP-1) 175, 176
Radioplane 174, 176, 235, 236, 249, 252, 253, 258, 260, 265, 269, 277, 280, 283, 284, 287
Radioplane Company 237, 238, 239, 242, 245, 247, 249, 252, 254, 260, 261, 270
Radioplane Flotation-1 (RF-1) 247
Radioplane-14 (RP-14) 243
Radioplane-15 (RP-15) 243
Radioplane-16 (RP-16) 243
Radioplane-18 (RP-18)246
Radioplane-19 (RP-19) 246, 247
Radioplane-2 (RP-2) 176, 177, 288, 289
Radioplane-26 (RP-26) 252

Radioplane-3 (RP-3) 177, 292
Radioplane-4 (RP-4) 236, 237, 238, 239, 300, 301, 302, 303, 304
Radioplane-5 (RP-5) 239, 305
Radioplane-5A (RP-5A) 241
Radioplane-5A (RP-5A) 310
Radioplane-71 (RP-71) Falconer 259
Radioplane-8 (RP-8) 241, 242
Radiorocket 253
Radioship 178, 253
Radiotank 178, 253
Rae, Lawrence 9
Raiders of the Lost Ark 285
Ramo, Simon 285
Rand, Ayn 246
Ratcliffe, E. J. 47, 148
Rath, E. J. 147, 153
Rathbone, Basil 173, 175, 232, 234, 241
Rawlins, John 241
Ray, Al 160
Ray, Bernard "B. B." 173
Rayton, Velma 307
Reagan, Ronald 240, 245
Realart Pictures 24
Rebecca 236, 239, 279, 298, 299
Reckless Age, The 32, 33, 93
Red Hot Speed 146, 148, 158, 190
Red Skelton Hour, The 258, 262
Reed, Donna 241, 308
Reggie's Robot 314
Reginald Denny Hobby Shop 166, 223, 224, 249, 267
Reginald Denny Industries 165, 174, 235, 237, 238, 260, 261
Reid, Wallace 32, 38
Reisner, Charles 155
Remember Last Night? 173
Remick, Lee 262, 320
Republic Pictures 176
Reville, Alma 236
Reynolds Diaz-Albertini, Stockwell "Tiny" 127
Reynolds, B. F. 94
Rialto Theatre 33, 38, 132

Rich, Lillian 29, 136, 137
Richard III 23, 157
Richest Girl in the World, The 169, 170, 171
Richter, Paul Jr. 42, 104
Righter, Walter 171, 174, 175, 176, 177, 179, 180, 236, 237, 247, 300, 302, 305
Ring at Blackfriars 8
Riviera Country Club 155, 156, 215
RKO Theatre 163, 170
RMS Aquitania 133
RMS Benegaria 127
RMS Olympic 11
RMS Titanic 10, 11
Roach, Hal 173
Robert Montgomery Presents 250
Robertson, John S. 24, 25
Robin Hood 129
Robin, Louis B. 271
Rockwell, Helen 50
Rogell, Albert 159
Rogers, Will 155
Rogue Song, The 154
Rolling Home 48, 49, 53, 114, 115, 116, 117
Romeo and Juliet 45, 175, 232, 233, 234, 241
Rooney, Mickey 166
Roosevelt Hotel 148
Rosalind 16
Ross, Nat 29
Roth, Lillian 154
Round Five: The Taming of the Shrewd 27, 76
Round Four: A Fool and His Honey 27, 75
Round One: Through the Looking Glass 26, 72
Round Six: Whipsawed! 27, 77
Round Three: Payment Through The Nose 27, 74
Round Two: With This Ring I Thee Fed! 26, 73
Roxy Theatre 169
Royal Academy of Dramatic Art 168
Royal Air Force 18, 41, 66, 131, 240, 278, 315

Royal Canadian Air Force 19, 275, 278
Royal Flying Corps 18
Running Springs 43, 138, 198, 199, 200, 201, 202, 203
Rutan, Burt 285
Ryan, Don 242, 243
Ryan, Robert 258
Ryan, T. Claude 285

S

Sabaka 258
Sadler's Wells Theatre 5
Safety Last 35
Salford Palace 132
Sanders, George 179, 236
Santa Monica Airport 42
Santa Monica Civic Auditorium 253, 271, 272, 277
Savage, Courtenay 153
Savoy Hotel 128
Schenck, Joseph 22, 50, 155
Schertzinger, Victor 157
Schulberg, B. P. 176
Scott, Mabel Julienne 30, 89
Scott, W. 132
Scrooge 6
Seasongood, Mayor Murray 49, 114
Secret Life of Walter Mitty, The 248, 312
Secretary of Defense 255, 257, 258
Seegar, Miriam 154, 205
Seiter, William 33, 39, 46, 47, 52, 53, 54, 56, 59, 94, 123, 124, 133, 135, 136, 140, 141, 153, 166, 167, 169, 170, 171, 240, 272, 273, 281
Selznick, David O. 236, 239, 248, 279
Serrano people 174
Seven Sinners 238
Shakespeare 16, 23, 157, 175
Sharkey, Sailor 141
Shaw, George Bernard 16, 130, 132, 140, 153, 252, 259, 262, 273
Shea, Gloria 169
Shearer, Norma 27, 154, 155, 175, 214
Sherlock Holmes 27, 241

Sherlock Holmes and the Voice of Terror 241
Sherriff, R. C. 170
Shubert, Lee 22, 24, 49, 50
Shuberts 10, 23
Sidney, George 176
Silvia, Sydney 321
Simmons, Craig 249
Simmons, James 238, 249
Sinatra, Frank 269, 274
Six, Bert 94
Skinner's Dress Suit 47, 48, 53, 111, 112, 113, 137, 138, 147, 273, 281
Slow Down 56
Smallwood, Cecil 166
Smith, Ferris M. 237
Smith, George 131
Smith, Leigh 158
Smith, Paul Gerard 168
Snell, Earle 135, 136, 142, 147, 150
Something For Nothing 87
Song of the Open Road 241
Sono Art-World Wide Pictures 153, 154
Sopwith Snipe 18, 19, 128, 132, 133, 134, 149, 268, 269, 274, 275, 278, 326, 327
Sound of Music, The 277
Soutar, Andrew 182
Southern, Ann 258
Spensley, Dorothy 51
Sporting Youth 31, 32, 41, 91, 92
Sprague, Rear Admiral C. A. P. 242
Spring Parade 238
Sproul, Norman 36
SS Barbarene 34, 46, 49, 98, 149
St. Barbe, F. E. N. 133, 183
St. Clair, Malcolm 180, 241
St. Francis Xavier College 7
Stack, William 133, 183
Stag Lane Aerodrome 132, 183, 184
Stahl, John 158
Standard Capital 175
Standing, Sir Guy 176
Stanford Theatre 36
Stanwyck, Barbara 258

Star Wars 285
Staub, Ralph 176
Stein, Eddie 32
Stella the Star-Gazer 147, 149, 150
Stephens, Moye 248
Stephenson, Henry 238
Stepping Out 155
Sterling, Robert 258
Stevenson, Hayden 26, 135
Stevenson, Robert Louis 250
Stiefel, Isabelle 137, 142
Stout Metal Airplane Company 106
Strange Justice 157
Strife 9
Strike Father, Strike Son 82
Suhrawardy, Prime Minister Huseyn Sha-heed 323
Sullavan, Margaret 159, 160, 240
Sullivan, Arthur 5
Summerville, Slim 148, 152
Sunday Night at the Trocadero 176
Sunderland, Brigade General Archibald Henry 177
Swanson, Gloria 157

T

Take It From Me 52, 53, 120
Tales from Hollywood 257
Tales of the 77th Bengal Lancers 262
Talisman Studios 175
Talmadge, Norma 22
Tangier 248
Tanner, James Tolman 9
Target Drone Denny (TDD-1) 239, 246, 250, 279
Target Drone Denny-2 (TDD-2) 241, 310
Target Drone Denny-3 (TDD-3) 242, 243
Tarkington, Booth 151
Taylor, Sam 173
Tead, Phil 158, 161
Technicolor 157
Telephone Time 261
Temple Theatre 31
Tesla, Nikola 7, 164

Thalberg, Irving 154, 155, 167, 175, 234
That's My Daddy 136, 137, 139, 140, 158, 167, 186
Theatre 250
Theatre Royal 250
Thew, Harvey 31, 53
They All Want Something 153
Thiele, Lieutenant Colonel C. M. 175, 176
Thiele, Wilhelm 173, 176
Third Party, The 140, 152
Thomas, Evan 297
Thomas, Faith 158
Those Three French Girls 155, 210
Thunder Birds: Soldiers of the Air 240
Tierney, Gene 241
Tinee, Mae 48, 54, 61
Tinkley, Allen 271
Tobin, Genevieve 173
Todd, Arthur 153
Todd, Arthur Mrs. 150
Todd, Michael 261, 279
Tomaine, Paul 325
Tomick, Frank 134
Tone, Franchot 161, 173
Topper 258
Torrence, Ernest 10
Tower Productions 158
Transcontinental Bus 161
Triart Pictures 25
Tropical Love 25, 26, 71
Trotti, Lamar 240
Twentieth Century Fox 155, 173, 179, 180, 240, 241
Twin Beds 15
Two in a Crowd 174
Tyron, Glenn 145

U

U. S. Air Force 177, 252, 253, 258, 268, 269, 318, 325
U. S. Air Force Museum 327
U. S. Air Force XQ-1 252
U. S. Army 174, 175, 177, 242, 246, 247, 252, 253, 257, 325

U. S. Army Air Corps 177, 37, 238, 293, 300, 301, 303

U. S. Army Air Corps Special Weapons 177, 235

U. S. Army Antiaircraft Forces 177

U. S. Army OQ-1 238

U. S. Army OQ-14 242

U. S. Army OQ-16 243

U. S. Army OQ-19 247

U. S. Army OQ-2 239

U. S. Army OQ-3 241

U. S. Army OQ-3 310

U. S. Marines 253, 316

U. S. Navy 239, 240, 242, 247, 253, 264, 265

Uncle Tom's Cabin 45, 136

Underhill, Harriette 35

Unger, Ivan "Bugs" 42

United Artists 155, 241

Universal City Studios 27, 30, 36, 45, 48, 52, 53, 56, 57, 58, 137, 175, 281

Universal Film Company 26

Universal Film Manufacturing Company 26, 27

Universal Pictures 36, 37, 39, 47, 49, 50, 52, 55, 133, 134, 135, 136, 137, 139, 140, 141, 146, 151, 158, 159, 167, 173, 174, 238, 240, 241, 248

Universal Weekly 36, 37, 45, 52, 54, 56, 60, 141, 142, 145, 146, 148

Uptown Theatre 52, 53, 54, 60, 142

USS Shangri-La 242

V

Vagabond Lady 173

Valley Music Theater 272, 329

Valli, Virginia 109

Van Nuys Metropolitan Airport 149, 237

Van, Beatrice 37

Vaudeville Theatre 6

Veir, Martin "Pete" 249, 267

Venuta, Benay 321

Vidor, Charles 176

Vine Manor 179

Vita Temple Theatre 133

Vitaphone 141

Vitograph Company 10

Vreeland, Frank 51

W

Waggner, George 248

Wagstaff Gribble, Harry 240

Waldrop, Oza 65

Wallace, Richard 171

Wandering Two, The 30, 84

Wanger, Walter 179

Warner Bros. 130, 141, 167, 240, 248

Warner, H. B. 180

Warner, Jack 167, 168, 278

Watt, Nate 94

Wayne, John 238

We're in the Legion Now 175

We're Rich Again 166, 169, 170

Weeks, George 158

Wellman, William A. 240

West, Adam 274

Westside Civic Light Opera 271

Whale, James 167, 173

What A Man 153, 154, 205, 206

What Every Woman Knows 8, 14

What Happened to Jones 46, 47, 53, 107, 108, 147

When Kane Met Abel 81

When the Devil Was Sick 147

Where Was I? 39, 98

Whistler, The 258

White House, The 116

White Lodge 127, 128, 132, 136, 167, 168, 230, 240, 251

Whittier, Olive 165, 221

Whittier, Paul 165, 168, 174, 216, 221, 235, 236, 237, 238, 242, 289, 300

Whole Town's Talking, The 55

Widower's Mite, The 30, 85

Wightman, Wing Commander David P. 275

Wilbur, Crane 175

Wiles, Gordon 176

Wilkes, Charles 325

Williams, Barbara 272

Williams, H. L. 132

Williams, Lt. William 149
Williams, Valentine 159
Wilson, Harry Leon 34
Wilson, Tom 37, 38
Wilson, Woodrow 173
Wings 134, 149
Winter Garden Theatre 23
Winter, Phillip 297
Winwood, Estelle 253
Withers, Jane 166
Without Children 173
Witwer, H. C. 26, 27
Wizard of Oz, The 179
WMGM Radio 325
Wolper, Isaac 25, 26
Women of Glamour 176
Wonderland 8
Wood, Sam 158
Wood, Vernon 150, 168
World Film Studios 23
World for Ransom 255
World Moves On, The 161, 170
Worth, Barbara 57, 135
Worthy Deceiver, The 157

Wray, Fay 169
Wright Brothers 18
Wright Patterson Air Force Base 260, 269, 293, 327
Wrigley, William Jr. 33
Wynn, Keenan 262, 320
Wynyard, Diana 167

Y

Yeomen of the Guard, The 5
Yerger, Waldon 160
You've Got To Fight 148
Young King Cole 29, 78
Young, Gig 248
Young, Loretta 179
Young, Robert 173
Young, Roland 27, 154, 208
Your Show Time 250

Z

Zanuck, Darryl 29, 240
Ziegfeld Follies 158
Zinnemann, Fred 241
Zukor, Adolph 146

ABOUT THE AUTHOR

THE GRANDDAUGHTER OF LEGENDARY ACTOR and unmanned aviation pioneer Reginald Denny, Kimberly Pucci was a natural in the world of Hollywood from the start. At her baptism, godmother Pat Hitchcock had to keep *"The Birds"* away from the sacred blessed water bowl while holding Kim during the ceremony. Her first backstage visit was at age two when she was held in the arms of Julie Andrews during the original Broadway run of *My Fair Lady*. A few years later, trips to Vegas were a regular occurrence where she hung out with the Rat Pack while her uncle Ed protected Frank Sinatra as his famed bodyguard. From there, Kim's life and professional career went on to include exciting passages surrounded by colorful icons in the worlds of music, film, television, and aviation. Following a decade of management roles within the airline and luxury hospitality industries, Kim launched her career in the entertainment industry as Senior Executive Assistant to high-profile chairmen of Hollywood's leading studios while at MGM, Columbia Pictures, Sony Pictures Entertainment, and eventually as Executive Vice President of Peters Entertainment at Warner Bros. With these prominent roles, Kim gained overall experience in film production as she managed celebrity lifestyles and orchestrated A-list entertainment industry events to elite luxury worldwide travel planning. Given her combined experience in the entertainment, event planning, and travel fields, Kim joined Paramount Pictures in 2007 as Executive Concierge where she was "house-mother" to the stars for ten years. Now semi-retired while spending her time as a world-traveler, Kim has come out with her latent role as writer. She brings several treasured projects to life including *Prince of Drones: The Reginald Denny Story*, the Hitchcockian psychological thriller *Interception*, and sci-fi apocalyptical thriller *I-Cetacea*.